Leadership Strategies for the Hybrid Workforce:

Best Practices for Fostering Employee Safety and Significance

Matthew Ohlson
University of North Florida, USA

Lakshmi Goel
University of North Florida, USA

A volume in the Advances in Human Resources Management and Organizational Development (AHRMOD) Book Series

IGI Global
PUBLISHER of TIMELY KNOWLEDGE

Published in the United States of America by
IGI Global
Business Science Reference (an imprint of IGI Global)
701 E. Chocolate Avenue
Hershey PA, USA 17033
Tel: 717-533-8845
Fax: 717-533-8661
E-mail: cust@igi-global.com
Web site: http://www.igi-global.com

Library of Congress Cataloging-in-Publication Data

Names: Ohlson, Matthew, 1974- editor. | Goel, Lakshmi, 1979- editor.
Title: Leadership strategies for the hybrid workforce : best practices for fostering employee safety and significance / Matthew Ohlson, and Lakshmi Goel, editor.
Description: Hershey, PA : Business Science Reference, [2022] | Includes bibliographical references and index. | Summary: "This book offers readers a collection of best practices on how to lead when people are working remotely or in a hybrid fashion, offering a blueprint on how to make people feel safe & significant in the workforce"-- Provided by publisher.
Identifiers: LCCN 2022004124 (print) | LCCN 2022004125 (ebook) | ISBN 9781668434536 (hardcover) | ISBN 9781668434543 (paperback) | ISBN 9781668434550 (ebook)
Subjects: LCSH: Leadership. | Virtual work teams--Management. | Telecommuting--Management. | Organizational change--Management. | Virtual reality in management. | Employee morale.
Classification: LCC HD57.7 .L43527 2022 (print) | LCC HD57.7 (ebook) | DDC 658.4/092--dc23/eng/20220202
LC record available at https://lccn.loc.gov/2022004124
LC ebook record available at https://lccn.loc.gov/2022004125

This book is published in the IGI Global book series Advances in Human Resources Management and Organizational Development (AHRMOD) (ISSN: 2327-3372; eISSN: 2327-3380)

British Cataloguing in Publication Data
A Cataloguing in Publication record for this book is available from the British Library.

For electronic access to this publication, please contact: eresources@igi-global.com.

Advances in Human Resources Management and Organizational Development (AHRMOD) Book Series

ISSN:2327-3372
EISSN:2327-3380

Editor-in-Chief: Patricia Ordóñez de Pablos, Universidad de Oviedo, Spain

MISSION

A solid foundation is essential to the development and success of any organization and can be accomplished through the effective and careful management of an organization's human capital. Research in human resources management and organizational development is necessary in providing business leaders with the tools and methodologies which will assist in the development and maintenance of their organizational structure.

The **Advances in Human Resources Management and Organizational Development (AHRMOD) Book Series** aims to publish the latest research on all aspects of human resources as well as the latest methodologies, tools, and theories regarding organizational development and sustainability. The **AHRMOD Book Series** intends to provide business professionals, managers, researchers, and students with the necessary resources to effectively develop and implement organizational strategies.

COVERAGE

- Organizational Learning
- Employee Communications
- Diversity in the Workplace
- Workplace Culture
- Talent Identification and Management
- Collaborative Method
- Outsourcing HR
- Executive Education
- Process Improvement
- Work-Life Balance

IGI Global is currently accepting manuscripts for publication within this series. To submit a proposal for a volume in this series, please contact our Acquisition Editors at Acquisitions@igi-global.com or visit: http://www.igi-global.com/publish/.

The Advances in Human Resources Management and Organizational Development (AHRMOD) Book Series (ISSN 2327-3372) is published by IGI Global, 701 E. Chocolate Avenue, Hershey, PA 17033-1240, USA, www.igi-global.com. This series is composed of titles available for purchase individually; each title is edited to be contextually exclusive from any other title within the series. For pricing and ordering information please visit http://www.igi-global.com/book-series/advances-human-resources-management-organizational/73670. Postmaster: Send all address changes to above address.

Titles in this Series

For a list of additional titles in this series, please visit:
www.igi-global.com/book-series/advances-human-resources-management-organizational/73670

Transgender Discrimination in the Workplace
Zafeiris Tsiftzis (OCL Solicitors, UK)
Business Science Reference • copyright 2022 • 315pp • H/C (ISBN: 9781799873129) • US $195.00 (our price)

Implementing Diversity, Equity, Inclusion, and Belonging Management in Organizational Change Initiatives
Abeni El-Amin (Fort Hays State University, USA)
Business Science Reference • copyright 2022 • 320pp • H/C (ISBN: 9781668440230) • US $215.00 (our price)

Handbook of Research on Challenges for Human Resource Management in the COVID-19 Era
Paula Cristina Nunes Figueiredo (ULHT - Universidade Lusófona, Portugal) Eduardo Luís de Campos Soares Tomé (ULHT - Universidade Lusófona, Portugal) and José Carlos Dias Rouco (ULHT - Universidade Lusófona, Portugal)
Business Science Reference • copyright 2022 • 450pp • H/C (ISBN: 9781799898405) • US $295.00 (our price)

Mainstreaming Diversity, Equity, and Inclusion as Future Workplace Ethics
Lukman Raimi (Universiti Brunei Darussalam, Brunei) and Jainaba M. L. Kah (Office of the President, Gambia)
Business Science Reference • copyright 2022 • 297pp • H/C (ISBN: 9781668436578) • US $240.00 (our price)

Developing Diversity, Equity, and Inclusion Policies for Promoting Employee Sustainability and Well-Being
Sónia P. Gonçalves (ISCSP-ULisboa, Portugal) Paula Cristina Nunes Figueiredo (ULHT - Universidade Lusófona, Portugal) Eduardo Luis Soares Tomé (ULHT - Universidade Lusófona, Portugal) and José Baptista (ISCSP-ULisboa, Portugal)
Business Science Reference • copyright 2022 • 330pp • H/C (ISBN: 9781668441817) • US $240.00 (our price)

For an entire list of titles in this series, please visit:
www.igi-global.com/book-series/advances-human-resources-management-organizational/73670

IGI Global
PUBLISHER of TIMELY KNOWLEDGE

701 East Chocolate Avenue, Hershey, PA 17033, USA
Tel: 717-533-8845 x100 • Fax: 717-533-8661
E-Mail: cust@igi-global.com • www.igi-global.com

Table of Contents

Detailed Table of Contents

As the COVID-19 pandemic hit every facet of our lives, GuideWell leaders quickly rose to the challenge to make sure our workforce was safe and prepared to navigate these uncertain times together. They did this by simply living out our great culture that already existed and putting their values into action. Their values influenced every decision they made, from quickly pivoting to working remotely and ensuring their members received affordable treatment and testing to championing vaccination efforts and giving back to communities in need. Their culture and values make them who they are and ground them in how they respond to any crisis situation. And most important, as a health solutions company, they led with action in a caring, compassionate way, not only for their workforce, but for their members and the communities they serve.

This chapter stresses the importance of expectations and their role in performance and accountability. In a hybrid work environment, unclear expectations can lead to adverse performance and difficulties with accountability. The chapter encourages the use of dialogue to establish expectations and strategies to that end. Overall, expectations are a process and are dynamic. They need to be revisited often. Shared expectations are a strong foundation that contributes to the clarity of tasks and can enhance performance. They outline accountability, and the practice of developing

leadership qualities became extremely important to determining an organization's success. Specifically, the ability of leaders to effectively communicate, be flexible with operational procedures, and to establish a culture of creativity all proved to be instrumental in determining an organization's ability to persevere through the many challenges they faced.

Section 3
Leading in the Digital Age

The pandemic has accelerated the need for organizations to embrace digital strategies for processes that are both internally as well as externally facing. The demand for innovation in how a firm serves customers, supports teams, and empowers employees has necessitated the adoption of digital solutions. In this chapter, the authors provide a framework for how organizational leaders can envision digital transformation in a way that is in alignment with business strategy. Digital innovation, while left to the IT enterprise in the past, is now elevated to the level of organizational strategy and can be instrumental to business competitiveness and continuity. Strategic digital transformation can help organizations build agility and resilience, capabilities that have proven to be essential in the face of unpredictable forces, such as those experienced during the COVID-19 pandemic.

Every company, regardless of size and industry, is in the digital technology business—whether they realize it or not. The authors define digital leadership as having practical skills to lead or guide other individuals, teams, or entire organizations. The main point they are making is that such leadership is impossible without a basic technical understanding of the impact of digital technologies on the business. This does not mean that digital leaders should be software developers, system integrators, or advanced data analysts. However, they should know what is technically feasible to shape and communicate their vision.

to better utilize the power of networking. This networked approach to knowledge work transcends geo-political boundaries which will shift employment into a more global ecosystem not just with business processing organizations (BPOs) but also into individual entrepreneurs. This extension of the ecosystem thus provides access or expands the pool of skilled knowledge workers without regard to the source of talent, relocation expense, or immigration quotas.

Preface

The global Covid pandemic brought about dramatic changes at home and in the workplace and has prompted leaders throughout the world to embark on the departure from the pre-Covid era and towards the "next normal." Countless researchers from institutions of higher learning including Harvard and Cornell have been examining the shift in the way we lead and the way we work in the way we make people feel safe and significant in their working environments. Powerful findings across numerous studies show the dramatic shift in people's perceptions of virtual learning, working remotely and how to recruit and retain the best employees.

Emerging from the countless studies examining the Covid era are the ideas that leaders need increased flexibility and safety. They also need to pay more attention to their employee's mental health, their overall wellness and take a closer look at the daily pressures faced by their staff. In addition, there needs to be an increased focus on the significance of women in leadership roles as well as the importance of harnessing technology to increase collaboration and communication. Finally, there is clear need for deliberate decision making that allows employees to feel both empowered and part of the policy and practices of an organization.

Yet, few resources offer clear examples of how to put these recommendations into action. This powerful text harnesses the experiences and best practices implemented by some of the highest performing businesses and organizations as they navigated the Covid era and made significant changes in the areas of communication, staffing, production and leadership. Rather than looking at isolated case studies or the theoretical, Leadership Strategies for the Hybrid Workforce: Best Practices for Fostering Employee Safety and Significance equips the reader with proven strategies for enhancing policies and practices that allow organizations to emerge from the covid era with the skills and resources needed to thrive in this "Next Normal."

Leaders from a variety of fields from around the globe have generously agreed to document their lessons learned and spotlight the ways that effective leadership has transformed organizational outcomes and helped people thrive despite mask mandates, shutdowns, and global economic turmoil. This text will truly serve as a catalyst for positive and change and we are excited that you are now part of this learning community. After reading this book, please reach out to us to share some of your own best practices and success stories. We hope to emerge from the pandemic more effective, more adaptable and more capable as we help to make others feel safe and significant in the workplace.

ORGANIZATION OF THE BOOK

Chapter 1: As the COVID-19 pandemic hit every facet of our lives, GuideWell leaders quickly rose to the challenge to make sure our workforce was safe and prepared to navigate these uncertain times together. We did this by simply living out our great culture that already existed and putting our values in to action. Our values influenced every decision we made, from quickly pivoting to working remotely and ensuring our members received affordable treatment and testing, to championing vaccination efforts and giving back to communities in need. Our culture and values make us who we are and ground us in how we respond to any crisis situation. And most important, as a health solutions company, we led with action in a caring, compassionate way, not only for our workforce, but for our members and the communities we serve.

Chapter 2: This chapter stresses the importance of expectations and their role in performance and accountability. In a hybrid work environment, unclear expectations can lead to adverse performance and difficulties with accountability. The chapter encourages the use of dialogue to establish expectations and strategies to that end. Overall, expectations are a process and are dynamic. They need to be revisited often. Shared expectations are a strong foundation that contributes to the clarity of tasks and can enhance performance. They outline accountability and the practice of developing can make the evaluation of performance easier. As more employees ask for flexible work and more employers are trying to meet these needs, expectations are crucial in establishing environments that maximize performance and accountability.

Chapter 3: In today's business environment, professionals are often pulled in multiple directions and can easily be distracted from their primary objectives. From high volumes of emails, Teams™ messaging and social media swiping, to business travel, meetings, and office politics, there are countless ways to get pulled away from the core focus of any job role. Add in a typical work from home environment and the list of distractions grows exponentially. In most cases, the onus falls on leadership to create an environment of accountability and high performance for the organization. To hold a business team accountable, leaders must gain a deep understanding of each team member's "why," utilize pertinent metrics to measure progress, and maintain clear and consistent lines of communication with each individual and the team.

Chapter 4: This chapter combines facts, nuances, and implications of the Turnover Tsunami and Great Resignation phenomena. The author provides important insights that connect changes at social and generational levels—notably regarding stress and burnout, engagement and commitment, and socio-technical work trends such as virtual work and the metaverse—to current and future employment challenges. The chapter is designed to open lines of sight into the most complex and dynamic times ever seen in the employment realm. The author infuses personal strategy (e.g., Know Your People), commentary (e.g., collective collusion), and applied theory (e.g., cognitive dissonance) to open pathways of thought, understanding, and exploration into mid-post pandemic employment issues.

Chapter 5: This chapter provides an in-depth behind the scenes look at how the COVID-19 pandemic changed the sports - and golf - landscape in 2020. At the employee level, the TOUR had no choice but to develop a plan that had no playbook. Utilizing leadership traits and transparent communications that were frequent, the TOUR persevered through the toughest challenge of its 50+ year history. At the same time, the organization underwent a massive transition to a new campus, breaking down barriers and embracing change.

Chapter 6: Some people are great leaders because they choose to be. Fire Chiefs are great leaders because they have to be. They are experts in developing innovative ways to foster employee safety and significance. This chapter presents the framework, process, and strategy that fire-service and public-safety executives use to help firefighters reach their full potential as leaders, innovators, and change makers. Firefighters define leadership as the things a person does and says that inspires others to take action. Like most things in life, leadership is a skill anyone can learn. Yes, becoming a highly-respected leader is easy for some people and difficult for others; but with hard work, and the right framework, anyone can achieve leadership excellence.

Chapter 7: This chapter per the author describes many of the specific challenges faced by workers as a result of the hybrid environment created by the COVID-19 global pandemic. Leaders of organizations are also struggling with many of the same personal challenges and the requirement to meet organizational goals regardless of the environmental factors affecting their employees. This chapter discusses practical management strategies to help leaders at all levels strike a balance between life and work from home so they can lead with authenticity, empathy for the human experience and a mindset of productive compassion. Employees want to feel valued and significant. How leaders approach the challenges of the hybrid workforce determines whether or not an employee feels empowered, included and ultimately significant.

Chapter 8: This chapter examines the impact COVID-19 has had on the world of sports, and the critical leadership traits that emerged during this challenging time. Sports leagues around the world were dramatically impacted by the global pandemic, and as they navigated the many "new norms" that were created during this time, certain leadership qualities became extremely important to determining an organizations success. Specifically, the ability of leaders to effectively communicate, be flexible with operational procedures and to establish a culture of creativity all proved to be instrumental in determining an organizations ability to persevere through the myriad challenges they faced.

Chapter 9: The pandemic has accelerated the need for organizations to embrace digital strategies for processes that are both internal as well as external facing. The demand for innovation in how a firm serves customers, supports teams, and empowers employees has necessitated the adoption of digital solutions. In this chapter, the authors provide a framework for how organizational leaders can envision digital transformation in a way that is in alignment with business strategy. Digital innovation, while left to the IT enterprise in the past, is now elevated to the level of organizational strategy and can be instrumental to business competitiveness and continuity. Strategic digital transformation can help organizations build agility and resilience, capabilities that have proven to be essential in the face of unpredictable forces, such as those experienced during the COVID-19 pandemic.

Chapter 10: Every company, regardless of size and industry, is in the digital technology business—whether they realize it or not. We define digital leadership as having practical skills to lead or guide other individuals, teams, or entire organizations. The main point we are making is that such leadership is impossible without a basic technical understanding of the impact of digital technologies on the business. This does not mean that digital leaders should be software developers, system integrators, or advanced data analysts. However, they should know what is technically feasible to shape and communicate their vision.

Chapter 11: To stay relevant in a world set on fast forward, organizations need to ensure they have all the critical components in place to stay relevant. More than just great products and services, organizations need to ensure they have the right mix of strategy, culture, leadership and agility; the modern building blocks required for today's business continuity. This chapter will address how these components are interdependent and all contribute to creating an environment where people real Connected and inspired.

Chapter 12: Although there are classical and modern leadership styles, from a historical perspective, hybrid leadership practices have been the norm. It is essential to state that the idea of hybrid leadership is not new, nor has it resulted from hybrid working conditions. This chapter analyzes hybrid leadership from different perspectives, tracing its origins, the start of publications in the field, and its evolution. A short bibliometric analysis is included to provide a general background about how the study of hybrid leadership has evolved. The different leadership styles and models connected to hybrid leadership will be analyzed, as well as its main characteristics. The goal is to present an overview of hybrid leadership and how it has been applied in different contexts.

Chapter 13: The pandemic has accelerated the rate of change for knowledge workers from the traditional office work environment to a more remote or digital environment. In the "resignation era" – more than money, people are looking for more flexibility and control over their lives. All these factors seem to suggest a trend towards a hybrid model or virtualization in the workforce. This suggests that we need to view knowledge workers as nodes on a network, capable of accomplishing appropriate outcomes from virtually anywhere. This requires different recruitment, management, and leadership styles to better utilize the power of networking. This networked approach to knowledge work transcends geo-political boundaries which will shift employment into a more global ecosystem not just with business processing organizations (BPO's) but also into individual entrepreneurs. This extension of the ecosystem thus provides access or expands the pool of skilled knowledge workers without regard to the source of talent, relocation expense, or immigration quotas.

Matthew Ohlson
University of North Florida, USA

Lakshmi Goel
University of North Florida

Section 1

Culture and Collaboration Through the COVID-19 Era

Chapter 1
Living Our Values and Culture During Extraordinary Times

Amy Ruth
GuideWell, USA

ABSTRACT

As the COVID-19 pandemic hit every facet of our lives, GuideWell leaders quickly rose to the challenge to make sure our workforce was safe and prepared to navigate these uncertain times together. They did this by simply living out our great culture that already existed and putting their values into action. Their values influenced every decision they made, from quickly pivoting to working remotely and ensuring their members received affordable treatment and testing to championing vaccination efforts and giving back to communities in need. Their culture and values make them who they are and ground them in how they respond to any crisis situation. And most important, as a health solutions company, they led with action in a caring, compassionate way, not only for their workforce, but for their members and the communities they serve.

HOW COVID-19 SHOWED OUR TRUE COLORS

When I was asked to write this chapter and share how GuideWell has lived up to our values during the first global pandemic of our time, my first thought was "Holy COVID!" But all kidding aside, as a company, we have learned what we are truly made of during this extraordinary time.

GuideWell is a health solutions company, and includes companies like GuideWell Health, which provides health care to patients, as well as Florida Blue, Florida's Blue Cross and Blue Shield plan. Our family of forward-thinking companies

DOI: 10.4018/978-1-6684-3453-6.ch001

touches the lives of more than 15 million consumers and interacts with nearly 500 non-profits to fulfill our mission of helping people and communities achieve better health (GuideWell, 2022).

During the pandemic, we have grappled with caring for our employees, communities and customers through unprecedented challenges, at a time when they needed our services more than ever to stay healthy. And we have learned the answer to the question every company asks of itself during times of crisis, "Are we who we say we are?"

The answer, thankfully, is yes.

For us, the story starts long before COVID-19 became a household name. It starts with our values, the values we share with every new employee on their first day at orientation:

- Respect
- Integrity
- Inclusion
- Imagination
- Courage
- Excellence

At GuideWell, our values aren't just talk. We live them every day. Our values guide the decisions we make. They set the tone for how we treat our employees and customers and how we shape our culture. We want to attract and keep employees who feel strongly about these values, too.

Together with our mission statement, "To help people and communities achieve better health," we let our values drive us every step of the way when we learned the new coronavirus was spreading in the United States in early 2020. Because our values are embedded so deeply into the fabric of our organization, our response to COVID-19 wasn't about bottom lines; it was about caring for the people and communities we serve. And that always starts with our employees.

We believe employees are our greatest resource and that the better we take care of them, the better they can take care of our members. And at no time in our company's history has this ever been more important than during the COVID-19 pandemic, when our members and the communities we serve have needed our support the most. Our values of excellence and imagination guided us, because if there is any time to bring your 'A game' as a health solutions company, it's when people's lives are at stake.

We are dedicated to our customers, who we keep at the heart of everything we do. COVID-19 didn't change that one bit. In fact, the pandemic heightened this commitment to take care of our members. We made changes to make sure they could get the care they needed, from offering $0 copays for COVID treatment to expanding virtual care options, and more. And although we closed our Florida Blue Centers in 2020 and for much of 2021, our nurses and staff were still supporting members on the phone to help them get through a really challenging time.

The values of excellence and imagination our employees bring to work every day have also sparked new innovations and ideas that are changing our organization and health care for the better.

And, last but never least, our values of inclusion, integrity and excellence guided us to support our communities in any way we could. We developed a partnership with Feeding Northeast Florida to help provide food to people in need. We also led the way to promote COVID-19 vaccinations across the state of Florida, not only to protect people from getting sick, but also to help bring this pandemic to an end.

These are just a few of the ways GuideWell rose to the challenge of COVID-19 and showed its true colors during these unprecedented times. In the next section, I will share more about what we have done to lead with our values first to make sure we are protecting our employees, helping members get the care they need and supporting the communities in which we all live and work.

WE'RE IN THIS TOGETHER: CARING FOR OUR EMPLOYEES DURING A PANDEMIC

In December 2019, the first case of COVID-19 was reported in China (World Health Organization, 2020). At the time, to us here in Florida, it was a world away. In fact, our communications team published a blog in January 2020 telling our members not to worry about COVID-19, because it probably would not spread here. But spread it did.

By March 1, 2020, Florida reported its first known cases of COVID-19, and we knew we were facing an emergency unlike one any of us had ever seen before (Cutway, 2020). We're used to planning for hurricanes, not viruses. But even though it was new to us, we knew our first priority was keeping our employees safe and healthy.

Two weeks later, on March 15, after it became clear that COVID-19 was spreading across Florida and the U.S. as a whole (Cutway, 2020), we made the decision to transition most of our employees to remote working. Our CEO, Pat Geraghty, along with our Emergency Operations Center, sent a communication to let our employees know we were moving to remote working and how that transition would take place.

Moving our teams off-site wasn't as simple as sending employees home with laptops. Although GuideWell already had many remote workers and systems in place to help facilitate remote work, we were not prepared to have most of our workforce working off-site at the same time. Would our systems hold up? We weren't sure how it was going to go, but we knew we needed to make it happen. And not all of our employees were prepared to work at home. In some cases, we had employees who didn't have internet access at home or who didn't have a space to work. On top of that, schools were closed, so many of our staff members also had to care for their children and learn how to home-school — all while keeping up with their jobs.

With an incredible amount of work behind the scenes, and within a few weeks, we found a way to get employees all the resources they needed, and nearly all of our employees were successfully working remotely.

For those employees whose work is so critical to our infrastructure that they must do their work on site, we launched efforts to keep them as safe as possible while they were in their offices. We required they wear masks and we socially distanced their workspaces. Our cafeterias were closed, so we brought in lunch for our teams who were working in the office. And we kept up a rigorous cleaning schedule to ensure our facilities were sanitized and safe. Offices were deep-cleaned nightly, and sanitizer and wipes were available to employees working on site.

But ensuring employees were safe in their physical environments wasn't the only change we needed to make to address the concerns our team members had during the pandemic. One of the first questions we considered was what we should do if and when one of our employees were to get sick. We established a policy giving employees two weeks of sick time if they contracted COVID-19, and we made sure every employee who got sick and reported it received a care package. These care packages included: homemade soup, hot rolls, a dozen cookies, tissues, lozenges, a blanket and cozy socks.

We also changed a few of our HR policies to keep up with the changing situation. As lines became blurred between working from home and our normal work-life balance, we restricted meeting times so they would last under one hour and asked teams to no longer schedule meetings during lunchtime, from noon to 1 p.m. Secondly, we ensured our employees had more flexibility with their work hours, allowing modified work schedules and adding 30 minutes of personal time employees could use to help children who were at home doing school online during the early part of the pandemic, when schools were closed. Employees could use this time to take care of any personal needs that arose during the day, regardless of whether they had children at home or not.

Because we care about our employees and want them to feel engaged and have what they need to do their jobs, we implemented frequent pulse surveys to gauge our employees' needs, and find out, in general, how they were doing. Our regional presidents who lead our offices in Jacksonville, Miami, Orlando and Tampa also held regular check-ins with leaders to share best practices and find out how employees who traditionally worked in their regional offices were faring.

And perhaps most importantly, we established clear lines of communication with our team members early. We knew from past emergencies that maintaining regular communications with our team members is crucial. Because this was such an uncertain time, we decided not only to send frequent updates to our employees about the rapidly changing situation from the Emergency Operations Center, but also to have Pat reach out to them as well.

Prior to the pandemic, Pat's typical line of communication with our teams was a regular blog. But we realized quickly that our employees needed to feel supported and connected. There was fear, uncertainty and anxiety about COVID-19 and what the pandemic would mean for our daily lives. So, instead of a written blog, we began to produce weekly videos where Pat could update employees and share his thoughts about what was going on. These videos let our employees know we were all in this together, and employees voiced their appreciation for this direct line of communication from the CEO.

One employee wrote in an email to Pat, "I really appreciate getting these updates each week. It shows the level of dedication that you and all our leaders have for members and employees. It's clear that people are our business." While another said, "Thank you very much for creating these videos. It is uplifting to hear from the head of our company and to be kept up to date on what is happening. I really enjoyed hearing how we are using our kitchen equipment and staff to assist the community." (P. Geraghty, Personal communication, June 1, 2020)

One of the most important messages Pat conveyed to our team members in 2020 was not to worry about going back into the office. We committed at the beginning to listen to the science and the feedback from experts at the Centers for Disease Control & Prevention. And we made a commitment to our employees that we would not plan to reoccupy our campus until there was a vaccine or a treatment for COVID-19.

Soon, these videos from Pat became weekly conference calls where employees could ask Pat questions directly. Eventually, these calls became video Q&As. How we communicated to our employees during the heat of the pandemic and how we moved forward with communications has definitely evolved in a positive way.

Another issue we faced was to help our team leaders adjust to managing remote teams. Although GuideWell already had a policy for employees to work remotely if they wanted to do so and their jobs allowed for it, many of our managers had never managed remote employees before. Despite the physical distance we now faced, it was equally important to make sure our teams stayed connected.

To help, our HR teams provided a lot of support to our managers to make this transition as seamless as possible. We created talking points leaders could use with their team members to help them understand what things were changing and why. We also provided resources and tips leaders could use to help manage the stress they may be feeling, as well as the stress their employees were feeling. Many of our managers held more frequent meetings with teams, just to give them space to share any concerns they had about what was going on.

As the pandemic wore on, we also started to encourage our employees to be ambassadors for safe behavior, too. We encouraged employees to wear their masks in public, and once the vaccines began to roll out, we not only encouraged employees to get their shot, but also gave them two hours of personal time off just for getting it.

After the vaccines became available to all adults, we started to develop plans to return to campus in July 2021. But we let all employees know they did not have to return to the office if they did not want to work on-site. And we started bringing people back in slowly. Due to the surge of the COVID Delta variant in the summer of 2021, some of these plans were halted. While some of our employees have returned to the office — often finding calendars still turned to March 2020 in their workspaces— most of our staff remains remote as of January 2022.

One of the things we learned very early in the pandemic is that remote work did not slow our employees down at all. We have maintained the same level of pre-pandemic productivity throughout 2020 and into 2021 and beyond, despite the obstacles we have faced. We also, thankfully, never had to make layoffs as a result of this crisis. This is great news considering the past two years have been a trying time for our members, too. Our employees have continued to show their dedication to taking care of our members and putting them first. It's what we like to call living our mission.

HELP WHEN YOU NEED IT MOST: SUPPORTING OUR MEMBERS TO GET THE CARE THEY NEED

As mentioned earlier in this chapter, our customers are truly at the heart of everything we do, and for us, this dedication to the people we serve is definitely a point of pride. So, just as we committed to taking care of our employees at the start of COVID-19, we were equally dedicated to making sure it was as easy as possible for our members to get the care they needed during the pandemic.

Living through a global pandemic is challenging enough. But some of our members were also losing their jobs due to closures or worrying about who was going to take care of their children while they worked. We didn't want our members to also worry about the cost of COVID-19 treatment or how to get the care they needed safely.

One of the first changes we made was to waive the cost of COVID treatment for our members. Until September 2021, our members had a $0 cost-share for COVID-19 treatment. This was a relief for one of our members, Sharon[i], who talked to one of our nurse care managers, Betty Khan, while she was still in the hospital recovering from COVID-19. Betty could tell how worried Sharon was about the bill for her six-day stay in the hospital and was able to reassure her there would be no cost-share for her hospitalization. (B. Khan, Personal communication, March 29, 2021)

"She made me feel as though I was part of the Florida Blue family; a family that cared about me and a family that wanted me to quickly recuperate and make it out of the hospital safely," Sharon said. "I was relieved when she called me and thankful to God for Betty" (B. Khan, Personal communication, March 29, 2021).

But we also needed to make sure our members were able to still get the regular, everyday health care they needed at a time when they may not want to leave their homes to be around people. This was especially true for our members who are older or who have health conditions that put them at greater risk for complications if they were to get COVID-19.

Enter virtual care.

Many of our health plans already included some access to virtual care before the pandemic. But not all members were aware of how virtual care works or how to get it. Our communications team put special emphasis on this in the communications we created for members, letting them know how to access virtual health care through virtual health providers, like Teladoc, and through our GuideWell Health doctors and through their local doctors who began offering virtual care.

For our Medicare members, specifically, we added the virtual health provider Teladoc as a benefit to our 2020 Medicare Advantage plans. And our 2021 Medicare Advantage plans included more virtual health benefits than ever before.

And perhaps most importantly of all, we took immediate steps to make sure our members could keep their health plans, even if they were facing financial struggles due to the pandemic. We immediately offered payment extensions for our individual/family and group plan members. We expanded the available options members had to pay their bill and even offered a $500 incentive to help members pay their premium. (Florida Blue, 2020)

One of the most crucial steps we took to make sure our members felt cared for was to send out frequent communications to our members throughout the pandemic. At such an uncertain time with misinformation swirling around, we wanted them to feel informed and know they could count on us.

Because we wanted our members and the public to know they could trust the information we were sharing with them, we relied on our medical team to begin sharing information with the public in a new way. Throughout the pandemic, three of our doctors have taken the lead on holding interactive webinars to help educate the public and answer their questions about COVID-19.

Dr. Kelli Tice, M.D., our senior medical director, led webinars and other outreach efforts to help people understand a variety of COVID-19 related issues. Dr. Elizabeth Malko, M.D., our vice president for Medicare Solutions, has led webinars and answered questions about COVID-19 for our Medicare members, while Dr. Nick Dewan, our vice president for behavioral health, has led webinars to help answer members' questions about their emotional health and coping during the pandemic.

Although we closed our Florida Blue Centers to the public through July 2021, our team of social workers was still working remotely, taking calls and helping our members in any way they could. Some of these queries have been as simple as helping a member understand more about COVID-19 and how long it could stay on surfaces — a big concern early in the pandemic — to finding resources for food, transportation and more.

Aside from helping our members on a personal scale, we also have led campaigns to help support the health of our communities as a whole. In the fall of 2020, we launched the #GetMaskedFL campaign to encourage people to protect themselves, their families and community by wearing a mask in public. We launched a social media campaign to let people know that wearing a mask wasn't just about protecting yourself, but about protecting the people you love. We wanted to encourage people to do their part to slow the spread of COVID-19. So, we shared photos of CEO Pat Geraghty wearing a mask and encouraged others to show their masks, too. (Florida Blue, 2020)

Thankfully, by early 2021, a COVID-19 vaccine was available. We strongly believe the vaccine is the best available weapon against COVID-19. The vaccine provided a way to get back to living and sharing moments with our families and friends. And we think everyone should have equal access to getting their vaccination. That's why we played a significant role in vaccination efforts across our state of Florida. Our GuideWell Health facilities administered up to 15,000 vaccines a week, to members and non-members. (GuideWell, 2021) We also have held COVID-19 vaccination events at some of our office locations to make it convenient for our team members and their family members to get vaccinated.

Some of our members could even earn a $10 gift card from us just for getting their vaccine. We also worked to bring vaccines to homebound older adults, held vaccine events in historically underserved communities and offered transportation to a vaccine appointment for our Medicare members. Our members in many individual under 65 plans also could use a Lyft benefit to get to their vaccine appointment.

One of our main goals throughout this pandemic has been to ease the worry our members were feeling. This pandemic has lingered longer than any of us hoped, and it has been difficult for everyone. As leaders and employees, we know how it feels because we have been going through the same things. So, hopefully, our efforts have helped to take some of the burden off our members' shoulders.

Next, I will share what we have done to give back to our communities in what has been an unprecedented time of need.

PAYING IT FORWARD: GIVING BACK TO OUR COMMUNITIES IN A TIME OF NEED

As I mentioned earlier in this chapter, our values are deeply embedded in our company's culture. So, naturally, as we thought about how to best help our employees and members through this crisis, our thoughts also turned to the communities in which we live and the health care providers we work with. Not only did we want to support individuals, but also we needed to care for the communities we're part of and the hospitals and other health care organizations we rely on to keep us well.

Early in the pandemic, after most of our employees had switched to remote work, we closed our cafeterias on our Jacksonville campus. Unfortunately, that meant there was no work for our food service staff. We came up with an innovative solution to keep our workers employed and help people in Northeast Florida at the same time. We partnered with Feeding Northeast Florida to produce meals for older adults in need. Our food service employees prepared nearly one-half million meals, which were distributed to seniors. (GuideWell, 2020)

Every year, we hold a United Way campaign and match what our employees contribute to help support nonprofits in the communities in which our employees live and work. During the pandemic, we upped our match, initiating a \$2-for-\$1 match because we knew our local nonprofits needed the extra support. (GuideWell, 2020)

Additionally, we have been working closely with health care providers and hospital systems throughout the pandemic to help prevent a cash flow crisis for these institutions. In 2020, revenues were down for many hospital systems, but their costs were very high as they dealt with an influx of patients who needed complex care to treat COVID-19 (American Hospital Association, 2020). We also actively advocated for our state and federal governments to do their part to maintain the integrity of our health care system during a time when all of us need it the most.

Our community investments during the COVID-19 pandemic totaled in the millions. And again, for us, this time of crisis wasn't about bottom lines; it was about doing whatever we could to help the people and communities we serve to achieve better health. There has never been a more important time to make sure all Americans have access to high quality and affordable health care. Not only has the pandemic caused catastrophic health challenges, illness and death in our communities, many people lost their health care coverage in 2020 due to closed businesses, job losses and layoffs. (Cox, 2020)

While health disparities already existed in many of our underserved communities, where higher proportions of Black families live, COVID-19 worsened them (Peace, 2022). Black adults are twice as likely to die from heart disease as white adults and are 50 percent more likely to have high blood pressure, according to the Centers for Disease Control and Prevention (CDC, 2017). Our mission is to help people and communities achieve better health, which cannot happen without addressing the drivers of health (or social determinants of health) that affect our communities.

We are strongly committed to taking bold and measurable action to promote diversity, equity, inclusion and belonging among our employees, customers, partners and communities. And we are advocating for change across the health care industry as a whole. The health care industry must expand its focus to factors outside the traditional health care model that can impact health and costs. In doing so, we will be better positioned to provide a holistic approach to care and improve health outcomes in underprivileged communities.

In May of 2020, we established the GuideWell Equity Alliance, an enterprise-wide initiative focused on addressing systemic racism and health inequities for Black Americans in the communities we serve. As noted, we also made sure that vaccines reached underserved communities by holding vaccination events within those communities and making it easier for people to get the vaccine by offering transportation to vaccine appointments and events.

While we have worked hard to take care of the people and communities we serve right now, we have also kept an eye on improving health care outcomes in the future. Throughout this crisis, we have remained a hub for innovation by tackling many of the health care challenges that affected our communities during the pandemic.

In July 2020, GuideWell, in collaboration with XPRIZE, OpenCovidScreen, several Blue Cross Blue Shield plans and other innovative organizations, announced a $5 million XPRIZE Rapid COVID Testing competition. This competition was used to accelerate the development of high-quality COVID-19 testing that is low cost, easy to use, and quick-reporting, paving the way for more frequent testing. (GuideWell, 2020)

Also, as we began navigating the COVID-19 pandemic, the GuideWell Innovation team launched a national effort to develop a COVID-19 Health Innovation Collaborative to bring entrepreneurs together to address major challenges our health care system was facing. And just as our country was experiencing a new level of racial reckoning, the team hosted a virtual health equity challenge and well-being forum.

In addition, living through a pandemic and working remotely sparked new ideas from our teams during our annual innovation challenge in 2020. Our employees thought of novel ways to improve how we conduct business and the service we offer to our customers.

STAYING SAFE IN OUR "NEW NORMAL": SAFETY IS OUR TOP PRIORITY FOR OUR EMPLOYEES, MEMBERS AND COMMUNITIES

As we move forward, we will continue to lead with our values. It's what we have always done at GuideWell. Our values guide us and show us what is truly important, and what our priorities should be, whether it's a time of crisis or not.

Our goals and priorities remain the same. We want our employees to be safe, healthy and engaged throughout this crisis and beyond. We want to help our members and the communities we serve achieve better health. And we want to do our part to make sure health care is available to everyone.

But some things will change — they have to — and that has been an important lesson for all of us. The past two years have required us all to be flexible, to adapt to change quickly and respond to new science and recommendations. As new information emerges, we will continue to change and evolve to meet the needs of our employees, members and communities. This is probably the most important promise we can make to the people we serve.

In early 2021, we put together a plan to allow employees to return to campus if they were vaccinated and wanted to be back in the office. In July, phase 1 of our re-occupancy plan launched, with 10 percent of our workforce returning to our campuses.

However, we remain firmly committed to allowing all employees who can work at home to remain remote if they choose. In fact, we have polled our employees and 70 percent of them want to remain remote long term. And they showed us very early in this pandemic that not only can they work remotely, but they can do it extremely well. Because of the great amount of respect we have for our team, we want them to be in the environment that works best for them.

As of January 2022, we are still doing most things remotely. But we have put together guidance to help our teams navigate this when the time comes. We have determined how to best hold on-site meetings and events so our remote employees can keep the flexibility they value while also being able to attend meetings and events in person, when needed, so we can retain the culture we've built that our employees love.

Aside from remote work, one of the other things that rose to new heights during this pandemic was the use of telehealth, or virtual care. The pandemic forced us to deliver care in new and different ways. As people seek to return to normal, we may not continue to use telehealth as much as we did during the past two years, but telehealth is sure to grow. Patients who at one time were reluctant to try virtual care quickly became advocates, given how easy and convenient it is. Providers also embraced telehealth. And, as our tech-savvy younger generations grow up, they likely will want to have telehealth available as an option.

And we will continue to tackle the issues that make health care too expensive for some people to afford. Prior to COVID-19, we were already facing a health care affordability crisis. The urgency of the pandemic has brought these issues to the forefront. We applaud the administration's effort to get more people the health care coverage they need and deserve through the Affordable Care Act (ACA) Special Enrollment Period. Enhancing the ACA will be an important next step toward increasing access for more people.

None of us expected to be in this situation this long, but here we are. We have been tested and challenged in ways we never anticipated. However, we have to look at what we have learned during this time and what we will take away.

We have learned to be flexible. We have learned the importance of resilience.

And most importantly, we have learned that whatever the future holds, we will get through it by respecting each other's values and by nurturing a corporate culture built on these values. At GuideWell, our employees, members and the communities we serve will always be our top priority. As long as we put them first, we can overcome just about anything.

REFERENCES

American Hospital Association. (2020, June 30). *New AHA Report Finds Losses Deepen for Hospitals and Health Systems Due to COVID-19*. Retrieved from https://www.aha.org/issue-brief/2020-06-30-new-aha-report-finds-losses-deepen-hospitals-and-health-systems-due-covid-19

Centers for Disease Control and Prevention. (2017, July 3). *African-American Health article*. https://www.cdc.gov/vitalsigns/aahealth/index.html#:~:text=African%20Americans%20ages%2018%2D49,high%20blood%20pressure%20than%20whites

Cox, C. (2020, December 9). *How Has the Pandemic Affected Health Coverage in the U.S.?* Kaiser Family Foundation. https://www.kff.org/policy-watch/how-has-the-pandemic-affected-health-coverage-in-the-u-s/

Cutway, A. (2020, September 25). *Timeline: The spread of coronavirus in Florida*. https://www.clickorlando.com/news/local/2020/03/20/timeline-the-spread-of-coronavirus-in-florida/

Florida Blue (2020). *Rewards to Help You with Premium Payments and Medical Expenses*. Retrieved from https://www.floridablue.com/blog/rewards-to-help-you

Florida Blue [@floridabluehealth]. (2020, September 4). #GetMaskedFL [Status update]. On *Facebook*. https://fb.watch/d69PU2i-eQ/.

GuideWell. (2020). *2021 GuideWell Social Impact Report*. Retrieved from https://www.floridablue.com/binaries/content/assets/floridablue/misc/2021-guidewell-social-impact-report.pdf

GuideWell. (2021). *Grand prize winners selected in $6M XPRIZE Rapid COVID Testing competition to create fast, frequent, cheap and easy-to-use solutions*. Retrieved from https://www.guidewell.com/tags/blog/xprize

GuideWell. (2021). *Pat Geraghty Full Transcript: Moments of Hope Show We're Turning a Corner*. Retrieved from https://www.guidewell.com/blog/pat-geraghty-full-transcript-moments-hope-show-were-turning-corner

GuideWell. (2022). *Who We Are*. Retrieved from https://www.guidewell.com/who-we-are

Peace, L. (2022, February 27). Florida health equity experts reflect on progress, setbacks two years into COVID. *The Tampa Bay Times*. https://www.tampabay.com/news/health/2022/02/27/florida-health-equity-experts-reflect-on-progress-setbacks-two-years-into-covid/

World Health Organization. (2020). *Archived: WHO Timeline - COVID-19*. https://www.who.int/news/item/27-04-2020-who-timeline---covid-19

KEY TERMS AND DEFINITIONS

Affordable Care Act (ACA): The Affordable Care Act is a comprehensive health care reform law enacted in March 2010 (sometimes known as ACA, PPACA, or "Obamacare").

Blue Cross Blue Shield: Since 1929, Blue Cross Blue Shield (BCBS) companies have provided health care coverage to members, allowing them to live free of worry, free of fear. In every ZIP code, Blue Cross Blue Shield offers a personalized approach to health care based on the needs of the communities where their members live and work.

COVID-19: Coronavirus disease (COVID-19) is an infectious disease caused by the SARS-CoV-2 virus.

COVID-19 Vaccine: The COVID-19 vaccine is designed to prevent COVID-19 infection or reduce a person's risk of severe illness.

Florida Blue: Florida Blue, the leading health insurer in Florida, has been providing health insurance to residents of Florida for more than 75 years. Driven by its mission of helping people and communities achieve better health, the company serves more than 5 million health care members across the state. In total, Florida Blue and its affiliated companies serve 16 million people in 29 states. Headquartered in Jacksonville, Fla., it is an independent licensee of the Blue Cross and Blue Shield Association.

Florida Blue Centers: Florida Blue Centers help our members navigate their health care and talk to someone face-to-face in their community. Each of our Florida Blue Centers offers a variety of programs, classes, and events.

GuideWell: GuideWell and its family of forward-thinking companies are focused on helping people and communities achieve better health and are at the forefront in the transformation of health care. The not-for-profit mutual holding company includes Florida Blue, GuideWell Connect, GuideWell Health and Diversified Service Options, Inc.

Medicare Advantage: Medicare Advantage plans include all the same benefits covered in Medicare Parts A and B, and many of these plans offer additional drug, vision, hearing, dental and wellness coverage.

Pat Geraghty: Patrick "Pat" Geraghty is president and chief executive officer (CEO) of GuideWell Mutual Holding Corporation, Florida Blue and GuideWell Group, Inc.

Virtual Care/Telehealth: Virtual care, or telehealth, allows patients to have health care visits with their doctors and other providers using technology.

ENDNOTE

1 Name changed to protect privacy.

Chapter 2
Setting the Stage for Performance and Accountability Through Expectations

Justin M. Sipes
University of North Florida, USA

ABSTRACT

This chapter stresses the importance of expectations and their role in performance and accountability. In a hybrid work environment, unclear expectations can lead to adverse performance and difficulties with accountability. The chapter encourages the use of dialogue to establish expectations and strategies to that end. Overall, expectations are a process and are dynamic. They need to be revisited often. Shared expectations are a strong foundation that contributes to the clarity of tasks and can enhance performance. They outline accountability, and the practice of developing can make the evaluation of performance easier. As more employees ask for flexible work and more employers are trying to meet these needs, expectations are crucial in establishing environments that maximize performance and accountability.

"I am just getting back into the fold of things, and I am immediately overwhelmed. I am being asked to do more with far less. Our full-time professional staff was reduced with the expectation of filling those gaps with part-time employees. I can barely staff my area to do our basic suite of programs, let alone any new ones. It is beyond frustrating. Not only am I dealing with this, but I also have multiple people in my life with significant COVID-related issues. I have long haul COVID effects

DOI: 10.4018/978-1-6684-3453-6.ch002

that I am struggling with and trying to make sure that my son is safe too. Being able to do more of a hybrid approach would ease many of these burdens but that is not an option for me. I am looking for other opportunities as I feel there are too many limitations restricting me and making it far more difficult than necessary."

This is paraphrasing a recent conversation that I had with a colleague, Ryan, and is likely similar to what many are experiencing. This person returned to an in-person environment and was met with numerous challenges further compounded by issues many of which are out of this individual's control. More frustrating is that this person really felt helpless and was not sure of what to do based on the circumstances. We chatted for a bit more and it became clearer that the colleague was concerned with performing at the same level pre-pandemic and being held accountable if things did not work out, even when some of the issues were out of the individual's control. Moreover, the colleague was looking for flexibility. Ideally, a transition to a hybrid work environment might have been conducive to his situation and could have eased some of the burden. Through an extensive literature review, Baker (2021) found remote work provided numerous prospective advantages including increased retention, productivity, and work satisfaction.

Reflecting on this conversation, it dawned on me that there was a misalignment of expectations that needed resolution. This dissonance was creating unease around performance standards and concerns for accountability. To explore what this might mean in the current and post-pandemic environment, it is important to consider the current literature and emerging research on expectations, performance, and accountability in hybrid work environments. Mahfoodh et al. (2021) ask a most prescient question in light of the shift to hybrid workspaces, "How might we implement a trust culture based on employees' accountability and credibility performance of tasks?"

LEADERSHIP

Before diving deeper into these concepts, a brief aside about leadership in hybrid workspaces. Baker et al (2007) suggested a management culture of support and trust is essential for effective and successful work from home (WFH) arrangements. Neufeld and Fang (2005) determined crucial to WFH productivity was managerial attitudes and beliefs about WFH and in turn how these attitudes and beliefs were influenced by social interactions with colleagues, managers, and family members. van Dyne et al (2007) found managers want to monitor employees which is easier to achieve when employees report to an office, therefore, support for WFH can be negated by managers who are negative about team workers working remotely.

Additional research (Baker et al., 2007; Peters & den Dulk, 2003) found national cultures can affect the acceptance of WFH and a manager's willingness to delegate trust and power. Furthermore, van der Lippe and Lippenyi (2019) found managers rate team productivity higher when co-workers WFH no more than one day per week, yet rated overall team performance as inferior.

Leadership challenges are magnified in a hybrid environment with implications for communication, trust, collaboration, socialization, overall team effectiveness, and recognition of employee individuality (Baker, 2021; Pauleen, 2004). Critical leadership actions are maintaining communication, establishing relationships, and managing conflict (Zander et al., 2012). Furthermore, Bentley et al (2016) suggested providing peer, organizational, and technical support as these are factors to simultaneously promote work satisfaction and performance while also diminish adverse impacts on remote work including stress, social isolation, and work/family conflict. Kronfli (2021) states "employers have a responsibility to create and foster an environment that is healthy and safe – both physically and psychologically" (p. 14).

Absence of face-to-face contact leads to problems in communication and relationship development, lack of trust, cultural mismatch, and complex conflict handling (De Paoli & Ropo, 2015). Further research (Dose & Klimoski, 1995; Ferris et al., 1995; Maclagan, 1983) showed the importance of managerial trust for satisfaction, wherein trustworthy individuals are likely to respond negatively to controlling managers. Moreover, Bjorn and Ngwenyama (2009) find that "communication breakdowns related to a lack of shared meaning at the lifeworld level often becomes more salient when the participants are co-located than when geographically distributed" (p. 227). In a report by Barnakova and Krupp (2021), they identify a communication paradox in hybrid workspaces in balancing informational and intimate. They go on to suggest communicating early, often, and transparently, listen actively and openly, and to model an open, caring culture by being vulnerable.

In the De Paoli and Ropo (2015) study, managers stressed the need for teams to meet face-to-face at the beginning of the project and to develop a joint understanding of goals and tasks, especially when people have not previously met and when the task is complex and demanding. This face-to-face interaction was seen as important for motivating people, sharing information and integrating knowledge, getting a feeling of the project and, as a leader, getting a grasp of how things are going. Furthermore, investing additional resources mental health and wellness can lead to "more engaged, motivated, and supported employees; reduced absenteeism, presenteeism, and drug and disability claims; improved productivity and performance; better health outcomes … and help attract and retain talent" (Kronfli, 2021, p. 14).

A suggested solution to hybrid workplace issues is adapting leadership styles and roles. De Paoli and Ropo (2015) found literature to support the use of distribution and delegation of leadership functions and responsibilities (Bell & Kozlowski, 2002) through self- and shared leadership (Davis & Bryant, 2003; Muethel & Hoegl, 2010; Zigurs, 2002), emergent leadership (Kirkman et al., 2004), and transformational leadership (Joshi & Lazarova, 2005; Mendenhall et al., 2012). Alternatively, a traditional leader-centric approach with focus on the abilities of the team leader (Pauleen, 2004; Wakefield et al., 2008; Zhang & Fjermestad, 2006) could also be used in hybrid settings. Barnakova & Krupp (2021) recommend that "leaders who create new paradigms for how we work can create thriving cultures with high engagement and performance, a critical advantage in an exploding war for talent" (p. 2). Baker (2021) found that WFH might have consequences for individual-level performance, and it is imperative on the leader to consider how employees impact each other and how they utilize each other's knowledge and skills.

According to Barnakova and Krupp (2021), people have been getting more done with more autonomy and less time spent commuting with a stronger focus on key business priorities and more accountability. Baker (2021) suggested to focus on what is right for the people, the business, and the work environment. Barnakova and Krupp (2021) highlight five paradoxes for employers to consider for hybrid work environments: (a) inclusion; (b) communication; (c) career development; (d) productivity; and (e) innovation.

For purposes of this chapter, the first four are the most relevant to further examination and will be addressed at different points in this chapter. At the same time, it is important to note that almost everyone at some point is in the position of being an employer and employee and often holds these identities simultaneously. The following chapter will often switch between the two to emphasize certain points, but the dominant tone is that of the employer.

EXPECTATIONS

Expectations are vital to relationships. They establish what the involved parties are willing to do and contribute to make the relationship work. Expectations might be interpreted as job descriptions, job responsibilities, ethical statements, policies, regulations, strategic plans, and so forth. They might seem like a contract but in reality, expectations should be more pliable than an authorized document from legal counsel. Where these documents will have a part to play in expectations, and should help to ground expectations, expectations they are not. More often than not, these documents tend to be theoretical, but can become more practical when integrated with feedback (Mahfoodh et al., 2021).

Furthermore, frequent communication and relationship development is more important in hybrid environments (Zigurs, 2002) because the focus tends to be more on the task and technology than relations (De Paoli & Ropo, 2015). This is why expectations **should** be a dialogue. The results of that dialogue might be written down to document the conversation, but the actual process of forming expectations **should** be a dialogue.

If you had not noticed, **should** is bolded for emphasis because this is often not what goes down. Unfortunately, expectations are often dictated and there is no process. It is simply a transaction.

"Here are the expectations. Thank you for your time. See you at your next performance appraisal or when you fall short, whichever comes first. By the way, there will probably not be any feedback along the way, so the first time you will find out you are not meeting expectations will be at the mandated performance appraisal. You know, the one that I am begrudgingly participating in only because I consistently receive threatening emails from human resources, so I am already completing it in a negative space which I then take out on you. Have a great day and see you at our next human resources mandated meeting!"

Though the text might be facetious, it is not. Ultimately, this approach robs both the supervisor and supervisee of what could be a transformational opportunity. Treating expectations as a dialogue creates the chance to form trust, build a relationship, and have the employee feel and be heard and included. Often in the literature, the importance of communication and trust is stressed in professional environments (Aubert & Kelsey, 2003; De Paoli & Ropo, 2015; Hoegl et al., 2012; Jarvenpaa & Leidner, 1999; Krebs et al., 2006; Zigurs, 2002).

This takes dedicated time and energy. The initial dialogue is a starting point. What this means is that expectations are meant to be dynamic. Unlike the documents listed previously that are rigid and usually based on a specific timeframe, expectations should be revisited often. This requires checking in and taking more time to continue to engage in meaningful dialogue around the topic. It requires a deeper investment in the employee. Costikyan (2021) recommends 30 days for new hybrid work arrangements and at least one annual review.

More importantly, in today's environment, this dialogue should happen sooner rather than later. Operating under old (pre-pandemic) expectations is setting up employees for failure. Conditions have changed significantly even if things feel as if they are going back to "normal." There are new challenges that exist and an absence of dialogue about expectations is doing a disservice to all parties involved. As more workplaces consider hybrid environments, the importance of clearly defined roles, duties, and rights becomes even more crucial to employee performance and accountability (Mahfoodh et al., 2021).

Not too long ago in the height of the pandemic, I was in a virtual training with colleagues on ethical practices in the workplace, where an audience question confounded me a bit. The individual, Anna, asked if there was an organization policy for timely response to emails. The presenters did not have an official response beyond what they would recommend. Without prompting Anna continued, it became clearer that they believed the employer should have a universal policy established. There was frustration that a policy was established for that unit, and it was not similar across all units, therefore, making it more difficult to hold employees in Anna's unit accountable.

Anna's question might seem trivial in the grand scheme of things, and arguably it very much is. An email response within 24 hours compared to 48 hours, often is not a make-or-break proposition. In addition, if it is an emergency situation, email typically is not the best way to communicate a need for expediency. Nevertheless, the question was laid bare before the presenters and attendees. After providing some more feedback, the presenters opened it to the audience for their suggestions. I waited a beat to see if anyone else was going to chime in. Silence permeated the space. I unmuted and said,

"We have a 24–48-hour expectation in our unit and it is something we all agreed to as a collective staff as reasonable and appropriate for our area. If at any point in time in the future, we deem it is not working for whatever reason, we will revisit that expectation. Where it can be frustrating that other units do not have a similar expectation, we also understand that our unit is different compared to others. Therefore, I cannot expect those units to respond to us in the same fashion. Their day-to-day goals are different than ours, so we need to respect that and work with it."

There were head nods of those with cameras on demonstrating some tacit acceptance and agreement with the response. Anna's head did not move.

To me, it seemed that Anna set a policy for the employees of that unit without a conversation with the employees and expected others throughout the organization to do the same in alignment with what Anna believed to be best. It is important to note Anna wanted a policy.

Policies are rigid, formal, restrictive. They often are not practical or oriented to the people they affect or who implement them (Mahfoodh et al., 2021). Costikyan (2021) suggests "policy as the platform and guidelines as the scaffolding, which ensure that both processes and outcomes are: (1) equitable, (2) without bias or favoritism, (3) job appropriate and driven by business needs, (4) net-neutral or net-positive in effect, (5) dynamic and responsive to change, and (6) documented for accountability and to inform larger institutional decisions" (p. 1). It is good to have parameters, but hard and fast rules or policies can often become excuses that hamper change. More importantly, policy makes it easier to say "no" and often neglects the realities of day-to-day situations. Again, Costikyan (2021) suggests it is best to "provide broad guidelines that enable 'local' discretion combined with clear accountability" (p. 3).

So, the question becomes how to have a dialogue about expectations. Like most things in life, practice makes the process easier. First, it is understanding what dialogue is and what it is not. Bohm (2008) authored an excellent book, On Dialogue, which can assist with education on the topic. It is highly philosophical and extremely dense, yet an amazing and relatively short read. In synopsis the goal of dialogue is a way for each person to share their perspective with one another. It is not an attempt to prove one party is right and the other wrong. If it results in someone's changed opinion, then great but not the purpose. The purpose is the process of trust and active listening. It requires openness and care which often seem difficult to provide especially in the high-paced, results-oriented world. The catch is that taking the time to create the conditions for actual dialogue will result in a better product over time.

There is no official script to the dialogue of expectations. Inherently, it will be different for each interaction as each employee is different. Their needs and wants are unique. The lingering effects of the pandemic also enter the fold. Now that many have experienced the opportunity to work from home, expectations around flexible work environments are in demand with increased desires for hybrid situations. Obviously, the capacity to work from home will fluctuate based on the field and industry. Nonetheless employees are looking for the ability to have more control of their schedules and create a harmonious life-work situation.

And who can argue? With the evolution of technology, work has become more ubiquitous, permeating more aspects of our lives. We are constantly surrounded by and to a certain degree immersed in it. As technology advanced, our relationship to work also changed. Expectations were often negotiated without employee input and the new norm shifted to "one is always working." To a certain degree, the pandemic forced employers to revisit this unspoken contract as employees were coping with previous demands and responsibilities in new ways. Kronfli (2021) finds this includes "dealing with fatigue as employees juggle professional and family responsibilities, promoting social connections while maintaining physical distancing, managing performance and productivity remotely, virtually supporting employee mental health, and much more" (p. 5).

Now is not the time to revoke alterations and go back to the old patterns. "Organization successes forged during the crisis need to be hardwired into the new operating model; and leaders must ensure their organizations do not revert to old behaviors and processes" (De Smet et al., 2020, p. 2). It is an opportunity to determine a new path forward that is respectful of employees needs while balancing the needs of the employer. These do not need to be in competition with one another and in fact can operate in harmony. Furthermore, Baker (2021) suggested finding a balance of how much time employees should spend remote and, in the office, when implementing a hybrid workplace, where Bentley et al (2016) found managers perceived 1-3 days of remote work as a suitable balance of flexibility and promoting interaction among colleagues. Costikyan (2021) offers that in making these transitions one of the things to keep in mind is guarding against the signaling of constant work.

A blanket approach is no longer acceptable. This is a benefit of dialogue in crafting expectations. A household with children might need the capacity to work from home if there is a quarantine situation at the school. An employee with elderly parents might need to be cautious in the work environment and reduce the number of in person meetings when possible. People quickly transitioned to hybrid workspaces and for many it was a better fit for their life. It "requires making permanent structural changes that can sustain speed in ways that will inspire and engage employees" (De Smet et al., 2020, p. 2).

Challenges presented by the pandemic are not evaporating before our eyes. The pandemic brought to light issues of equity that were always present, lying in wait just below the surface. Now, they are standing before us and there needs to be a rational, empathetic response.

A recent TedTalk from Angela Garbes (2021) highlights these changes from the perspective of working parents. In fact, Baker (2021) hypothesized a hybrid workplace might be enticing to employees with young children, since it can be sustainable and flexible enough to meet the demands of their familial situation. What Garbes (2021) talks about are not new issues, but ones that have become more prominent in the pandemic: paid family leave, open environments to talk about children, and work that gets done versus tracking time. For the latter, Angela talks specifically about the hours of 5PM to 8PM being crucial to families and that sending an email at 8:30PM is more conducive to the life-work harmony for many working parents. Is the "normal" 9AM – 5PM still the most advantageous traditional working hours for many? Does that really produce one's best work?

In light of recent work from home orders and seeing employees still be productive, my team agreed to continue to work from home one day a week in accordance with an existing but not well-known human resources policy. This has not hampered productivity in any way, and anecdotally, I believe it has been more beneficial to the organization and employees. It provides employees the freedom to take care of errands and schedule appointments on work from home days. It can be extremely helpful to throw a load of laundry in the washer in between meetings or to start cooking at 4:30PM instead of 5:30PM after commuting home. Sitting in a chair in an office simply to clock hours does not actually help anyone.

This is where the advancement of technology has created conditions to provide flexibility and ultimately better productivity. For example, DeFilippis et al (2020) found hybrid employees may have generated more flexible schedules to accommodate for daily disruptions that contribute to increases in the productivity and duration of the average workday. Granted not all work environments can provide that level of plasticity to their employees, as noted by Boell et al (2016) that it will depend on the nature of the work, but employers should start figuring out how and where they can provide these options to employees. More employees are seeking these options.

Not to pick on Anna, but at another meeting in discussing characteristics and qualities for a new president, Anna declared that we are losing qualified staff to other area institutions because we cannot offer similar financial compensation and work flexibility compared to those campuses. It was deemed a responsibility for a new president to sort out, but in actuality it is not. It is up to Anna. It is easy to jump to external factors for employee dissatisfaction. It is more difficult to reflect on one's own responsibility in that equation that led to an employee leaving. Where there are limitations for financial compensation, then what is the environment created to retain employees? What opportunities were explored for more flexible work? Did the employees feel valued? Did they feel like they belonged? This is a new challenge for employers to face as employees are more open to switching companies to seek upward mobility and different conditions that promote more harmonious life-work situations, such as hybrid workplaces.

In both of these situations with Anna, I believe they had more control of the outcomes than what they believed they did. This speaks to connections between expectations, performance, and accountability. Sound expectations lead to clear evaluation of performance which contributes to a shared accountability.

At the end of the day, having a dialogue about expectations does not mean that the employer needs to acquiesce to every need of an employee. It simply means listening to what an employee needs and then balancing that with the needs of the employer in a way to optimize employee contributions. It means finding where there are opportunities to provide flexibility, but also having a clear understanding of what is not possible. This latter statement requires conversations with human resources and other managers to determine what and where those breaking points are.

It also means presenting to the employee rationale beyond a simple "no." "No" is easy. There is no effort expelled to say "no." If it is a human resources issue, then dig a little deeper to provide the rationale for the "no." Perhaps, the "no" does not need to be a "no." It simply is something that has never been a question before, or it is an issue that needs to be revisited. Even if the answer is still a "no," at least the investigation prompts a good faith effort for the employee and can deepen the level of trust in the relationship. The employee knows that you are willing to ask questions on their behalf. Again, trust is vital to a strong working relationship. The more trust one can build, the increased likelihood of employee retention and satisfaction (Baker, 2021).

What is often forgotten about expectations is that they are more than what the employee will do for the employer. They are also about what the employer will do for the employee. This is why it is vital for expectations to be facilitated by dialogue and not decree. The expectations should also lay out what is expected of the employer. Again, this information may be found in some human resources documents or onboarding practices. However, it is more about the actual process of dialogue between the employee and employer. Expectations go both ways.

As the employer, you lay the groundwork for the conversation. You determine how to make this happen. As the employee, you cannot hope that the employer will do this. It is important to figure out where the opportunities present themselves to engage in meaningful dialogue around expectations. If you do not believe the employer is broaching the issue, then plan to discuss it in a future meeting or request time to have that chat. It is important to the long-term success of both parties.

The employer-employee dynamic is just that, dynamic. It changes based on the people, and it changes over time. Because organizations are people dependent, it is innate that they will change as new people enter and leave and move throughout the organization.

If and when you find yourself in the employee role with an employer who is not open to dialogue around expectations, then the task falls to you. The likelihood of having a meeting solely about expectations is farfetched, so find ways to seamlessly introduce the conversation in other ways. "Hey Tim, I know we have that meeting coming up Friday for the new project, could we take a few minutes either before or after to chat about flexing my time a bit to accommodate some changing responsibilities?"

This is a way to open the door to what you need while staying focused on what the employer needs. It can create an opportunity for future discussions that eventually lead to having a set of expectations without having a full sit-down meeting. After each conversation, it is important to follow-up in writing about what was discussed so that a fuller picture of the expectations can be developed. This is vital for the performance and accountability aspects of the employer-employee relationship. An appreciative follow-up can help to encourage the employer to seek further opportunities to engage in similar conversations in the future.

Once expectations are established in one session or over time, it is important to determine how and when to revisit them. As previously mentioned, Costikyan (2021) recommends 30-days for new hybrid work arrangements, which seems a reasonable period for an initial check. As the employer, engage the employee by asking what they believe to be the ideal number of meetings to have specific time to revisit the expectations. If your industry has natural cycles, then it might be best to adapt these expectation check-in meetings to those rhythms. If not, then go with whatever is agreed upon between the two parties. What is most important is that the meetings occur. If you are the employee, then ask if you can have pre-determined check-ins to discuss expectations. If the employer is hesitant, again, think about natural ways to incorporate these chats into other meetings and always follow-up in writing, outlining what was discussed.

To facilitate the check-in meeting, think about what you need to know from the employee about their experience to that point. Provide a couple questions in advance for the employee to have the opportunity to reflect and feel prepared coming into the meeting. "What is working? Not working? What are some barriers you are experiencing? What is your favorite part of being a part of the organization?" These simple questions can elicit a lot of information with proper follow-up questions.

Ultimately, you want to understand if the expectations are working for both parties and what adjustments might need to be made. By asking the previous questions, you can get to these answers in a more organic way. Bookending the conversations with questions asking about positive experiences is important to steer the conversation in a productive manner. You want to know the bad and ugly, but there also needs to be focus on what is going well and how to further accentuate the positive aspects. In this scenario, you want to be spending more time on the first and last question and hopefully little time on the middle two.

So, you have LOTS of employees and have no way of doing this with them all. That is a practical consideration as the process as laid out takes time. It is not a one-and-done event. It is a process and all processes require investment of additional resources; in this instance, primarily, it is a commitment of time. When you are responsible for numerous employees this can be daunting. Focus on your primary reports and building a culture of dialogue around expectations. Engage them in the process so it becomes an expectation they do the same with their employees and so on. Establishing the culture will make it easier for the behaviors to permeate throughout the system and work environment. As the employer, you are in a position to set the tone so decide how you want that to happen and act accordingly.

Even if you have hundreds of people directly reporting to you, then find more formal and structured ways of hosting dialogues around expectations. Maybe it cannot be done in one-on-one interactions. Perhaps, it needs to be done in smaller groups. Utilize technology to collect large amounts of information earlier in the process. Then use that feedback to structure the expectations dialogue. This can make it easier to understand what majorities of the employees are experiencing and what needs they might want addressed. It provides a helpful framework to engaging in dialogue and might make the process seem less daunting.

If you have control of the process, then designate certain periods of time in your calendar to have these dialogues. Whether it is weekly, monthly, quarterly, whatever makes most sense, it is important that they are scheduled and part of your routine. Block out the time necessary and make sure others understand that it is a priority for you. Again, set the tone if and when you have the ability to do so. If you make it clear that it is important, then others will respect that even if they might be skeptical. The process itself will lead to results that will justify the means.

Why is so much space dedicated to expectations? The simple response is because they are that important. They set the tone and dictate how to evaluate performance and determine measures for accountability. Without sound expectations, the next two sections become murky and present a quagmire for both employee and employer. Clearly established expectations ensure there is no confusion. When they are revisited often, it provides feedback to employee and employer about the relationship, opportunities for growth, and successes.

PERFORMANCE

Now that the concept of expectations has been addressed, performance can be evaluated. Extensive research shows remote work has a positive impact on productivity (Baker, 2021; Baker et al., 2007; Bentley et al., 2013; Bloom et al., 2015; Coenen & Kok, 2014; Collins, 2005; DeFilippis et al., 2020; Felstead & Henseke, 2017; Kazekami, 2020; Lister, 2021; van der Lippe & Lippenyi, 2019; Neufeld & Fang, 2004, 2005; Vitterso, 2003). More specifically, the literature showed increased life satisfaction (Kazekami, 2020; Madsen 2003), work satisfaction (Baker et al., 2007; Bentley et al., 2013; Bloom et al., 2015; Felstead & Henseke, 2017), work engagement (Felstead & Henseke, 2017; Lister, 2021), and less turnover (Bloom et al., 2015). Furthermore, Neufeld and Fang (2004) found remote work productivity to be positively associated with attitudes and beliefs and situational and social factors. In addition, Bentley et al (2016) found managers had high levels of satisfaction with their hybrid employees.

Research by DeFilippis et al (2020) found that the average workday increased by 48.5 minutes for WFH employees. Kamouri and Lister (2020) found remote workers spend approximately half the time they would have otherwise spent commuting actually working and saved an additional 35 minutes a day due to less interruptions at home. Furthermore, Bentley et al (2016) found by not commuting multiple days a week, employees saved on various costs (transportation, parking, dry cleaning, food) that increased work satisfaction. Finally, Kazekami (2020) found the productivity increase is larger for employees who experience lengthy commute times (more than one hour) or use crowded public transportation (bus, train, subway) options.

On the other hand, there are instances were hybrid work and WFH arrangements can decrease productivity (Coenen & Kok, 2014; Felstead & Henseke, 2017; Kazekami, 2020; Knights & McCabe, 2003; Kotera & Vione, 2020; Moretti et al., 2020; The Balance Careers, 2020; van der Lippe & Lippenyi, 2019). For example, Felstead and Henseke (2017) found it challenging for WFH employees to establish boundaries between home and work, which according to Kazekami (2020) can contribute to too extensive work hours and detrimental to performance. Furthermore, Bentley et al (2016), Kotera and Vione (2020), Moretti et al (2020), and The Balance Careers (2020) all acknowledged detriments to productivity for those who WFH or hybrid, including social isolation, home and work boundaries, mental demands and fatigue, communication difficulties, and financial costs.

In addition, hybrid and WFH arrangements can limit productivity of teams. The work of van der Lippe and Lippenyi (2019) found the individual performance of a hybrid employee decreased based on the increased percentage of other employees in similar situations. Knights and McCabe (2003) acknowledged that working together gets more challenging when colleagues cannot readily exchange information. This was also seen by Felstead and Henseke (2017), where they determined remote work leads to intensification of workload burdening the employee to use their individual knowledge and skill since co-workers are not always immediately available.

To evaluate performance, there should be a shared expectation of how that will happen and what will be measured. This stems back to expectations. Costikyan (2021) suggests that to manage teams in hybrid environments it is imperative to "set expectations and measure performance outcomes, set goals and timetables and define deliverables clearly, and assess the quantity, quality, and timeliness of work" (p. 2). Part of a managerial work ideology is that problems can be solved with "strong governance principles" and "commercial business techniques" like "budgetary control, quality assurance, and performance accountability" (Clarke & Newman, 1997; Winter & O'Donohue, 2011, p. 6). This removes the human aspect of the equation and can further complicate hybrid workspaces.

Surprising an employee at an annual performance appraisal with a negative review does not help anyone. First, the employee will likely have some questions, concerns, and confusion. Second, it creates distrust, and it has been stressed continuously that building trust is important, so anything to deteriorate that is inherently negative. Third, human resources will want to know what is happening. Not only should an employee never be surprised but HR also falls into that same boat. Essentially, many red flags are being raised at the same time, when all could have been avoided simply by providing regular, consistent feedback to the employee. In fact, Baker et al (2007) found task identity and providing feedback to be the most consistent and significant factors contributing to work satisfaction and productivity.

There are a couple of things to unpack. If there are issues stemming from performance, then they need to be brought to someone's attention sooner than later. Waiting does not fix anything, and only provides more opportunity for unwanted habits to form. The idea of nipping it in the bud. A problem stems from delaying the conversation, but furthermore, the process suffers from not having a shared language to approach the issue.

This is where expectations can make things easier. Because they are shared, agreed upon, and grounded in work responsibilities, it makes it easier to point out when someone is not living up to their end of the bargain. Expectations establish mutual understanding and can help to remove ambiguity which might plague performance. If expectations are visited often, this further removes ambiguity as there are regular checkpoints to determine what might still be in the gray areas or what new tasks require additional clarity.

Secondly, there should always be an effort towards building trust. Again, expectations are a foundation for trust. Each party agrees to what they will do and trusts that the other party is upholding their end. When one side falters, this can negatively impact performance. It is important to figure out how to rectify the issue quickly and appropriately, so ideal work conditions can be reinstated. Bentley et al (2016) and Pichault and McKeown (2019) found less professional support reinforces the feeling of social isolation and stress/strain. This in turn can lead to increased probability of managerial control through bureaucratic controls, performance targets, and accountability, eroding any possibility of discretion in daily work practices (Evetts, 2014).

Finally, if there are persistent and pervasive performance issues even after revisiting expectations, then this is where human resources should be consulted. Document previous attempts to work with the employee and provide that information to HR. The hope is that it does not progress to this level, but unfortunately, every once in a while, it might.

In the lead up to the pandemic, I had this situation. Eventually it got to the point where the situation was no longer tenable, and the employee was let go during their probationary period. Consistently, the employee did not meet the expectations we established and after multiple conversations and opportunities the situation did not change. The issues were pervasive in multiple areas of the employee's performance and various attempts to coach and retrain did not produce different results. In addition, when work from home orders were issued and things transitioned to virtual, this exacerbated previous issues to the point that the employee's shortcomings were affecting the other employees in the organization.

It was an extremely difficult decision to make and further compounded by the reality of the pandemic, but nonetheless was the right decision for the organization and the other people in the office. The employee's performance regularly affected the ability for others to do their work effectively and efficiently. Once the situation became detrimental to others in the organization then the options to retain the employee became far more limited and ultimately the probationary period provided avenues to terminate the employment.

In this scenario, even though the transition to virtual and working from home contributed to the release of the employee, it is important to note that an employee requesting to work from home does not mean that performance will suffer. Again, with clear expectations in place, there are guardrails to promote positive working conditions that contribute to success.

Around this same time period, two other employees were hired and brought into the organization. It was rocky early on as everyone was adapting to new modalities of working and also trying to create bonds that are easier to form through informal interactions in an in-person environment. In this instance, taking the time to establish expectations and revisit them frequently in the early phases of these employees' tenures with the organization paid off dividends.

These check-ins allowed me to understand what they needed and how to optimize the environment and conditions to be more conducive to their work. It was a work in progress as each employee had different needs to promote their productivity. However, the ability to revisit the expectations made this process easier and assisted with the transition back to in-person work. Performance never wavered throughout this period and often exceeded expectations.

This scenario associates well with the fourth issue from Barnakova and Krupp (2021) around productivity, where the paradox is control versus empowerment. The primary recommendation is to design fit-for-purpose solutions, where the nature of the work should define the way of working. Subsequent suggestions include reinventing performance management to track outputs with objective measures and leverage data to monitor work dynamics and integrate into decision-making processes. Finally, within this paradox, ask your employees how they would measure productivity and maintain accountability to create fit-for-person solutions that assess the tradeoffs of limiting commuting and physical office seat time.

Another component of performance in the hybrid environment was taking time to celebrate small wins, and it is ever more crucial in the current state of being. People want to feel valued and that they belong. There is a whole burgeoning research area in higher education on college students' "sense of belonging" and how that impacts their experiences and outcomes. In summation, a lack of sense of belonging is typically bad. Students who feel a lack of sense of belonging underperform academically and are less likely to graduate. Why would we believe that this changes after college?

Therefore, employees are seeking to belong. In addition, they want to feel their contributions matter and that they are valued. This is not rocket science. We can all think of work environments that we have thrived, and it is more than likely contributing factors to our success were based on belonging and value. We were likely to work harder for the people that made us feel that way. It was not about the organization, but the people of the organization.

If an employee does something great, find ways to reward the behavior. If we are looking to promote positive performance, then we always want to find opportunities to reinforce actions, deeds, or words that support the conditions and environments we want to create. It can be more difficult in the current environment but nevertheless there needs to be an effort made to do it. There are numerous ways to reward performance that reinforce the culture we want to shape and maintain. Find out how the employee wants to be recognized and then figure out how to make that happen when possible and appropriate.

These latter points speak to the third paradox introduced by Barnakova and Krupp (2021). The third paradox is associated with career development and the dichotomy of networked and proximate. Again, frequent check-ins are proposed. In addition, leaders should deliberately orchestrate networking connections and be prepared to build "leader as coach" capabilities and skills. Lister (2021) found remote work forces managers to manage based on what is achieved versus perceptions of achievement. However, there is the adage, "out of sight, out of mind." As the leader, it is imperative to share the good works of the employees in your area, especially those working in hybrid environments, as the lack of visibility can often be perceived as lack of productivity. These sentiments are supported by the work of Bloom et al (2015), who found that WFH employees had lower promotional rates conditional on performance, and McCloskey and Igbaria (2003), who found that WFH employees had greater career advancement concerns.

ACCOUNTABILITY

Expectations are made. Performance is evaluated. The employee is falling short, what now? All that trust you have been building becomes vital at this stage in the process. According to Heath et al (2002) and Bjorn et al (2009), accomplishing accountability by people being able to see and monitor each person's contributions. Furthermore, the knowledge that others are monitoring one's actions can reinforce social norms and adjust actions of employees for fear of sanctions (Bjorn et al., 2009; Erikson & Kellogg, 2000).

Therefore, communication and use of productivity tools in the hybrid environment are based on expectations and mutual accountability (Costikyan, 2021). Furthermore, "everyone working on a team must be clear about what needs to get done by whom, when, and why. Employees must also be equipped with the right skills and mindsets to solve problems, instead of waiting to be told what to do. And there must be disciplined follow-up to make sure actions were taken and the desired results achieved" (De Smet et al., 2020, p. 4). However, it is important to clarify what is meant by accountability.

Accountability is often seen as something that happens after the fact and a negative. An employee did something wrong, therefore, they need to be held accountable. Where that is a component of accountability, it is only one facet of it. Accountability is about meeting expectations and creating the conditions for that. So similar to expectations where the employer has a role to play, that is also the case for accountability. If the employer is not following through on what is expected of them, then there also needs to be accountability. Accountability is a shared responsibility. It is important for both parties to hold each other to account.

The fear of this is that accountability inherently has power attached to it. In moving accountability to a shared responsibility, this requires one to relinquish some of the power in the relationship. To be effective, it requires a deeper trust among the parties. It requires the person relinquishing some of their power to be comfortable with that proposition and not all are.

If we treat accountability as a regular function of the organization and not a one-off when things go awry, then it builds a culture where it is okay to innovate, try new things, and at times fail. For example, check-in meetings for expectations are essentially accountability meetings. It is an opportunity for both parties to revisit and hold each other to account for the expectations. These frequent opportunities to hold one another accountable make the occasional mistake and misstep easier to endure. If accountability is a normal part of the organization, then it is easier to treat failure as a learning opportunity.

It does not mean there is absolution of consequences for mistakes, missteps, or failures. What it should do is create the space for employees to feel that it is okay to take chances that can be beneficial to the employer and the clients. Pichault & McKeown (2019) state effective professional support through group norms, which can be an accountability measure, give employees more discretion and thus autonomy in work practices.

EQUITY AND INCLUSION

It would be difficult to have a chapter on performance and accountability and ignore equity and inclusion. Lister (2021) found remote work compels managers to manage by what people achieve and not hours in the office. However, there are extensive studies and data on biases in workplaces that spread from employee evaluations to salaries to promotions to appearances to hiring and so forth. These biases, whether explicit or implicit, run counter to creating spaces where employees feel a sense of belonging. Furthermore, to foster inclusiveness, it is imperative to approach expectations seriously as this is the foundation for the working relationship.

Revisiting the work of Barnakova and Krupp (2021), with inclusion, the paradox is balancing personalization and harmony. Suggestions include getting to know team members as people, creating flexibility, reaching out to colleagues on a regular basis, and connecting actions to organization purpose. Because the formation of expectations is an individualized process of agreements between the employee and employer, inherently, this becomes an inclusive process. It also is the underpinning for performance and accountability. As Costikyan (2021) points out, "equitable does not mean the same or even similar outcome between two individuals" (p. 1). Hybrid work environments require recognition that employees are individuals with diverse habits and needs (Baker, 2021).

It also would be remiss to have a chapter on these topics and not mention generational differences and impacts. First, many entering the workforce are of Generation Z; the oldest Millennials are in their late thirties and early forties. It is important to note this as there are differences in attitudes and beliefs between these two generations that often get lumped together. Generation X and Boomers (though decreasing) are in positions of power throughout organizations and their management style might be of a different era. This can create dissonance and reinforces the importance of developing expectations. For example, Baker (2021) suggested that newer employees are less likely to be trusted to work remotely when compared to longer tenured colleagues.

The problem is that the starting perspectives might be further apart on a continuum and there is a larger chasm to bridge. In addition, receptiveness to these dialogues might be icy at best, and could be outwardly antagonistic. This is where strategies to integrate these conversations into existing structures is important. It also means that actual dialogue might be limited. Take advantage when opportunities present themselves, and frame the conversation in ways that are constructive, productive, and demonstrate the employer benefit. At the end of the day, both parties, employer and employee, should gain something from the interaction.

There can often be a mentality that one must be seen to be perceived as being productive (i.e., performance) (Bloom et al., 2015; Lister, 2021; McCloskey & Igbaria, 2003). In an article for BBC (2020), Sijbrandij believed a hybrid model removed egalitarian benefits promoted by a fully remote workforce and the advantageous interactions of fully in-person work that can lead to innovation; furthermore, those in the office more frequently will have a perceived advantage over those who are not. This is a farce. It is a misleading proposition, as we can all identify at least one person whose productivity and contributions are questionable at best but are extremely visible. However, this can be a generational mindset because of traditions surrounding "seated" time versus actual completed work. Again, this will vary with industry, but these notions can be pervasive and often rooted in previous ways of being that are difficult for people to break.

It is not to say that generational differences are bad and in fact are important to diverse and inclusive work environments. There is informal knowledge transfer that both creates vibrancy in the workplace and is fundamental to an organization. Comradery is created through these interactions. New ideas and opportunities are generated. It becomes easier to create a sense of belonging when people are able to physically interact with each other. Information transmits between employees in ways to broaden organizational knowledge among colleagues. This leads to deeper understanding of the organization and can allow for better collaboration and working environments across and within units. It can increase opportunities and likelihood of positive performance and the ability to reinforce those behaviors in public settings.

Generational workplace culture often is pitted against each other, where it should not be. It is an extension of the people and what they view to be conflicting needs. This harkens back to dialogue about expectations. If dialogue were to occur about these differences, then there would be opportunity to see the perspectives of each party. This can lead to further understanding and help people to see that the perceived chasm might not be as wide as it actually is.

CONVERSATION REDUX

Revisiting the initial conversation at the top of this chapter, the question remains about what is next for my colleague. There are decisions to be made about how to approach the situation. Part of that decision is how the employee communicates needs to the employer in a productive way. What is the relationship between the two parties and how can the topic of expectations be introduced? It is incumbent on the employee to figure out how to make this happen considering it seems to be out of the purview of the employer. A hybrid situation would be helpful to my colleague Ryan and there are many others who could benefit from a similar situation. Research shows that employees can maintain high performance standards and remain accountable; it is incumbent on the employer to promote a conducive environment for hybrid work through clear expectations.

These are challenges many of us will continue to face moving forward. At this time, uncertainty is the only certainty. We are all adjusting to changing conditions and environments. Since people are the heart of every organization, this demands that approaches to expectations, performance, and accountability need to be dynamic endeavors.

REFERENCES

Aubert, B. A., & Kelsey, B. L. (2003). Further understanding of trust and performance in virtual teams. *Small Group Research, 34*(1), 575–618. doi:10.1177/1046496403256011

Baker, D. (2021). *The future of work is hybrid: Could covid be the catalyst for organizations to implement a hybrid workplace model?* Academic Press.

Baker, E., Avery, G. C., & Crawford, J. D. (2007). Satisfaction and perceived productivity when professionals work from home. *Research and Practice in Human Resource Management, 15*(1), 37–62.

Barnakova, Y., & Krupp, S. (2021). *The work anywhere paradox: Love it or hate it, how leaders can optimize it.* Heidrick Consulting.

Bell, B. S., & Kozlowski, S. W. (2002). A typology of virtual teams: Implications for effective leadership. *Group & Organization Management, 27*(1), 14–49. doi:10.1177/1059601102027001003

Bentley, T. A., Teo, S. T. T., McLeod, L., Tan, F., Bosua, R., & Gloet, M. (2016). The role of organizational support in teleworker wellbeing: A socio-technical systems approach. *Applied Ergonomics, 52*, 207–215. doi:10.1016/j.apergo.2015.07.019 PMID:26360212

Bjorn, P., & Ngwenyama, O. (2009). Virtual team collaboration: Building shared meaning, resolving breakdowns and creating translucence. *Information Systems Journal, 19*(3), 227–253. doi:10.1111/j.1365-2575.2007.00281.x

Bloom, N., Liang, J., Roberts, J., & Yin, Z.-J. N. (2015). Does working from home work? Evidence from a Chinese experiment. *The Quarterly Journal of Economics, 130*(1), 165–218. doi:10.1093/qje/qju032

Boell, S. K., Cecez-Kecmanovic, D., & Campbell, J. (2016). Telework paradoxes and practices: The importance of the nature of work. *New Technology, Work and Employment, 31*(2), 114–131. doi:10.1111/ntwe.12063

Bohm, D. (2008). *On Dialogue*. Routledge Classics.

British Broadcasting Corporation. (2020). *Why the future of work might be hybrid.* https://www.bbc.com/worklife/article/20200824-why-the-future-of-work-might-be-hybrid

Clarke, J., & Newman, J. (1997). The managerial state. *Sage (Atlanta, Ga.).*

Coenen, M., & Kok, R. A. W. (2014). Workplace flexibility and new product development performance: The role of telework and flexible work schedules. *European Management Journal, 32*(4), 564–576. doi:10.1016/j.emj.2013.12.003

Collins, M. (2005). The (not so simple) case for teleworking: A study at Lloyd's of London. *New Technology, Work and Employment, 20*(2), 115–132. doi:10.1111/j.1468-005X.2005.00148.x

Costikyan, N. (2021, August). *Conversation with Nancy Costikyan, Director of Work/Life at Harvard University.* Boston College Center for Work and Family. http://hdl.handle.net/10713/16574

Davis, D. D., & Bryant, J. L. (2003). Influence at a distance: Leadership in global virtual teams. *Advances in Global Leadership, 3*(1), 303–340. doi:10.1016/S1535-1203(02)03015-0

De Paoli, D., & Ropo, A. (2015). Open plan offices – the response to leadership challenges of virtual project work? *Journal of Corporate Real Estate, 17*(1), 63–74. doi:10.1108/JCRE-08-2014-0020

De Smet, A., Pacthod, D., Relyea, C., & Sternfels, B. (2020). *Ready, set, go: Reinventing the organization for speed in the post-COVID-19 era.* McKinsey & Company.

DeFilippis, E., Impink, S. M., Singell, M., Polzer, J. T., & Sadun, R. (2020). *Collaborating during coronavirus: The impact of COVID-19 on the nature of work.* National Bureau of Economic Research (Working paper; 27612). doi:10.3386/w27612

Dose, J. J., & Klimoski, R. J. (1995). Doing the right thing in the workplace: Responsibility in the face of accountability. *Employee Responsibilities and Rights Journal, 8*(1), 35–36. doi:10.1007/BF02621254

Erickson, T., & Kellogg, W. A. (2000). Social translucence: An approach to the designing systems that support social processes. *ACM Transactions on Computer-Human Interaction, 7*(1), 59–83. doi:10.1145/344949.345004

Evetts, J. (2014). The Concept of Professionalism: Professional Work, Professional Practice and Learning. In S. Billett, C. Harteis, & H. Gruber (Eds.), *International Handbook of Research in Professional and Practice-Based Learning* (pp. 29–56). Springer International Handbooks of Education. doi:10.1007/978-94-017-8902-8_2

Felstead, A., & Henseke, G. (2017). Assessing the growth of remote working and its consequences for effort, well-being and work-life balance. *New Technology, Work and Employment, 32*(3), 195–212. doi:10.1111/ntwe.12097

Ferris, G. R., Mitchell, T. R., Canavan, P. J., Frink, D. D., & Hopper, H. (1995). Accountability in human resources systems. In G. R. Ferris, S. D. Rosen, & D. T. Basman (Eds.), *Handbook of human resource management* (pp. 175–196). Blackwell Business.

Garbes, A. (2021). *What working parents really need from workplaces*. TED Series: The Way We Work. https://www.ted.com/talks/angela_garbes_what_working_parents_really_need_from_workplaces

Heath, C., Svensson, M. S., Hindmarsh, J., Luff, P., & Lehn, D. (2002). Conðguring awareness. *Computer Supported Cooperative Work (CSCW) International Journal, 11*, 317–347.

Hoegl, M., Muethel, M., & Gemuenden, H. G. (2012). Leadership and teamwork in dispersed projects. In P. W. G. Morris, J. K. Pinto, & J. Söderlund (Eds.), *The Oxford Handbook of Project Management* (pp. 483–500). Oxford University Press.

Jarvenpaa, S. L., & Leidner, D. E. (1999). Communication and trust in global virtual teams. *Organization Science, 10*(1), 791–815. doi:10.1287/orsc.10.6.791

Joshi, A., & Lazarova, M. B. (2005). Do 'global' teams need 'global' leaders? Identifying leadership competences in multinational teams. In D. L. Shapiro, M. A. Von Glinow, & J. L. C. Cheng (Eds.), *Managing Multinational Teams: Global Perspectives* (pp. 281–301). Elsevier. doi:10.1016/S0747-7929(05)18011-1

Kamouri, A., & Lister, K. (2020). *Survey reveals 76% of global office workers want to continue working from home post-COVID-19.* Global Workplace Analytics. https://globalworkplaceanalytics.com/brags/news-releases

Kazekami, S. (2020). Mechanisms to improve labor productivity by performing telework. *Telecommunications Policy, 44*(2), 101868. doi:10.1016/j.telpol.2019.101868

Kirkman, B. L., Rosen, B., Tesluk, P. E., & Gibson, C. B. (2004). The impact of team empowerment on virtual team performance: The moderating role of face-to-face interaction. *Academy of Management Journal, 47*(2), 175–192.

Knights, D., & McCabe, D. (2003). Governing through teamwork: Reconstituting subjectivity in a call centre. *Journal of Management Studies, 40*(7), 1587–1619. doi:10.1111/1467-6486.00393

Kotera, Y., & Vione, K. (2020). Psychological impacts of the new ways of working (NWWW): A systematic review. *International Journal of Environmental Research and Public Health, 17*(14), 5080. doi:10.3390/ijerph17145080 PMID:32674518

Krebs, S. A., Hobman, E. V., & Bordia, P. (2006). Virtual teams and group member dissimilarity: Consequences for the development of trust. *Small Group Research*, *37*(6), 721–741. doi:10.1177/1046496406294886

Kronfli, C. (2021). *Mental wellness in the workplace: A playbook for employers*. Ontario Chamber of Commerce.

Lister, K. (2021). *The business case for remote work – for employers, employees, the environment, and society*. Global Workplace Analytics. https://globalworkplaceanalytics.com/whitepapers

Maclagan, P. W. (1983). The concept of responsibility: Some implications for organizational behaviour and development. *Journal of Management Studies*, *20*(4), 411–423. doi:10.1111/j.1467-6486.1983.tb00216.x

Madsen, S. R. (2003). The effects of home-based teleworking on work-family conflict. *Human Resource Development Quarterly*, *14*(1), 35–58. doi:10.1002/hrdq.1049

Mahfoodh, H., Aleid, K., Bahzad, A., Matar, S., Shubbar, Z. S., & Mattar, E. (2021) *Sustaining work continuity through hybrid work environments: Tracking systems*. 2021 International Conference on Innovation and Intelligence for Informatics, Computing, and Technologies (3ICT), Zallaq, Bahrain. 10.1109/3ICT53449.2021.9581371

McCloskey, D. W., & Igbaria, M. (2003). Does "out of sight" mean "out of mind?" An empirical investigation of career advancement prospects of telecommuters. *Information Resources Management Journal*, *16*(2), 19–34. doi:10.4018/irmj.2003040102

Mendenhall, M. E., Reiche, B. S., Bird, A., & Osland, J. S. (2012). Defining the 'global' in global leadership. *Journal of World Business*, *47*(1), 493–503. doi:10.1016/j.jwb.2012.01.003

Moretti, A., Menna, F., Aulicino, M., Paoletta, M., Liguori, S., & Iolascon, G. (2020). Characterization of home working population during COVID-19 emergency: A cross-sectional analysis. *International Journal of Environmental Research and Public Health*, *17*(17), 6284. doi:10.3390/ijerph17176284 PMID:32872321

Muethel, M., & Hoegl, M. (2010). Cultural and societal influences on shared leadership in globally dispersed teams. *Journal of International Management*, *16*(1), 234–246. doi:10.1016/j.intman.2010.06.003

Neufeld, D. J., & Fang, Y. (2004). Predicting telecommuter productivity. *Proceedings from 37th Annual Hawaii International Conference on System Sciences*. 10.1109/HICSS.2004.1265160

Neufeld, D. J., & Fang, Y. (2005). Individual, social and situational determinants of telecommuter productivity. *Information & Management, 42*(7), 1037–1049. doi:10.1016/j.im.2004.12.001

Pauleen, D. J. (2004). An inductively derived model of leader-initiated relationship building with virtual team members. *Journal of Management Information Systems, 20*(3), 227–256. doi:10.1080/07421222.2003.11045771

Peters, P., & den Dulk, L. (2003). Cross cultural differences in managers' support for home-based telework: A theoretical elaboration. *International Journal of Cross Cultural Management, 3*(3), 329–346. doi:10.1177/1470595803003003005

Pichault, F., & McKeown, T. (2019). Autonomy at work in the gig economy: Analysing work status, work content and working conditions of independent professionals. *New Technology, Work and Employment, 34*(1), 59–72. doi:10.1111/ntwe.12132

The Balance Careers. (2021). *The pros and cons of a flexible work schedule.* www.thebalancecareers.com/advantages-and-disadvantages-of-flexible-work-schedules-1917964

van der Lippe, T., & Lippényi, Z. (2019). Co-workers working from home and individual and team performance. *New Technology, Work and Employment, 35*(1), 60–79. doi:10.1111/ntwe.12153 PMID:32214593

van Dyne, L., Kossek, E., & Lobal, S. (2007). Less need to be there: Cross-level effects of work practices that support work–life flexibility and enhance group processes and group-level OCB. *Human Relations, 60*(8), 1123–1153. doi:10.1177/0018726707081657

Vittersø, J., Akselsen, S., Evjemo, B., Julsrud, T., Yttri, B., & Bergvik, S. (2003). Impacts of home-based telework on quality of life for employees and their partners. Quantitative and qualitative results from a European survey. *Journal of Happiness Studies, 4*(2), 201–233. doi:10.1023/A:1024490621548

Wakefield, R. L., Leidner, D. E., & Garrison, G. (2008). A model of conflict, leadership and performance in virtual teams. *Information Systems Research, 19*(4), 434–455. doi:10.1287/isre.1070.0149

Weinert, C., Maier, C., Laumer, S., & Weitzel, T. (2014). Does teleworking negatively influence IT professionals? An empirical analysis of IT personnel's telework-enabled stress. *Proceedings of the 52nd ACM Conference on Computers and People Research*, 139–147. 10.1145/2599990.2600011

Winter, R., & O'Donohue, W. (2011). *Understanding identity construction in hybrid organisations: A work ideologies perspective*. Australian National University.

Zander, L., Mockaitis, A. I., & Butler, C. L. (2012). Leading global teams. *Journal of World Business*, *47*(4), 592–603. doi:10.1016/j.jwb.2012.01.012

Zhang, S., & Fjermestad, J. (2006). Bridging the gap between traditional leadership theories and virtual team leadership. *International Journal of Technology, Policy and Management*, *6*(3), 56–78.

Zigurs, I. (2002). Leadership in virtual teams: Oxymoron or opportunity? *Organizational Dynamics*, *31*(4), 339–351. doi:10.1016/S0090-2616(02)00132-8

Chapter 3
Creating a Culture of Accountability and Performance

Ben Hippeli
University of North Florida, USA

ABSTRACT

In today's business environment, professionals are often pulled in multiple directions and can easily be distracted from their primary objectives. From high volumes of emails, Teams™ messaging, and social media swiping to business travel, meetings, and office politics, there are countless ways to get pulled away from the core focus of any job role. Add in a typical work from home environment and the list of distractions grows exponentially. In most cases, the onus falls on leadership to create an environment of accountability and high performance for the organization. To hold a business team accountable, leaders must gain a deep understanding of each team member's "why," utilize pertinent metrics to measure progress, and maintain clear and consistent lines of communication with each individual and the team.

Understanding what drives each team member to show up each day is a critical element in holding a team accountable for performance

With the pressures of day-to-day business, it is easy for leaders to only focus on productivity and the bottom line while forgetting that the team members responsible for achieving the desired results are themselves humans with their own thoughts and needs.

While focusing on the bottom-line, many new leaders often learn the hard way that neglecting the human element of their team hinders long-term success. Although

DOI: 10.4018/978-1-6684-3453-6.ch003

seemingly counter-intuitive, the more personal and consistent the care leaders apply to their team, the better the overall team performance will be. (Jones, 2017). In his book *Start with Why: How Great Leaders Inspire Everyone to Take Action*, Simon Sinek discusses the importance of understanding each team member's "why." Sinek explains that the goal is to understand what drives and motivates each individual team member to empower him or herself to perform at his or her best. (Sinek, 2009)

To accomplish this goal, corporate coaches at Benchmark Training utilize an effective tool called The F-Bomb, which is designed to help leaders get to know what drives individuals on their team. While the name may initially catch leaders off guard, participating in the F-Bomb assessment uncovers a trove of information that can be utilized to foster a supportive work environment and a cohesive, driven team. Three simple words, not four letters, come together to create the synergy needed for individuals to charge through self-imposed limits, which may hold them back from achievement.

Working one-on-one with individual team members to help them Focus on their Futures, Face their Fears, and Fuel their Fires is the beginning of a team's success journey.

When implementing the F-Bomb, leaders should follow the following steps during a one-on-one meeting with each of their direct reports:

FUTURE

The first step is to help direct reports clearly define their future. Having clear long-term and short-term goals is certainly a best practice when it comes to being successful in just about anything. Leaders should encourage their employees to focus on their

Figure 1.

long-term goals, both professional and personal, within the next one-to-two-year span. Leaders should begin by asking their employees to write down the vision that they would like to see unfold within the next one to two years. The intention is to mentally position this vision front and center. It is essential to keep self-limiting beliefs, or self-proposed fears, out of this part of the exercise. For now, the focus is simply on the desired future. Once employees have a clear picture of where they want to be in the designated time frame, leaders should ask them to note one or two steps they can take each day to Focus on their Future. Together, leaders and direct reports can now use this information as an action plan to help employees take steps towards achieving their goals.

FEARS

Next, leaders should guide their employees through the process of identifying what might scare them into inaction. Fear of failure? Fear of embarrassment? This step is often where things get a little tough; most people don't like to admit what their fears are, and that's a big problem. Allowing employees to ignore their fears may result in stress and anxiety, lack of initiative, feelings of inadequacy, or distraction from work responsibilities, all of which often culminate into an overall lack of achievement potential in the workplace. By guiding employees to acknowledge fears, leaders can help bring actions more freely to fruition. Defining fears creates tangible opportunities for improvement, which promote taking steps towards conquering fears. Once employees are focused on fears, leaders should ask employees to list one or two actions they can take to face those fears. For example, if an employee fears public speaking, the employee might consider joining an organization such as Toastmasters®, which can be a productive first step in facing that fear.

To use a quote from the movie, *The Usual Suspects*, "The greatest trick the devil ever pulled was convincing the world he didn't exist." Leaders should not let their employees' fears be the devil that holds employees back from being the best they can be.

FIRE

The final step in igniting employees through the F-Bomb is to help them define what charges them up. After creating a future-statement and identifying those lurking fears that could hinder achieving that desired future, leaders will complete this one-on-one meeting by helping employees uncover their driving force and asking them what fuels them. This step is all about understanding each employee's "why" so that leaders can help the employee fuel that fire along the way. As the culminating step, understanding this "why" is an essential part of the success formula but is also, unfortunately, where many leaders drop the ball. Not only can it be difficult to define an individual's fire but ot is also easy to neglect it and allow that fire to smolder. Leaders should ask employees what they can do each day to Fuel their Fire to assure that this fire burns strong through the toughest storm, both in and out of the workplace. Helping them tend this fire is easy to do if follow-up conversations are integrated into monthly or quarterly one-on-ones.

In sports, the objective is to score more points than the opponent. The goal is clear, and the team's leadership is focused on building a strategy that will outperform competitors by recruiting and developing the best players. Ultimately, however, it's up to the players to perform on the field to execute the strategy.

In business, winning can mean something different for each company; therefore, leadership must first design what winning means to the company. When the stakeholders of the business agree on their definition of winning, only then can leaders begin to develop the strategy they feel is best to achieve that win. With the main target or targets defined, departmental leaders are responsible for leading their team through the day-to-day challenges of achieving their specific objectives.

To orchestrate all these moving parts, it's key for leaders to set clear targets for the year and work together with their team members to break down those annual targets into quarterly and monthly objectives. By breaking annual corporate objectives into smaller objectives, it can be easier for the team to stay on track. These targets are considered lagging indicators of performance, meaning they show the results after they have occurred. For example, if a sales department's goal is to bring on 10 new clients each month, leadership would clearly need to track the number of new clients brough on throughout the month. As members of the team track this number, they are noting the current status of their goal and cannot predict future outcomes with just that number. Therefore, while lagging indicators are useful to show current or historical status to the goal, they do not help leadership influence activities that will help deliver the results.

Metrics that help leadership measure activities that are likely to deliver the results needed by the company are called "leading indicators." Once the monthly objectives are clearly defined, leadership must then work together with team members to define the activities necessary to achieve the defined monthly objectives and measure these leading indicators on a real-time basis.

To help explain why real-time measurement is important, let's look at a hypothetical scenario in which you and coworkers play softball in a corporate league, and you've made it to the finals, which means you must play the rival team that happens to be a competitor in your industry. Just as the game starts, the scoreboard breaks and there's no way for any of the players or coaches to know what the official score is, what the current inning is, or what ball the player is on. You've got coaches doing their best to track the data, players trying to scream information across the field, and everyone arguing about the status of the game. Finally, both teams become disengaged from the game, and everyone walks off the field disheartened and frustrated.

While this example in sports is unlikely to occur, a very similar parallel occurs month after month in business when leaders fail to provide a clear scoreboard for their team. Professionals in business need the same visibility of their progress as professional athletes need. That's why it's important for leadership to define and track Key Performance Indicators (KPIs) for all levels of the company, starting with the company as a whole and then moving to each department and ultimately to everyone.

Effective intradepartmental and interdepartmental communication can create a competitive edge within any company. Leaders can better understand the value of effective communication for a team by considering the effects of poor communication in an organization.

For example, consider two companies with the same technical capabilities, market presence, and financial resources competing in the same market. Company Type A created a culture that promotes effective communication across departments, and company Type B has not.

Table 1 anecdotally shows the likely outcomes of different common business scenarios based on how each company does or does not effectively nurture and promote effective communication within the company as a whole and within each department.

KEY INGREDIENTS

In order to build and nurture a culture of effective communication, regular communication must be structured both one-on-one and in strategic teams, take place on multiple mediums with consistent and appropriate frequency, and be held both formally and informally.

Communication Structure

Leaders should utilize both one-on-one meetings and team meetings as tools to build open lines of communication because each of the two structures will provide a different benefit. Team meetings provide an opportunity for the team to discuss complex challenges and solutions that affect multiple people and/or departments, to share the accomplishments they are responsible for, and to gain an understanding of the full team's and company's status. One-on-one meetings are better utilized by leadership to provide individual feedback and coaching to team members and to

Table 1. How effective communication creates a competitive advantage for an organization

Scenario	Type	Communication Culture	Business Result
Customer service is receiving a pattern of similar complaints about product problems	A	The customer service director has established effective communication with the operations team and shares feedback using both formal and informal communication. Both teams share feedback on what is considered mission critical feedback and what is not.	When the customer complaints started, the operations team looked into the problem early enough to fix the problem immediately. They even proactively reached out to customers to minimize the effects of the problem before customers even noticed, resulting in an increase in brand loyalty.
	B	The customer service director has shared feedback in the past but feels that his feedback falls on deaf ears. As a result, he no longer channels information upward.	What starts out as a controlled product problem, spreads further into the market and the company doesn't learn about the problem until a high percentage of customers have switched to a competitor.
The SE Regional Sales Team is continuously breaking sales records while the other regions are struggling to hit goal	A	The VP of Sales has nurtured open lines of communication with each regional director through regularly scheduled one-on-one meetings as well as open dialogue across regions through effective regularly scheduled team meetings	The SE Regional Director shares best practices that are helping her team exceed goal each month. Because of the relationships built over time, the regional directors are open to hearing ways to improve from their trusted peers.
	B	The VP of Sales reaches out to the directors whenever things are not going well and reviews lagging indicators to motivate the directors to push their team accordingly. He holds only two team meetings a year in order to avoid wasting the directors' time with too many meetings.	The SE Regional Director does not share her best practices with her peers because she feels as if she's in competition with them and because they never asked.
Based on the outcome of extensive market analysis, the executive leadership team restructures the organization to better compete in the dynamic marketplace	A	The VPs and directors of each department take the time to understand the "why" of each of their direct reports and require their direct reports to do the same for their team. Every quarter, leaders meet one-on-one with each of their team members to support the personal and professional goals of each team member.	When departments and job roles changed, team members were open to the change because they knew their personal and professional goals would remain a priority to their leadership team and that they were an important part of the entire team's success.
	B	VPs and directors focus on key metrics with their teams and provide additional training as needed when outcomes fall below expectations. No other discussions around the individual team member's personal or professional goals are notated outside of the one box that is included as part of the annual review.	When departments and job roles changed, team members felt mistreated and as though leadership was changing the rules for them personally. Many of the top performers left the company to find jobs with companies that appreciated them as individuals.

enable individual team members to communicate field and other pertinent information upward to leadership. With an understanding of the purpose and use of each meeting type, leaders are better equipped to create a stronger culture of communication when both types are used appropriately.

Communication Mediums and Frequency

For decades, leaders have navigated various complexities of team environments. From the less complex situations of having all team members in one room at the same time, to the extreme complex situations of working with teams spread throughout the globe covering various time zones. As communication technology improves, leaders have access to better options, and communicating with team members around the world becomes much more instant and life-like. Consider, for a moment, kings and military generals communicating with their lieutenants via a messenger traversing hundreds of miles on a horse as compared to sending a Teams™ message or jumping on a virtual video call such as Zoom™ or WebX™.

With these additional tools to which leaders now have access comes the challenge of knowing what tools are best used for each type of communication. For example, while texts are fast, they lack tone and body language to help provide the context of a message. And while in-person meetings are best for tone and context, in many cases they are too expensive and/or require too much time for travel.

To help better understand which communication tools are best used for specific needs, leaders should consider two factors: complexity and urgency. In simple terms, when a topic is more complex, the most in-person-like communication is the best option. When a topic is more urgent, the fastest method of communicating is best (see figure 2).

Communication Cadence

In addition to utilizing the appropriate communication medium for the desired outcome, leaders should also create a consistent cadence for one-on-one and team communication. Best practice for setting up the appropriate cadence is based on many factors including the complexity of the efforts required from the team and individuals, the experience level of the team and individuals, and the stability of the environment during the specific period.

In situations where complexity is high and/or the environment changes quickly, a higher frequency of team and individual meetings is more appropriate. The same is true when the team and individuals are less experienced in their roles. Additionally, proximity of team members will also be a factor in necessary frequency of communication.

Figure 2.

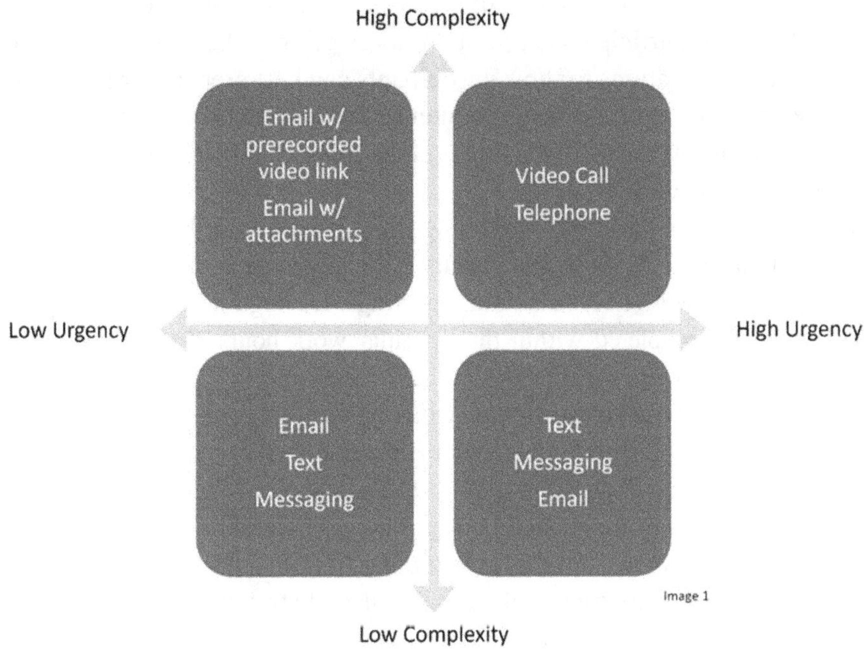

As events unfolded during the COVID-19 pandemic, the corporate coaches at Benchmark Training helped leaders in various types of organizations navigate the needs for the appropriate communication with teams that changed their work environment from working together in an office to working remotely with as little as 24 hours' notice. The coaches found that team members felt less anxious and were more productive when they communicated as a team with a frequency ranging between daily and three times per week as compared to just one time per week. As these same teams became more accustomed to the new work environment, meeting frequency was reduced to one to three times per week and achieved the same positive results.

Formal vs. Informal Communication

The final key ingredient to effective communication is combining the appropriate level of formal and informal communication.

Formal communication can be defined as communication that takes place with ample notice, has a structured agenda, and has a defined facilitator or facilitators. Formal communication can take place as team meetings as well as one-on-one meetings. To assure the best outcome for formal meetings, leaders should provide at least 48 hours' notice for the meeting, send the agenda out to the participant or participants at least 24 hours prior to the meeting start time, and set clear expectations for how participants can best prepare for the meeting to assure they are engaged in the content and the outcomes of the meeting. While formal meetings are effective and valuable, it's important to note that they can be overused.

In many organizations, formal meetings have been over utilized to the point at which participants at all levels of seniority of the organization find them spending over 50% of their work hours attending meetings, leaving minimal time to get the necessary work completed within their regular work hours. To avoid overusing meetings, leaders should consider the total cost of the meeting including calculating the hourly rate of each attendee. Including this expense helps weigh the value of each meeting and assures that only those who are actively contributing to the meeting are invited.

Informal communication can be categorized as communication that does not include the criteria noted for formal communication. In most cases, informal communication is impromptu and can take place between all levels within the organization. From watercooler talk to Teams™ messaging, to a phone call and any communication in between, informal communication takes place very regularly and has a big impact on how thoughts and ideas are shared throughout the organization.

Leaders can maintain open lines of communications by utilizing informal communication with their direct reports to help their team navigate unfamiliar and/or unstable environments and also gain up to date field intelligence that can be utilized in high level decisions.

CONCLUSION

With the demands of today's complex and highspeed business environments, there's more to leading a team than just measuring progress and providing motivation.

As leaders navigate new and complex work environments, creating a culture of effective communication and accountability will play a key role in the performance of their team.

By taking intentional action to better understand the human side of each team member, tracking pertinent metrics to measure progress, and by maintaining clear and consistent lines of communication with their teams, leaders can increase their chances of success in today's business environment.

REFERENCES

Jones, B. (2017, February 28). Great Leaders Show Genuine Care for Their Team. *Harvard Business Review*. https://hbr.org/sponsored/2017/02/great-leaders-show-genuine-care-for-their-teams

Sinek, S. (2009). *Start with Why: How Great Leaders Inspire Everyone to Take Action*. Penguin.

Chapter 4
The New Rules of Engagement:
Hearts and Minds in Turbulent Times

Dave Reed
University of North Florida, USA

ABSTRACT

This chapter combines facts, nuances, and implications of the Turnover Tsunami and Great Resignation phenomena. The author provides important insights that connect changes at social and generational levels—notably regarding stress and burnout, engagement and commitment, and socio-technical work trends such as virtual work and the metaverse—to current and future employment challenges. The chapter is designed to open lines of sight into the most complex and dynamic times ever seen in the employment realm. The author infuses personal strategy (e.g., know your people), commentary (e.g., collective collusion), and applied theory (e.g., cognitive dissonance) to open pathways of thought, understanding, and exploration into mid-post-pandemic employment issues.

INTRODUCTION

Let's face it, today's employment game is far and away the most complex and dynamic that the industrialized, technologized, and now digitized world has ever known. And it's only becoming more so. This chapter combines two lines of sight. The first follows a casual but factual overview of the current work situation with some nuances intended to get the mind of the reader thinking beyond the headlines, blogs, and social trends. The second looks at specific considerations of and for both employers and employees. One chapter cannot provide an answer for every question much less a solution for every problem or definitive crystal ball for every unknown.

DOI: 10.4018/978-1-6684-3453-6.ch004

You're better off with a Magic 8 Ball. But what it can do is offer our minds a flow of perspective to stir one's thinking toward comprehensions and solutions that are necessarily innovative yet fundamentally timeless.

THE KETTLE BOILS OVER

2021 brought a perfect storm for most employers. Companies who survived the previous year's onset of coronavirus were beginning to navigate their new realities with optimism for a soon-to-come, post-pandemic world. Most understood the workplace would be forever changed, but they nonetheless anticipated a return to some degree of normalcy. Yet concurrently, the outer bands of a "Turnover Tsunami" began shaking the already battered businesses. Researchers had been growing concerned about such an event, presciently predicting the now popularized "Great Resignation" as much as two years earlier (Klotz, 2001).

In September 2021, total non-farm employee quits in the U.S. rose to a record 3.0 percent, with over 4.4 million U.S. workers leaving their jobs (Bureau of Labor Statistics, 2021). This record month was merely the latest of many in an upward trend that began in April 2020, seventeen months before. Numerous factors, well beyond the pandemic, may be attributed. Nearly 20 years before, employment experts already were pointing to changes in career attitudes across the different generations now working together in the same organizations. Employee loyalties that once focused solely on companies have been shifting to broader professions and even now (with Generation Y) purely to oneself supported by ad hoc projects across numerous organizations and pop-up businesses (Barclays, 2013). Most recently, digital transformation has become the top priority of most CEOs, guaranteeing further changes in the workplace ladened with new challenges for the workforce and its management. These and many more dynamics were swirling when the coronavirus hit, creating a perfect storm. In fact—and we need to be clear on this—while the pandemic brought its tornadic forces, the main affect was to stoke numerous already simmering fires to full blaze.

The news, social, and business media all have a great much to say about the situation as one would expect. Reports of massive worker burnout, refusals to leave home, and plans to quit jobs abound. Surveys show employees becoming disengaged and disenchanted often blaming company cultures, bosses, pay, and lack of interest in returning to office life. U.S. unincorporated self-employment reached record highs in the Fall of 2021. A growing entrepreneurial spirit and unprecedented technological expansion provided opportunities for nearly 9.5 million people to take control of their work lives rather than suffer in traditional employment with its stress, disconnect, mandatory vaccination requirements, health compromises, and other real and perceived burdens. Such workplace motivation and engagement issues receive most of the attention from commentators and researchers. Importantly we must not forget the obviously related yet ironically underemphasized element of organizational commitment, which as aforementioned has already been in generational decline.

The good news is that conventional motivation and commitment theories still hold their water, even in changing times. Autonomy and empowerment, for example, have long been evidenced to influence motivation, satisfaction, engagement, and so on. It thus should come as no surprise that people greatly value self-determination in their work even as that value *appears* to have suddenly, dramatically increased. (More on this later.) Is the need so high that it must be satisfied by taking the reins of self-employment? Certainly, a self-owned small business has no greater probability of success than it did 10 or 20 years ago. Of the over 800,000 small businesses started between April 2019 and March 2020, almost 20 percent are already closed, falling right in line with the norms of the last 25 years (Bureau of Labor Statistics, 2021a). If those norms remain true, 70 percent will have failed within the coming 8 years.

Does this mean then, that the best way to obtain career fulfillment is by picking up projects online, selling on eBay and Amazon, or day-trading with Robinhood? One would hardly call those common paths to assured career success. Yes, there are countless examples of genuine success in these activities. You can read about them every day. News articles and blogs don't just celebrate the stories of these winners but will convince you that everybody's doing it. And this of course only adds fuel to the furnace, as media influencers are prone to do. I'd observe however that someone greatly suffering from stress and burnout in traditional employment may want to talk to most small business owners or people trying to make ends meet on eBay or anyone supporting a family on stock picks—talk to them about stress and burnout. Stress is stress, and burnout is burnout; I'm not trying to compare what different people experience. I'm simply saying that while leaping from the frying pan into the fire may seem the ultimate experiential expression of the self-directed work life, in the long run, most people will feel the burn at whole new levels in whole new places. Unless one has endless savings to drain or huge basements of parents in which to make a peaceful home, given time, most new work-for-self balloons will become find-a-job realities.

A CAUTIONARY PROPHECY

Let's be clear, however, not everyone quitting jobs are leaving the traditional employment workforce. People quit for different reasons. For example, the big September 2021 quit numbers included an 82 percent increase in the arts, entertainment, and recreation sector. Naturally, states with high concentrations of workers in those areas saw the greatest increase in quits, i.e., the highest increase in numbers of quitters. When experts and pundits trumpet how these quitters are leaving jobs for better working conditions and/or pay, it's no great stretch to expect one can do better than arts, entertainment, and recreation in the middle of a pandemic. But there's also a more insidious phenomenon worth noting.

As the trend of waning organizational commitment and increased job-hopping became more prominent, particularly with more and more millennials coming into the labor market, the interest in talent management and related implications naturally rose as well. In recent years, to keep their supplies of human capital flowing and turnover ratios intact, companies have been forced to find ways of meeting the unique expectations and requirements of a novel generation of worker. A negotiation between employers and labor began taking place, as newer workers took the position of "do it our way, or we will stay home". Firms were thus confronted with an unprecedented refusal-to-be-employed sense of entitlement on top of the increasingly common and accepted job-hopper mentality.

Observing recent social trends and attitudes, and notably, those playing out in the small investor space, I believe the next step beyond hopping and entitlement will be systematic collusion. More specifically, don't be surprised if a movement arises calling on workers to purposefully maximize job-hopping and/or workforce nonparticipation to force wage and benefit offerings higher for all. This is power to the people, sticking it to the corporations, etc. Of course, those costs to the companies are passed through in price increases to consumers (including the colluding parties, themselves), and the economic dominos fall from there. Some might be reminded of a union on strike. Not ironically, I hold the belief that firms have not seen many union workers caught in the plague of burnout, quitting, hopping, etc. Informal conversations have supported this theory, though I've yet to conduct or see any formal studies on the matter at the time of this writing.

We can certainly entertain the differences between job types, people types, and company types relative to the union wrinkle. We could also look at differences in motivation and fulfillment. And a full understanding of such contrasts might produce insightful information for the problem at hand. Without completely ignoring them, we may at least here for our purposes surmise that organizational commitment is alive and well in unions, where it is not elsewhere, and note that the reasons deserve investigation. I would also suggest that the pandemic once again has only served to expose and amplify growing differences already well in the making.

THREE CRITICAL TRUTHS

Getting back to changes in what organizations have been doing and offering to attract and retain employees, many firms are taking these tactics to new extremes in the Great Resignation. Unable to find workers, they are further increasing pay and benefits offerings and finding other shiny objects to dangle in front of progressively discriminating workers. While many of these changes are positive responses and approaches to a changing world, others simply reflect desperate times calling for desperate measures. This is not a bad thing unto itself given the nature of demand and supply—what I will confusingly refer to as the demand for labor versus the demands *of* labor. However, we are seeing a point where the dog is giving itself over to be wagged by the tail, which brings us to three critical truths.

The first truth returns to my collusion theory, namely that if people as a social collective will quit enough or stay on the sidelines enough, employers will cave into the demands of the labor supply. (Again, when I say labor, I'm not speaking of unions, even though there's a familiar union ring to what I'm saying.) With western culture devolving from a mosaiced melting pot into stark neo-social groupthink armies, such patterns of collusion are becoming increasingly evident. This said, I do not want to discount the fact that changes such as those demanded by the labor supply can be very necessary and good—especially when employers have fallen behind in meeting the needs and desires of their employees as they can be wont to do. And we may presume the existence of a natural economic need to reach a new and mutually viable equilibrium, which brings us to a second truth. While turnover churn may prove sustainable for firms in the brave new world, workers staying on the sidelines out of the workforce is not.

One of the mysteries of the Great Resignation is not turnover—the rate of employees leaving and being replaced. It's the number of employees leaving without being replaced. Along with the people finding ways to employ themselves, many have quit altogether to the sidelines, sitting out of the workforce. Some of this can be blamed on health concerns, and some can be pegged to government subsidies (most pointedly, monies provided above and beyond established levels of welfare and unemployment support). As referenced previously, what stands out is the number of people claiming and blaming stress and burnout. One cannot be so thick as to believe that the pandemic has not significantly influenced stress and burnout. But we also now have an epidemic of people telling one another that they *should* feel stressed and burned out.

A recent post on social media by a senior executive shared about her discovery of how unready she was to return to work and how she instead dropped out—not for good—but only until she could feel like she could give it her all. She was immediately celebrated for telling her story and making such a difficult decision with heroic bravery (an odyssey and decision that we all share and too should be making if we too could be so brave) and serving as an inspiration to so many caught in the same epic struggle. Before the pandemic, going to work despite not feeling up to it was considered common and necessary—a strength, maturity, and discipline required by adults going through the trials of life. It now is an unfair imposition. An email recently reached my inbox from a major university empathizing with students greatly suffering from and stressed by the switch to daylight savings and offering them concern, advice, and support. I do not discount the fragile mental, emotional, and in many cases physical state of our people after nearly two years of pandemic. However, when one feels ashamed to say, "I'm doing well, thank you," some other sickness has taken hold. An insistence that we all must crumble together and that anyone bearing up and standing up is obtusely insensitive... well, this presents a problem when we talk about the likes of motivation, satisfaction, fulfillment, and commitment. But it also brings us to the third and most important truth.

The fact is that everything we know about motivation, satisfaction, fulfillment, and commitment are not null and void just because of what people may be experiencing, feeling, telling themselves, telling each other, and—perhaps even more to the point—what they may be believing they want and deserve. We cannot in the same sentence complain about being disengaged from and feeling disconnected with our organizations while refusing to go back to the office, shopping on Amazon during team Zoom meetings, and monitoring job alerts every other minute while working on company projects. I believe that oftentimes part of today's stress and burnout is the result of cognitive dissonance, i.e., the struggle over inconsistent and contradictory thoughts, actions, feelings, and understandings, especially relative to our environment and to change. We believe one thing e.g., I can't give up my freedom and go back to work—when somewhere deep inside, we yearn for something different—I need to be a part of something, involved with other people, having meaningful interaction, giving satisfying contribution, achieving a greater purpose. Not everyone feels those stirrings. But not everyone feels inordinate stress, burnout, and disengagement from their jobs.

KNOW YOUR PEOPLE

Despite this third truth, employers and employees alike fall prey to the same old false beliefs. More money may entice people in the short run, but it will not *retain* people in the long run. There's absolutely nothing wrong with great pay and super benefits. But it will not keep an employee engaged, satisfied, fulfilled, and committed. Employees failing to receive such intrinsic meaning and purpose ultimately will go somewhere else for it, chase even better money and benefits elsewhere, sit on the sidelines, or find an alternative form of employment that at least produces alternative means to intrinsically satisfying outcomes and rewards. If they stay, they likely do so only because they feel honor-bound by a sense of obligation or reciprocal duty, or because they perceive the benefits of staying as outweighing the costs of leaving. The former is not the healthiest reason to stay, but at least it is pro-organizational. The latter (typically referred to as a mere continuance level of organizational commitment) results in more harm than good to all parties. What's eye-opening however is that most largescale employee surveys conducted in 2021 suggest that half of all U.S. employees fall into this latter continuance category. 50% of employees are ready, willing, hoping, and planning to leave—just hanging on until the right reason, opportunity, or predetermined departure date comes along. You can imagine what that does for stress, burnout, cognitive dissonance, and the celebration of quitting. You can further imagine what it does for job performance and morale in the workforce.

Growing scarcer is what researchers refer to as an affective level of commitment (Meyer & Allen, 1991). Think of it broadly as having affection for the place you work. To be a bit more specific it's an emotional attachment to and a self-identification with one's organization—what I would call an *affinity*. The more people become disengaged and disconnected (and notably while working virtually from home), the less affinity they have with their organization. I tend to view this in terms of involvement, satisfaction, and enthusiasm. When employees are involved, satisfied, and enthusiastic about their work they will experience high engagement. When they are involved, satisfied, and enthusiastic about their organization they will have a greater affinity with and commitment to the organization. When someone has both you're not likely looking at a person who's stressed, burned out, and ready to quit because of their work or organization, and you're also less likely looking at someone who's going to chase better dollars and benefits elsewhere at the drop of a hat. Even the old truism that people don't quit jobs, they quit bosses, is less of a factor if those people have high work engagement and a strong affinity with their company.

Organizations must come up with a program that I like to call KYP—Know Your People. We often attribute to Peter Drucker or sometimes Edwards Deming, the notion that you cannot manage what you do not measure, you cannot improve what you cannot measure, and various other combinations and versions, none of which either said. However, I'm certain that from gurus to good managers, everyone can agree on these principles. To know your people, you must measure their involvement, satisfaction, and enthusiasm for their work and for their organization. You cannot manage and improve what you do not measure. Such measuring can occur through HR surveys, a formal process between employee and manager, and other mechanisms. But the measure will only be as useful as it is accurate. You must capture the right information in the right ways. I'm a big proponent of two concepts in this regard: *internal* marketing and *internal* customers. Organizations need to know their internal customers, their people, with the same level of concern and effort that they seek to understand the wants and needs of their external customers. They even can employ the same types of assessments such as customer surveys, net promoter scores, customer effort scores, customer satisfaction scores, benchmarking, and what I call Obwa (Observing by walking around), as examples.

If you're at some level of management, do you know the chief aspirations, career attitudes, and communication preferences of your people? Do you know their levels of involvement, satisfaction, and enthusiasm for their work and for the organization? Are you prepared to do what's necessary to understand your people and ensure their engagement and connectedness? Or are you running on assumptions, presumptions, and a belief that it's up to the employee to be engaged and connected? Perhaps you don't have the time, desire, training, or tools. Perhaps that's just not your organization's culture, how you came up, or how the people to whom you report manage you, yourself. Or perhaps you don't have a compelling vision and the leadership skills to inspire your employees to pursue goals and achievements beyond their individual self-interests. Yes, we can point fingers at generational trends, pandemics, cognitive dissonance, and all kinds of things. But if the organization and its leaders and managers are not doing their part to understand their people, meet the needs and desires of their people, and lead their people to experience something greater than self, then the game is already lost.

Let's be clear, the world and people are changing. While older folks might shake their heads at ideas like a metaverse where people meet and carry out work as avatars, there's a whole generation of younger people who would find a metaverse far more comfortable and engaging than working face-to-face alongside someone. They get stressed out and burned out because they live in a virtual world, not a real world. As I've argued earlier in the chapter, deep down our humanness knows the difference between real and virtual, and I believe people struggle to resolve the cognitive dissonance that arises as a result. Virtual engagement is not real engagement. Virtual connectedness is not real connectedness. How many of us can sit in front of a computer, take a telephone call, and give the caller our full attention? How many of us won't even take the call because we'd rather spend 20 minutes texting when a 20-second call would've accomplished what we needed? What I'm saying is that the longing for real engagement and real connectedness will not go away. It will just get further from our experience as our preference for virtual life and virtual freedom grow. The cognitive dissonance created will always produce stress, burnout, and quitters every time the going gets tough because people haven't learned and prepared to live with reality when it doesn't align with their virtual world. Instead of dealing with reality, future workers will opt for the metaworld in which to live a virtual life including for their work. They will fully insist that reality must meet *their* demands and will not accept a world where they must meet the demands of reality. This can happen in a virtual world, but it doesn't happen in the real world. And so, they will stress out, burn out, and quit.

CONCLUSION

The challenge for the future is to know the human heart and mind; to understand that what truly motivates us and engages us is real, not virtual. We must know our people, learning and understanding how to reach and satisfy their real human needs. If we can give them something real—real motivation, real satisfaction, real engagement, real fulfillment—a real sense of purpose, growth, value, and belonging—then we will again see real affinity and commitment. Then we can stop dangling more money, benefits, and shiny objects. Yes, the pandemic changes everything, and yes, the metaverse will too. But neither can change what truly motivates people at work. If you don't know what that is—if you're not familiar with self-determination theory, Herzberg's two-factor theory, or the job characteristics model—look them up. They're not complicated. We just need to be innovative in how we apply them to the modern workplace and worker. If you've never learned about leadership as a two-way relationship requiring very deliberate thinking, communicating, and behaving, pick up a book on it. There are plenty out there. Find new ways to put those skills and knowledge to work in your organization. No one chapter can package all these things up and tie on a bow. But hopefully, this one opens the mental pathways needed to reclaim hearts and minds in turbulent times.

REFERENCES

Barclays. (2013). *Talking About My Generation: Exploring the Benefits Engagement Challenge*. Barclays.

Bureau of Labor Statistics. (2021). The Economics Daily, *Quits rate 6.6 percent in accommodation and food services in September 2021*. U.S. Bureau of Labor Statistics. https://www.bls.gov/opub/ted/2021/quits-rate-6-6-percent-in-accommodation-and-food-services-in-september-2021.htm

Bureau of Labor Statistics. (2021a). Business Employment Dynamics, *Establishment age and survival BED data for nation by major industry*. U.S. Bureau of Labor Statistics. https://www.bls.gov/bdm/us_age_naics_21_table1.txt

Klotz, A. (2001, May 30). *The Covid vaccine means a return to work. And a wave of resignations: For everyone exiting the pandemic feeling burned out, know you are not alone.* NBC News. https://www.nbcnews.com/think/opinion/covid-vaccine-means-return-work-wave-resignations-ncna1269018

Meyer, J. P., & Allen, N. J. (1991). A three-component conceptualization of organizational commitment. *Human Resource Management Review, 1*(1), 61–89. doi:10.1016/1053-4822(91)90011-Z

Section 2
Leading Within the Workplace

Chapter 5
From the Office to WFH to RTO . . . Kinda:
The New Normal for Golf's Pre-Eminent League

Kirsten Sabia
PGA Tour, USA

David Cordero
PGA Tour, USA

ABSTRACT

This chapter provides an in-depth behind-the-scenes look at how the COVID-19 pandemic changed the sports—and golf—landscape in 2020. At the employee level, the tour had no choice but to develop a plan that had no playbook. Utilizing leadership traits and transparent communications that were frequent, the tour persevered through the toughest challenge of its 50+ year history. At the same time, the organization underwent a massive transition to a new campus, breaking down barriers and embracing change.

OVERVIEW ON THE PGA TOUR:

By showcasing golf's greatest players, the PGA TOUR engages, inspires and positively impacts our fans, partners and communities worldwide. The PGA TOUR is a 501(c)6 membership organization.

DOI: 10.4018/978-1-6684-3453-6.ch005

The PGA TOUR, headquartered in Ponte Vedra Beach, Florida, co-sanctions tournaments on the PGA TOUR, PGA TOUR Champions, Korn Ferry Tour, PGA TOUR Latinoamérica, and PGA TOUR Canada (the "Tours"). Members on the PGA TOUR represent the world's best players, hailing from 28 countries and territories outside the United States (90 international members). Virtually all tournaments are organized as non-profit organizations to maximize charitable giving, and to date, tournaments across all Tours have generated more than $3.2 billion.

The Situation

As the world's premier membership organization for professional golfers, the PGA TOUR and its network of members, tournaments, partners, clubs, employees and fans, span the globe. With the arrival of the COVID-19 pandemic in the early months of 2020, the feared threat to live sports quickly became a reality. The PGA TOUR was forced to cancel its marquee event, THE PLAYERS Championship, and subsequently suspend play across all Tours for a 12-week period before resuming play in June 2020, ultimately becoming one of the first sports leagues to return to competition amid the pandemic.

The following chapter reflects on that time, in the moment, the days to follow and ultimately the 20 months that the PGA TOUR stood still, paused, rebuilt and returned to a "new normal." The authors look through the lens of the PGA TOUR's Communications Department and how the golf world's preeminent league's workforce was changed, likely forever.

In the Moment

David Revsine (2021), The Big Ten Network's lead studio host, said to *The Sporting News*, "Sports are a reflection of our society. They are important to us. For whatever reason, they resonate with us. We measure time by them. They bring people hope and joy and frustration and anger – every emotion there is – and that's part of their place with us."

This sentiment is all the more reason why the minutes and days that passed during that second week in March 2020 were so pivotal in American society. Moments in sports history were starting to happen, and then compound:

- On Wednesday evening, the NBA suspended its 2020 season when Utah Jazz player Rudy Gobert tested positive for coronavirus;
- After completing Thursday's first round of THE PLAYERS Championship in front of 20,000 fans, the PGA TOUR announced that Friday's round would be played without fans, an unprecedented measure;

- Also on Thursday, professional tennis, soccer, the NCAA's biggest conference tournament, and the NHL cancelled or suspended their seasons;
- And by the end of Thursday evening, Major League baseball cancelled spring training, the NCAA cancelled all remaining winter and spring tournaments, including March Madness, and, perhaps the biggest telltale sign, Disney World closed;
- While golf seemed like the perfect social-distancing sport, being played outside on hundreds of acres, after days of crisis communications, by 10 p.m. Thursday, THE PLAYERS was cancelled. A tournament had not been cancelled in such a manner since 9/11.

The world froze, including the golf world.

With competition across all Tours suspended, the PGA TOUR's executive leadership developed its response to the pandemic and built a business unit to safely and responsibly Return to Golf, a feat which impacted each of the 1,000+ employees who make up the TOUR's workforce.

THE EARLY HOURS AND DAYS OF COVID

One of the main tenets of Crisis Communications is to address the business problem first and the communications problem second.

The PGA TOUR Communications department is set up into four pillars to handle a multi-billion-dollar operation, including:

- Competitive communications, including international coverage;
- Player content;
- Editorial development;
- Internal communications.

Prior to COVID-19, save for a hurricane here and there, the biggest challenge faced by the internal communications pillar – albeit a positive one – was the messaging to the Northeast Florida TOUR staff surrounding an impending move from 17 individual buildings at the global headquarters in Ponte Vedra Beach, Florida, to one building on the edge of the TOUR's property - bringing a multitude of departments from their individual microcosms into one space. While the January 2021 move was met with enthusiasm from many, it was also met with resistance to change from others. As they say, change is hard.

COVID-19 was more change than anyone could have ever expected. The many elements of everyday life were entirely turned upside down and unfortunately, there was no playbook to reference how to quell fears and concerns of so many constituents.

The coronavirus forced the majority of the TOUR's workforce to work remotely for the foreseeable future, creating a number of business communication concerns. Unlike other organizations, this proved to be unchartered waters for the vast majority of TOUR employees who had only known a traditional, office-based work schedule. As a result, employees had to learn to communicate in a way that was unfamiliar. (Ramella, 2021)

Internal communications met around the clock during the first days of the pandemic with Talent & Culture (formerly Human Resources), Risk Management and In-House Counsel on employee communications. While those discussions mostly centered on the ever-evolving tournament changes (e.g. no fans, cancellations), they also spoke to employee expectations surrounding health and safety. The TOUR had previously dealt with this exercise when the original outbreak in Asia forced the temporary closure of TOUR offices in China, Korea, Japan and Malaysia, but that was a small portion of the workforce, less than 2%. The process in the United States. happened within hours:

- In the early hours of Thursday morning, March 12, just after midnight, the TOUR announced optional work from home for offices in London, New York and New Jersey (high-transmission areas)
- By the close of business that same day, the decision was made to arrange for Northeast Florida staff to work from home by request/collaboration with their supervisor. TOUR offices remained closed until the creation of a voluntary return to work process with a limited capacity in June 2020, and full capacity in February 2021.

The Formula

One of the ongoing challenges an internal communicator will face at a mid-to-large organization is the ability to effectively communicate with its remote workers. This task proved to be further magnified during a pandemic, where essentially all organizational staff found themselves working in a remote capacity.

At the PGA TOUR, this challenge was met with a combination of both consistency and transparency. Simply stated-- it was critical to maintain a steady flow of communication from all areas of the organization to not only quell the proverbial rumor mill, but to instill a high-level of confidence and strength in the employee base.

The Tools

The first tactic was to quickly deploy a video from PGA TOUR Commissioner Jay Monahan. It was important that the message struck the appropriate tone and included language of hope, togetherness and resilience to overcome what proved to be one of the toughest challenges in the more than 50-year history of the TOUR. (In many organizations, a top-down approach from the most senior person yields the biggest employee engagement).

Armed with a thoughtfully prepared script, Commissioner Monahan looked deeply into the camera lens and spoke to the heart of employees. He endeared himself and appealed to the raw emotions of others. While this message proved effective, it was only the beginning of what would become a consistent drumbeat of poignant and strategically timed employee communication.

Over the next several weeks, and as employees from all office locations began to realize the enormity of the virus, top-down communication continued to be a lifeline to an anxious employee base. Equally as effective as the first message, the team drafted weekly, company-wide email updates ranging from league competition updates, local pandemic statistics and guidance around remote work.

Speaking of remote work, the pandemic ushered in an entirely new era for the PGA TOUR. While the company does have a relatively high number of employees who travel from tournament to tournament, the backbone of the organization was comprised of "desk-bound staff" who had grown accustomed to a daily office culture. As a result, making the switch to remote work would not be seamless and would require strategic thinking and the use of existing (and untapped) technology.

Like most of the business world, the PGA TOUR relied upon video conference technology to replace face-to-face collaboration and attempt to salvage what would soon be a suffering culture.

Modern technology platforms including Microsoft Teams, ZOOM, Ring Central and SharePoint became the new normal for conducting regular business. For some employees, this technology was already a familiar tool in the toolbox. But for a company with an employee base spanning five generations, it was necessary to push frequent communication on how to use these video conferencing platforms and ultimately, "how to work remotely."

Leveraging IT and HR folks to build appropriate and easy-to-understand messaging was of paramount importance. Training seminars, FAQs and how-to videos needed to be quickly disseminated. Moreover, personal conduct tips on business calls (appearance, how to use mute function, lighting, ergonomic safety) was unilaterally provided.

THE NEW NORMAL

As pandemic life became the new normal and employees embraced full remote work, sustaining morale ascended to the top of the priority list. Establishing a healthy level of connectivity across all departments kept employees engaged in business goals, strategy and most importantly, with each other.

Below are a few examples of employee engagement tactics during the pandemic:

- To mitigate the loss of in-person interaction, managers were encouraged to host departmental virtual meet ups in effort to boost morale. These bi-weekly check-ins allowed employees to interact in a casual environment and make up for the "water cooler conversations" that had been so desperately missed.
- The on-site gym was also missed by the company's health-conscious employees. As part of the internal communication cadence, the Fitness staff was tapped to provide videos demonstrating how to exercise and stretch from home without the use of gym equipment. In conjunction with these fitness videos, employees were also equipped with recommendations on ergonomic safety while working in make-shift offices.
- From a financial standpoint, the TOUR leveraged partner Charles Schwab to provide webinars on how to manage personal assets in a time of economic uncertainty.
- Organizationally, the TOUR introduced a new internal communication franchise called "YOU Chats." These weekly "chats" were Microsoft Teams-driven roundtable discussions with department heads, senior leaders, employee resource groups and medical experts. The goal was two-fold: to be transparent; and to bring comradery and collaboration into the homes of employees. Subject matters included: sponsorship value during the 13-week halt to competition, the development of a new digital franchise when access to players was unavailable during quarantine.

RETURN TO WORK – PART 1 (OLD BUILDINGS: APRIL – OCTOBER 2020)

While daily, weekly and monthly communications came from the Office of the Commissioner, Talent & Culture and Internal Communications at the beginning of the pandemic and during the Presidential and State-ordered shutdowns, behind the scenes a sub-group of the TOUR's Crisis Screening Team convened a Return to Work (RTW) Committee in March 2020 and it is still active today.

Made up of Talent & Culture, Internal Communications, Legal, Security, Risk and Medical Advisors, the team met daily to develop the eventual plans for a RTW strategy. This included a phased approach (based on the various building sizes of those aforementioned 17 locations), staggered schedules, daily screening, use of masks and building operational considerations (traffic patterns, use of amenities – kitchen, Fitness Center, Café) and enhancements for building sanitation. Repeatedly, it was expressed the focus was putting the employees' health and safety ahead of all business considerations. It was not the flip of a switch and people were certainly not returning to the same offices they left in March 2020.

Phase I of RTW started as early as April, when some international employees began returning to the office, and in April, domestic employees who needed production equipment to effectively carry on business operations also returned, but the numbers were small. It was not until May 26, 2020, when the TOUR lifted the closure of its Northeast Florida offices, for limited business purposes, with 10 percent density levels for preassigned employees. The Talent & Culture team developed and trained a group of HR professionals as "Wellness Officers," who were assigned to track COVID cases, regardless if the employee was working from home. As surges, especially in Florida were happening, new precautions and policies were messaged.

A comprehensive RTW Employee Playbook was developed for the two Northeast Florida campuses (Headquarters and our Production facilities) which outlined all the "rules and regs" of working in our buildings during a pandemic with no vaccine available (at that time).

Phase 2 started in late-June with a lift to 25 percent building density, again, with preassigned employees. As months rolled by, facility protocol flexibility was created due to the fact very few employees were working from the office, thus allowing for plenty of social distancing. As the rest of the world learned to live with the pandemic, the TOUR did too with curbside delivery options from the employee café, use of the Fitness Center by appointment and other amenity spaces.

As all of this was happening, the TOUR had returned to playing golf without fans or Pro-Ams (both significant revenue generators) while accruing costly operational precautions. As a result, the organization was going through budget cuts, salary cuts and reduction of staff, all of which had to be communicated at a time of uncertainty with a delicate touch.

Finally, by early-October 2020, employees were all assigned to work from home due to the decommissioning of office space in preparation for a new Global Home, with a planned opening in January 2021.

The most important lesson during the early RTW phases was constant communication on where the TOUR was, where it was going and any red flags. Transparency was key, even when it was a challenging message to deliver.

RETURN TO WORK – PART 2 (NEW BUILDING – FEBRUARY 2021)

As stated earlier, amid coping with the pandemic, the PGA TOUR was on the precipice of transformational change: a move to a 187K square foot headquarters – the largest such building in St. Johns County, Florida.

In what was intended to be a time of celebration, our RTW team was tasked with making the transition to the new space as seamless as possible.

R&D (Research and Duplicate)

The PGA TOUR is obviously not the only large organization to experience a move of this size and scope. As a starting point, the TOUR leveraged corporate relationships both locally and nationally to serve as benchmarks and ultimately, better understand the "change management" process and delicate road ahead.

During this process, the TOUR connected with dozens of internal communication and HR professionals who were eager to share their methodologies. The team also found that aside from some employee communication nuances, the wheel did not need to be re-created.

It was through these "listening tours" where the idea to create "Global Home Ambassadors" was formed – a mix of employees with different backgrounds, ages and departments, who could rally around a central mission to provide a smooth move

Figure 1. PGA TOUR Global Home, May 2021, (Credit: Chuck Choi/Foster + Partners)

into the new building. Having a group of ambassadors of their own peers, proved to be an effective strategy, and helped create a "We are in this together" culture.

The caveat was the TOUR was moving to a new building in the middle of a pre-vaccine pandemic. This was not in the pre-planning documentation so again, patience, greater thought towards safety and wellness, and two plans were necessary.

The lesson here is not to be afraid to seek the advice of others, curate the best ideas and implement the ones that will advance your goals and objectives.

The next challenge was figuring out how to inspire enthusiasm from an employee base that had grown accustomed to working from home, to want to return to an office environment – during a pandemic.

As business operated in a "voluntary" return state, it was imperative that engaging content help "sell" the benefits of being together again in a new (and unfamiliar) building. This manifested in myriad ways:

1. The creation of a User Guide for working in the new building (non-pandemic) and in a pandemic (masks, some amenities temporarily closed, etc.).
2. Six Global Home videos were produced to spotlight amenity spaces such as the Fitness Center, employee café and other points of interest.
3. Global Home newsletters filled with Q&As, images, time-lapse videos and project updates were sent monthly.
4. Talent & Culture and the Facilities Department hosted department "roadshows" to answer questions directly from employees about the move.

Again, the concept was to inject a healthy dose of FOMO (Fear of Missing Out) to encourage employees to come back to the office.

Still, challenges remained. Now that employees were coming back at a higher frequency, there needed to be constant updates and messaging around the PGA TOUR's COVID-19 safety protocols.

This began with an education program around the vaccines. Understandably, employees were clamoring for more information on the virus, the vaccine and the TOUR's masking and social distancing policies.

It was incumbent upon Internal Communications to work quickly to ensure these questions were answered. Like other high-profile projects, this effort required immense collaboration with several departments. Once policies were created, communications strategy included witty content to cut through the noise of typical business operations, as well as local and national stories shared with employees to promote the efficacy of the vaccine.

Further, the TOUR's medical advisor addressed employee concerns around the virus via an in-person employee meeting. Using a third-party source proved to be an effective tactic. More information was provided through Q&A sessions.

Figure 2. PGA TOUR YOU Chat, May 2021 (Credit: PGA TOUR)

Nevertheless, as spikes ebbed and flowed, while transparent, Return to Work – Part 2 (new building) was met with a lukewarm response. Those who wanted to come in, did, felt safe and had a new shiny building to themselves. Those who didn't were still provided the flexibility.

RETURN TO OFFICE (RTO)

After multiple dates for the official, non-voluntary RTO were set – first for early-June 2021 - the date continued to be pushed, due to the Delta strain of COVID and the second biggest spike in the country in Northeast Florida. June went to September. To October. And finally, November 1 was the target after the TOUR developed policies to ensure safeguards at full capacity, beginning with a policy promoting but not requiring vaccination.

After an initial voluntary survey was completed by 98 percent of employees asking about vaccination status, it was found that 70 percent of employees reported they were vaccinated by early August. While a positive number compared to the local market at the time, the TOUR sought a higher percentage before returning to full capacity.

All employees who were vaccinated submitted proof of vaccination confidentially to Talent & Culture. As the records were being collected, Talent & Culture informed employees that while vaccinations were not mandatory (unlike other sports leagues or network partners like ESPN), strict protocols would need to be followed for those who were unvaccinated to come into the office, work at a tournament, or otherwise attend work-related events.

This policy helped raise the vaccination rate from 70 percent to nearly 93 percent by the November 1 return. Once an employee submitted their proof of vaccination, their responsibility was complete. But for the approximately 80 employees who chose to not be vaccinated, they would be required to adhere to additional health and safety protocols.

Through this entire process, the TOUR's internal leadership was a big proponent of transparency.

The Business

While attempting to forecast, stay ahead of the virus (as best as possible) and manage expectations with employees, the team also had to ensure its core tournament constituents felt heard and ultimately safe.

While headquartered in Ponte Vedra Beach, Florida, the PGA TOUR co-sanctions hundreds of professional tournaments across the globe and players hail from 28 countries and territories outside the United States. Throughout the pandemic, golf, both recreationally and professionally, thrived simply due to the inherent nature of the game. It is played outdoors and across acres of land – allowing participants to spread out and do their jobs in a socially-distanced manner.

Again, while not perfect, the PGA TOUR, one of the first sports leagues to return, was successful for the following reasons:

- A comprehensive health and safety program was created in consultation with the TOUR's Chief Medical Advisor, Dr. Tom Hospel, epidemiologists and doctors from the Mayo Clinic and Harvard. This plan was eventually shared and blessed by the CDC prior to the return to competition.
- An extensive education program ensued with players, caddies, staff, media, tournaments and vendors to ensure that everyone knew the expectations and responsibilities upon the return. It should be noted that success was possible because the players and constituents understand the magnitude of following the stated guidelines and taking personal responsibility. They understood the importance of staying in the bubble that was created at each tournament site. Eating in their rooms, not traveling together, wearing a mask and socially distancing from one another.
- Most notably, the TOUR partnered with the Mayo Clinic and Walgreens so anyone associated with tournament operations could get vaccinated. Remember, many of these individuals are constantly on the road, so the ability to go to a Walgreens for instance, in any town was of paramount importance.

Figure 3. Dr. Tom Hospel at PGA TOUR global home, May 2021 (Credit; PGA TOUR)

Once the vaccine became accessible and the player vaccination rate was deemed high enough, the TOUR decided it didn't have to mandate the vaccine and ultimately refrained from weekly, on-site testing.

THE NEW, NEW NORMAL

At the time of writing, the Global Home daily welcomes approximately 550 employees. International offices are returning to full operations. The PGA TOUR's medical advisors are keeping a close watch on ever-changing conditions globally. Thanks to the learnings of working from home for so long, the culture is different, but for the better. Instead of strict 9 a.m. to 5 p.m. constraints, the door is revolving. As a live sports and entertainment organization, much of the TOUR's business takes place outside of those hours. While no longer in leisurewear or pajamas hidden by the computer screen, the dress code has relaxed, organically, as has the expectation that employees must be tethered to their desk. With a state-of-the-art gym, employees can focus on their health and wellness during the day. Each of these variables have proven to produce an energetic, and therefore, more productive workforce.

The culture is different. Most are happy. Some are not. Some have even left. But this is normal – whatever that means.

As the PGA TOUR developed strategies for the hybrid workforce that fostered employee safety from the start of COVID-19, the team looked at this unfathomable crisis as a business problem, first. What would employees expect? How does the

TOUR characterize the potential red flags? Then it became a communications problem. Who is the sender? How is it delivered? What is the cadence of timing? How do we handle the feedback/the chatter of a very polarizing topic?

In the end, the authors are proud of the TOUR's leadership, being steadfast with its decisions, delivering precise messages and ensuring there was no ambiguity, and ultimately, returning to a new Global Home in a safe manner.

The authors will submit that the journey and subsequent return to normalcy was not perfect. With such a diverse employee base, feathers were ruffled along the way and difficult conversations were had. Lots of debate. Lessons were learned and of course, even more questions. But with time, employees and their health as the number one priority prevailed.

REFERENCES

Ramella, B. (2021). 5 Business Communication Issues in the workplace. *GetVoiP Blog*. Retrieved from https://gp1.com/5-business-communication-issues-in-the-workplace/

Revsine, D. (2021). 'What is going on here?': Three days in March 2020 when COVID-19 changed everything in sports. *Sporting News*. Retrieved from https://www.sportingnews.com/us/ncaa-basketball/news/covid-19-sports-march-2020/52218di40lv41vacngrwqofen

KEY TERMS AND DEFINITIONS

Global Home: PGA TOUR's campus.
RTO: Return to office.
Talent and Culture: PGA TOUR's Human Resources department.
WFH: Work from home.

Chapter 6
Excellence on Fire!
Leadership Lessons From Firefighters

Dan Stotz
The Leadership Collaborative (TLC), USA

ABSTRACT

Some people are great leaders because they choose to be. Fire chiefs are great leaders because they have to be. They are experts in developing innovative ways to foster employee safety and significance. This chapter presents the framework, process, and strategy that fire-service and public-safety executives use to help firefighters reach their full potential as leaders, innovators, and change makers. Firefighters define leadership as the things a person does and says that inspire others to take action. Like most things in life, leadership is a skill anyone can learn. Yes, becoming a highly respected leader is easy for some people and difficult for others, but with hard work and the right framework, anyone can achieve leadership excellence.

Some people are great leaders because they choose to be. Fire Chiefs are great leaders because they have to be. They are experts in developing innovative ways to foster employee safety and significance. During my 35-year career as an educator, I had the privilege of building leadership development programs for astronauts at NASA, scientists at the FBI Crime Labs, engineers at GE, and physicians at a highly-respected healthcare system. However, my all-time favorite experience was designing and teaching in a leadership program for firefighters. This chapter presents the framework, process, and strategy that fire-service and public-safety executives use to help firefighters reach their full potential as leaders, innovators, and change agents.

DOI: 10.4018/978-1-6684-3453-6.ch006

Leadership is what we do and say that inspires others to take action. Like most things in life, leadership is a skill anyone can learn. Yes, becoming a highly-respected leader is easy for some people and difficult for others; but with hard work, and the right framework, we can all achieve leadership excellence.

THE LEADERSHIP FRAMEWORK

Theory without practice may be irrelevant; but practice without theory is unsustainable. To foster employee significance, all leadership development programs need to identify and commit to a leadership framework that is validated by research and proven in practice. The Fire Chiefs, who were the executive sponsors of the new leadership program for firefighters called the United Leadership Program, agreed to use a leadership framework that was developed by professors and researchers from the Ross School of Business at the University of Michigan. This framework helped everyone better understand the what, why, and how of leadership excellence.

The leadership framework was developed by Michigan Professor Robert E. Quinn and his colleagues as a result of their research on organizational effectiveness. The framework was originally named the Competing Values

Framework because the researchers found that high-performing organizations knew they had to create and deliver value in different, and often competing, ways (Quinn, 2006). However, for the fire-service and public-safety professionals, it

Figure 1. The creating value framework

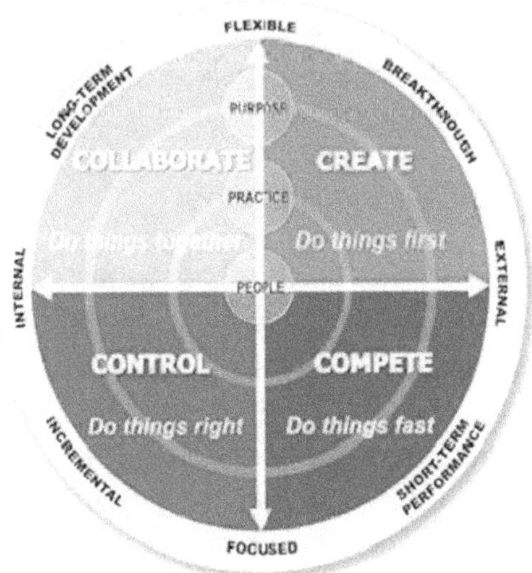

made more sense to rename it the Creating Value Framework to reinforce the fact that leaders have to continuously create and deliver value to the people they serve.

As seen in Exhibit A, the framework shows that high-performing organizations identify and clarify their higher purpose, the practices and processes they need to deliver on that purpose, and, most importantly, the people they need to get the job done. To achieve excellence, leaders must develop the knowledge, behaviors, and skills to create and deliver value in four ways—we have to do things fast, do things together, do things right, and do things first.

The leadership framework's four ways of creating value made a lot of sense to the firefighters. When they have to respond to an emergency, like a four-alarm fire, they have to do things fast, do things together, do things right, and, since every fire is different, they have to do things first—in other words, be innovative.

However, as the firefighters began to get promoted to lieutenant, captain, or assistant chief, they discovered that fighting fires was often easier than leading people, managing projects, or initiating organizational change. In order to become a highly-respected leader they needed to be more inspiring, caring, disciplined, and innovative.

Be an Inspiring Leader (Do Things Fast)

There's no such thing as a highly-respected leader who is great at building relationships but poor at getting results. When leading via the framework's "compete" quadrant, we are doing our best to inspire others to use focus and speed to drive results, exceed expectations, and achieve big goals. To be respected as an inspiring leader, the three most important things we need to do are:

1. Identify and communicate the BIG goal
2. Convert the BIG goal into SMART goals
3. Delegate as a way to develop others

Identify and Communicate the BIG Goal

To inspire others in a big way, we need a big goal! I have the privilege to be an executive and leadership coach to a newly-appointed Fire Chief for a city in the Atlanta area. His major challenge was his predecessor had lead in a way that created a negative and sometimes toxic culture. When asked to confidentially rate the fire department's culture, the new Fire Chief's senior leadership team rated the current culture as a 6.2 on a 10-point scale. Most leadership teams would shoot to improve the culture by a point or two; however, this team decided to pursue a Level 10 Culture!

Convert the BIG Goal Into SMART Goals

What does a "Level 10 Culture" look like? How will we get there? What success metrics will we use to track our progress? What's our deadline? To answer these questions we need to convert the BIG goal into SMART goals. The "S" stands for specific. The "M" stands for measurable. The "A" stands for assigned to one person. The "R" stands for realistic. The "T" stands for time-bound. Below is a partial list of what the fire-service leaders thought a Level 10 Culture might look like.

- High levels of trust; there's no "us and them" language
- Full spectrum competence
- Gains in employee retention
- Ownership at all levels
- Holding each other accountable
- Healthy communications; minimizing rumors and gossip
- Excellence in problem solving

Fire-service and public-safety leaders strongly believe that SMART goals are achieved by a team, not an individual. However, just one person needs to be clearly and publicly put in charge of the goal. That person will then recruit the team he or she needs to get the job done. Cleary identifying the person in charge, and giving the person responsibility and accountability, will increase the odds of achieving the goal.

Delegate as a Way to Develop Others

Effectively delegating to others accomplishes two things. We give other people the opportunity to develop new skills, and we free up our calendar to take on more strategic projects. This is the key to achieving goals faster. Although difficult for some of us, we need to delegate both the responsibility and the freedom to get it done in their own way. Excellent leaders know that we should tell the person "what" needs to be done and "why," but we should never tell them "how" to do it. As soon as we start telling someone how to do it; what they hear is; "You don't trust me." The odds are the other person just might do it better and faster than we could do it.

Be a Caring Leader (Do Things Together)

There's an old saying; "If you want to go fast, walk alone; if you want to go far, walk together." When leading via the framework's "collaborate" quadrant, we are doing our best to inspire others to use flexibility and empathy to attract and retain talent, reinforce core values, and build a positive culture. To be respected as a caring leader, the three most important things we need to do are:

1. Communicate with empathy
2. Ask great questions
3. Forge unbreakable trust

Communicate With Empathy

What is empathy? Empathy is the ability to feel another person!s experience. Respect is the ability to value another person!s experience. Excellent leaders understand the importance of both. What does empathy look like, and how can we become more empathic?

Dr. Helen Reiss, who teaches empathy at the Harvard Medical School, provides the answers by using each of the seven letters. I modified Dr. Reiss's teachings to better fit the fire-service and public-safety environment; and I highly recommend that you take the time to view Dr. Reiss's original TED Talk that was filmed in December of 2013 at TEDxMiddlebury.

The "E" stands for eye contact. Eye contact during a conversation shows attentiveness and interest. The "M" stands for muscles in your face. Facial expressions are a powerful way to show empathy and respect. Excellent leaders understand the importance and power of a smile. The "P" stands for put others first. Minimizing self-orientation is one of the best ways to build personal trust. The "A" stands for ask great questions. Highly-respected leaders ask insightful questions and then listen to understand—not listen to reply. The "T" stands for tone of your voice. How we say words will positively impact how the message is received. The "H" stands for hear the whole person. Leaders need to strive to understand the context in which people live; listen closely and be curious. And, lastly, the "Y" stands for your body language. Posture and body movements help us communicate what we are feeling. Using these seven recommendations will help any leader effectively communicate with empathy.

Ask Great Questions

If we want to truly connect with and care for others, we need to ask great questions and then genuinely listen. Excellent leaders ask the right questions, at the right time, and for the right reasons. It's our responsibility to ask questions where the person we're talking to will say; "That's a great question!" Examples include:

- What can I do to be a better leader?
- Is there anything you need from me?

- If you were running my department, what would you do differently?
- What process needs to be fixed or improved?
- How can I redesign your role to create what's next in your career?

We ask questions as a way to get feedback on how we can improve as leaders. It's important to always remember that feedback is a gift. And what do we say when we receive a gift? The answer is thank you—even if it's a gift we don't like.

Forge Unbreakable Trust

Communicating with empathy and asking great questions will help us build trusting relationships. What is trust? How do we earn someone's trust? David Maister, co-author of *The Trusted Advisor*, offers the best answer. He calls it the Trust Equation where trust = credibility + reliability + intimacy divided by self-orientation.

Credibility is typically earned through our content expertise, years of experience, college degrees and industry-relevant certifications, recommendations by others, and the accuracy of our work. Reliability is often measured by our dependability, the speed of our communications, our ability to keep promises, and exceeding the other person's expectations. Intimacy begins with our courage to talk about difficult topics, take emotional risks, and become a valued confidant. People don't care how much we know until they know how much we care. We need to care more about their needs and concerns than our needs and concerns (Maister, 2000).

Be a Disciplined Leader (Do Things Right)

As stated before, some people are great leaders because they choose to be. Firefighters are great leaders because they have to be. When leading via the framework's "control" quadrant, we are doing our best to inspire others to use focus and discipline to deliver high-quality services, increase stakeholder satisfaction, and continuously improve core processes. To be respected as a disciplined leader, the three most important things we need to do are:

1. Develop process maps
2. Improve processes using data
3. Embrace project management best practices

Develop Process Maps

Excellent leaders are continuously looking for ways to simplify, clarify, and communicate the organization's core processes. A core process is defined as any process that has a significant impact on the customer's experience. Of course, for firefighters, the word customer is not the correct word and it may not be the right word for you—the reader—so please replace "customer" with a word that best fits your environment (stakeholder, employee, colleague, student, patient, volunteer or donor).

A process map is an infographic that clearly shows the key steps in the process, who is responsible for each step, and how long it typically takes to complete the step. Showing the process map to another person helps us do a better job of understanding and managing their expectations.

For example, in the human resources context, the process map can help a colleague better understand why the hiring process takes longer than they think it should. The process map shows them why, in many cases, we need to "do things right" more so than "do things fast." Process maps can help us avoid and minimize the misunderstandings that negatively impact our relationships with others.

Improve Processes Using Data

The importance of continuous quality improvement has been proven time and time again by total quality management and lean six sigma experts from numerous industries. A process improvement idea often begins when a person uses their experience and intuition to evaluate the situation and identify an improvement idea. However, before implementing the person's idea, it is best to collect the data we need to validate the idea or improve the idea.

At the basic level, data comes in two forms—secondary and primary. Secondary data is information that has already been collected by another person or organization and the data is relevant to our situation. Reading books, articles, and case studies is a popular source of secondary data. Primary data is information that we gather ourselves in order to evaluate the idea. Focus groups, one-on-one interviews, benchmarking, and large-scale surveys are common methods for gathering primary data.

Embrace Project Management Best Practices

Almost every project we tackle in our professional lives, whether big or small, will be more successful if we use project management best practices. The Project Management Institute (PMI) provides the best information and training on how to effectively plan and implement a project. In fact, you can earn the popular Project Management Professional (PMP) certification if you are serious about improving your project management knowledge and skills. However, at minimum, leaders at all levels of the organization need to have a general understanding of project management processes, frameworks, and tools.

The Iron Triangle is a popular project management framework. To ensure we achieve the project's desired outcomes, we need to focus on three key factors—the project's scope, budget, and work schedule. Developing a reliable project plan begins by achieving clarity and agreement on the project scope. In fact, once approved, the project scope needs to be "cast in iron" because even minor changes in the scope can create major changes to the project's budget and schedule.

Be an Innovative Leader (Do Things First)

The recent COVID pandemic has challenged, or inspired, many leaders to be more adaptive, creative, and innovative. When leading via the framework's "create" quadrant, we are doing our best to inspire others to use flexibility and creativity to identify new products and services, lead positive change, and convert ideas into innovations. To be respected as an innovative leader, the three most important things we need to do are:

1. Develop an innovation process
2. Build a culture that embraces change
3. Sponsor and support risk-taking teams

Develop an Innovation Process

What is innovation? Innovation is anything we do that makes our organization better or new; and creates value for the people we serve. It's important to understand that we can innovate in all four quadrants represented in the Creating Value Framework. Some of our innovations will be small and deliver incremental improvements; and other innovations will be big and perhaps shake up an entire industry—as often done by Steve Jobs and his team at Apple.

For most organizations, how we innovate is what we innovate (DeGraff, 2009). We need to identify and commit to a proven innovation process. For example, numerous highly-respected innovative organizations use the Double Diamond process developed by the British Design Council. The first stage of the Double Diamond process is referred to as Discover—Define. The second stage is called Develop—Deliver.

In the Discover step we are "creating choices" and in the Define step we are "making the choice." In the Develop step we "build the plan" and in the Deliver step we "implement the plan." The Mayo Clinic Center for Innovation focuses on this process and creates three core teams; the Idea Team, the Data Team, and the Project Team.

Build a Culture That Embraces Change

Innovation and change almost always go hand-in-hand. It's like they are two sides of the same coin. For the fire-service leaders who are pursuing the BIG goal of achieving a Level 10 Culture, they realize that their prototype solutions will include innovations that may require major changes in structure, compensation, or policy. We need to do everything we can to build a culture that embraces change.

A common misconception is that people typically, or naturally, resist change. That's not true. What most people are thinking is: "How will this change initiative impact me and my team?" Therefore, we need to use our empathy skills and our communication skills to give people multiple opportunities to ask questions and share their concerns.

The earlier we do this in the process the better!

John Kotter, a Harvard professor and author of several books on the subject of leading change, offers a popular seven-step process that leaders can use to successfully implement change. The seven steps are titled; Understand, Enlist, Envisage, Motivate, Communicate, Act, and Consolidate. The major reason why most change initiatives fail to deliver the desired results is because leaders too often skip steps or don't spend enough "quality time" in some of the early steps.

Sponsor and Support Risk-Taking Teams

The core teams that are leading innovation and change will almost always have to take major risks in order to implement their ideas—therefore they need an executive sponsor. Gifford Pinchot, author of *Intrapreneuring in Action: A Handbook for Business Innovation*, said it best: "Sponsors support their people's ideas by protecting them from the "corporate immune system." They coach intrapreneurs, raising tough questions and then letting the intrapreneurs find their own answers. They help the group garner needed resources (Pinchot, 1999)." This is important advice from the man who invented the word intrapreneur—a person who acts like an entrepreneur inside of a larger organization. Intrapreneurs take a new idea and turn it into a profitable reality!

THE ABC APPROACH

The best way to become a highly-respected leader, and foster employee safety and significance, is to master the twelve leadership skills presented in this chapter. At the most basic level, we're talking about the ABC's of life—Adult Behavioral Change. According to Marshall Goldsmith, the world's most respected executive coach, there are two immutable truths of behavioral change:

1. Meaningful behavioral change is very hard to do.
2. No one can make us change unless we truly want to change.

In his best-selling book *Triggers*, Marshall states: "The good news is that behavioral change does not have to be complicated. Achieving meaningful and lasting change is simpler than we imagine. But simple is far from easy (Goldsmith, 2015)."

Firefighters, and other excellent leaders, are not afraid of hard work. They do their best to model the behavior they want to see in others. They follow the mantra—know yourself, grow yourself, be your best self. The Creating Value Framework reminds us that we have to continually develop new behaviors, skills, and habits that enable us to be a more inspiring, caring, disciplined, and innovative leader.

REFERENCES

DeGraff, J. (1999). How You Innovate Is What You Innovate: A Systematic Approach to Effectively Leading Enterprise Innovation. *The 2009 Pfeiffer Annual on Leadership Development*, 1-13.

Goldsmith, M., & Reiter, M. (2015). *Triggers: Creating Behavior That Lasts, Becoming The Person You Want To Be*. Crown Publishing Group.

Maister, D. H., Green, C. H., & Galford, R. M. (2000). The Trusted Advisor. Free Press, An Imprint of Simon & Schuster.

Pinchot, Gifford, & Pellman. (1999). Intrapreneuring In Action: A Handbook for Business Innovation. Berrett-Koehler Publishers, Inc.

Quinn, R. E., Cameron, K. S., Thakor, A. V., & DeGraff, J. (2006). *Competing Values Leadership: Creating Value In Organizations*. Edward Elgar Publishing, Inc.

Chapter 7
Employees Feeling Significant in a Hybrid Workforce

Douglas J. Dawson
University of North Florida, USA

ABSTRACT

This chapter per the author describes many of the specific challenges faced by workers as a result of the hybrid environment created by the COVID-19 global pandemic. Leaders of organizations are also struggling with many of the same personal challenges and the requirement to meet organizational goals regardless of the environmental factors affecting their employees. This chapter discusses practical management strategies to help leaders at all levels strike a balance between life and work from home so they can lead with authenticity, empathy for the human experience, and a mindset of productive compassion. Employees want to feel valued and significant. How leaders approach the challenges of the hybrid workforce determines whether or not an employee feels empowered, included, and ultimately significant.

INTRODUCTION

To feel significant is to feel important and valued. Prior to COVID-19, most people went to work at a physical location. Commutes included habits and routines that were disrupted when people were mandated to stay away from the workplace and work from home. Disruption of routines can create stress which can manifest in different ways. People began to feel differently about work once their daily routines and the social aspects of working with others was stripped away. Many in the workforce have become disconnected from the energy and synergy of the workplace and have begun to re-evaluate what they do when trading valuable time and talent for money. What workers do has become less important than why they do it and whom they do it for.

DOI: 10.4018/978-1-6684-3453-6.ch007

Supervisors who used to manage by walking around so they could provide instant praise and coaching are having a difficult time transitioning to a style that must include empathy, compassion and a large degree of trust that people are doing their jobs. Getting the work done became more difficult because the physical separation of work and life was gone. Supervisors were thrust into the personal lives of their employees and had to evolve into new roles that included; life-coach, resource provider, therapist and friend. The illusion of the professional separation between leader and employee vanished and their worlds became entwined. Some leaders were able to transform their style and approach to meet the needs of a remote workforce, but many have not. The inability to meet these needs has led to employees feeling undervalued and frustrated because their leaders are not able, or willing to help them work through the new challenge of work-life balance when both occur in the same physical space. It has been said that employees don't leave jobs, they leave the people they work for.

A great re-shuffling of the global workforce is happening as workers search for meaning in their work and a sense of significance. In this chapter we will discuss the dynamics at work that are creating an environment of dis-trust and feelings of insignificance with employees. We will examine the underlying emotional and mental health factors that will become the next healthcare crisis. The chapter will conclude with culture and leadership strategies that can keep employees engaged, feeling safe and valued in the hybrid work environment.

UNDERSTANDING THE DYNAMICS FOR EMPLOYEES

Prior to the global pandemic, the concept of work-life balance was straightforward. There was a clear delineation between time one spent physically at work and time at home. The pandemic, lockdowns, travel restrictions and on-going protocols have created a hybrid environment where workers now have great flexibility on how and where they do their work, but that comes at a cost. Working from home can be a benefit, provided some conditions prove to be true. These include, but are not limited to: the worker is a disciplined self-starter who requires minimal supervision; they are not dependent on the social aspect of a physical work environment with regular inter-personal interaction; and they have the appropriate tools and space at home to separates work-life from home-life. In the case of the last condition, there are many people who simply do not have adequate space to create a separate work environment. Rather, they are working from the dining room table, a spare bedroom, or worse...their own bedroom. Unfortunately, this last condition can be a challenge for many, as can the need for a social component.

Employees are used to break rooms, water cooler conversations, walking down the hall to get a question answered and interacting with associates in a 'live' environment. Today, however, many meetings and working groups take place as talking heads on an on-line platform. While information can be conveyed in this setting, there are more constraints. Much can be missed without body language and the unique energy and visual cues of a live environment. Additionally, people are less likely to have the side / water cooler interactions that they would in a traditional live environment. These unscheduled interactions are important because they help with relationship building, trust, and ideation.

As such, the new life-work amalgamation requires more from employees than ever before. Time-management is also critical. Work and home-life now need to be scheduled to maintain balance, focus and productivity. In a hybrid environment someone could be completing a project at home one minute, and then working from a cell phone and laptop the next while waiting in the car for a child to finish soccer practice.

THE PSYCHOLOGICAL IMPACT ON THE HYBRID WORKFORCE

A hybrid workforce is a disconnected workforce. Leaders and employees alike can experience a wide range of emotions due to an increase in non-work-related stimulus. These stimuli are generated because the work people are doing was not designed to be done from home. The paradigm of "leave it at the office" completely disintegrates once the office and home occupy the same physical space. This blurs the lines of what was once clear, creating a complex task for employee and supervisor alike as they attempt to weave together the new hybrid worker experience and deal with the emotional challenges that accompany it.

The nature of working from home in and of itself can create stress. Personal interruptions (e.g., family issues, pets, package deliveries, lawn mowers, and other disturbances) can result in anxiety, which left un-checked can result in depression and a steady degradation of performance at work.

The number of employees who are dealing with real symptoms of anxiety and depression are up significantly since the pandemic (Jernigan, PhD, 2021). Many workers feel more disconnected from each other, their leaders and their own families as they struggle to balance the new work from home model. The ability to juxtapose being fully present for work, and fully present at home is an insurmountable challenge for some. This can be more difficult for singles because there are no other demands on their time, and work can become all consuming.

A 2020 Study by the Centers for Disease Control cited by Dr. Jernigan in her article published by Psychology Today, 2021 found that almost 41% of survey respondents reported adverse mental or behavioral health conditions that include anxiety and depression. The interesting point here is that there is likely a much larger number of workers who are experiencing these issues but not reporting them. It is possible that almost half of the workforce from CEOs to front-line workers could be experiencing the debilitating effects of anxiety, depression, or any number of mental and emotional health issues.

The report continues to state that more than 26% of respondents reported that they had either started or increased the use of substances, including alcohol, in order to cope with the emotional stress caused by COVID-19 and the resulting social and workplace changes. Over 10% of respondents reported having seriously considered suicide within the past 30 days. Young people age 18 – 24 are impacted the most with almost 75% reporting symptoms, while less than 52% of workers age 25 – 44 reported symptoms. The study concludes that anxiety, depression and, or some form of Post-Traumatic Stress Disorder (PTSD) were the most common issues among almost half of the American workforce (Jernigan, PhD, 2021).

It is likely that if you work with 10 or more people, one of them may have contemplated suicide in the last thirty days; moreover, up to half may be attempting to cope with some type of emotional stress, mental or behavioral issue. These statistics are a direct result of the sweeping global change brought about by COVID-19. Poor mental health contributes to increased healthcare costs, missed workdays, higher turnover and under-performance. The increase in reported mental health and behavioral issue symptoms is staggering. Prior to 2019 only 11% of the American workforce reported symptoms; in 2021 the number is 42%. According to experts, mental health challenges will be the primary "non-virus related" health crisis in the wake of the pandemic (Jernigan, PhD, 2021)

CHALLENGES FOR LEADERS

Like workers, the role of leaders is more challenging than ever before because they have to understand what their personal challenges are along with those of their employees (e.g., those resulting from the hybrid work environment) in order to be effective. Leaders have to enter the personal lives of their employees in a way that is supportive and encouraging but not invasive and micro-managing. The paradigm of "keep it about business" is no longer valid. In a physically and socially disconnected workforce leaders must come out of the ivory tower, out from behind the desk and enter the lives of their people. They must strike the careful balance of accomplishing the goals of the organization they serve, while showing empathy for the people they serve.

Any perceived ingenuine empathy, lack of transparency or in-authenticity can lead to employee distrust. Trust and job satisfaction are closely related. Feeling valued and significant are critical in the process of accomplishing personal and organizational goals. Conversely, feelings of distrust brought about by a leader who cannot show vulnerability or demonstrate authenticity can result in adverse outcomes for the employee, the leader and the organization.

Leaders are not perfect humans, and are subject to many of the same life, emotional and mental challenges as their employees. It is important, therefore, for leaders to "put their oxygen mask on first" in order to be able to help others. A leader in an unhealthy headspace can become complicit in either creating or magnifying mental and emotional health issues for their employees. The CDC study cited in (Jernigan, PhD, 2021), did not make a distinction between employees and leaders, so it is likely that the same percentages apply to the total top-down workforce, to include top executives and CEOs. An argument could be made that people at the highest levels may experience these symptoms as much or more than their subordinates because they are ultimately responsible for keeping the business viable. The CDC Study predicts these mental health issues will persist long after COVID subsides (Jernigan, PhD, 2021). Additionally, a recent Microsoft Study found over 40% of the global workforce is considering leaving their job in the next 12 months to pursue more fulfilling work ("Survey: 40% of Employees Are Thinking of Quitting Their Jobs," 2021). If the information in these studies and surveys is accurate, the world is in for massive after-shocks to the economy. A global re-shuffling of the workforce and an increase in entrepreneurial ventures may be a likely outcome.

The concept of human capital is more important than it has been historically. Subsidies and alternatives to traditional work has led to labor shortages. Companies across all sectors are struggling to find employees. Therefore, leaders must understand their employees on a personal level and practice steward leadership, or leadership by serving others. The paradigm shift is this: employees do not exist as replaceable pieces in the game of business chess; rather, the leader exists to serve the people who make up the culture and produce results for the organization. Leaders must still demonstrate the qualities of leadership (e.g., coaching and mentoring), but they also need to understand each of their charges on a more personal level in order to be effective. Leading people by meeting them where they are, and understanding the unique challenges of each employee is critical to success in the hybrid work environment. The job must still get done, but the how and when of doing the work is the problem leaders and employees must solve.

REQUIREMENTS OF LEADERS IN THE HYBRID ENVIRONMENT

According to Premuzic and Berg, authors of "Fostering a Culture of Belonging in the Hybrid Workforce" (Chamorro-Premuzic & Berg, 2021), today's leaders must execute three critical strategies to prevent employees from feeling alone, and to make work more about what you do, and who you do it for… versus where you go every day.

The first of these is achieving a balance between the corporate culture that exists within the four walls of the company and Diversity and Inclusion initiatives that promote belonging and innovation from all stakeholders within a particular enterprise. An interesting thought from their article discusses a practice of people being recruited because they may challenge the status-quo, rather than just fitting in. Perhaps now is the time when culture needs to change, fresh perspective can be a challenge for many companies, but now may be the time when new ideas from diverse backgrounds can pay big dividends once the company gets through the pain of change. The flexibility that the hybrid environment provides has exposed weak spots in culture that was inclusive as long as the employee wasn't going to rock the boat. Now that many employees are seeing the work for what it is and not exposed to what this author would term "inside the castle culture," they are indeed feeling disenfranchised and are looking for meaning in what they do as shown in the ("Survey: 40% of Employees Are Thinking of Quitting Their Jobs," 2021). The real struggles many companies face are: will new ideas from a diverse workforce strip away everything that has been built? What does the future of company culture, product and go to market strategies look like? How can the core business be protected while innovating for the future?

Their second strategy is to find ways to maintain the social aspect of work. This is easier said than done because nothing can replace the social interaction and, to some degree, the social pressures of being in the same physical space. People naturally gain insight from body language and can somewhat sense the emotions of others. In the talking heads virtual environment, much of the information we need to effectively process communication is missing. Add greater diversity to the mix and a company has the perfect recipe for misunderstanding, mis-alignment and mis-communication, all of which can lead to a sense of disenfranchisement - which either begins or propels the cycle of poor performance that inevitably ends in turnover. Diversity within organizations can be a difficult change at first, but can produce long-term gains. The process of becoming more diverse must be skillfully managed to prevent lasting negative outcomes and create positive sustainable results. People desire meaningful connections in their personal lives and at work. Leaders must find new methods to engage employees who choose to return to the building while being inclusive of those who stay at home. Informal chat sessions between employees and leaders help to bridge gaps and re-create some of the missing casual conversation that formed workplace bonds.

The third part of this strategy involves having the courage to let the culture evolve. Cultures are not created overnight, and much thought, strategy and intentional actions repeated over time are necessary to create a great corporate culture. This is much easier to do when the effect on culture can be seen over time within a physical space. In the hybrid environment leaders find it increasingly difficult to maintain a culture, keep people engaged and measure the impact culture has on the work product and results.

Every crisis, to include COVID-19, presents an opportunity. Leaders can choose to just let it happen and clean up later, or to use the moment as a force to drive change, new ideas and innovation. The second strategy is more difficult, and gets harder the longer a company has been around. The leadership that made a company successful over time in the former environment may not have the appetite to embrace an opportunity to change and evolve in the current environment. Clayton Christensen, wrote about inertia in acclaimed book "The Innovators Dilemma", and how it can be a double-edged sword, (Christensen, 2013), explaining that companies build incredible inertia to become a success, but that same inertia can kill new ideas and innovation to protect what has been the core business. New ideas, however, need champions to implement them. If courage to make change is lacking, and legacy becomes more important than the future, companies and leaders will struggle to keep great people who bring new ideas and perspective.

Premuzic and Berg conclude their article with an interesting observation and a new generation identifier (Chamorro-Premuzic & Berg, 2021). "Offices may soon become our social and community nodes, rather the place you come in to do your work. They most likely will be important for internal networking, especially for *Gen C*, or "Generation COVID," the generation that will hit the job market after Gen Z. No matter what approach you choose, it is always important to make it explicit, to ensure that people understand the rationale, and to have the humility and data-informed mindset to evaluate what works, what doesn't, and to be ready to adjust accordingly."

DEVELOPING A STRATEGY THAT LEADS TO EMPLOYEES FEELING VALUED

"In the event of an emergency, please put your oxygen mask on first before assisting others." We hear this message on every commercial airline flight. As a pilot, this author can attest to these instructions being true along with the importance of knowing where the emergency exits are, how many rows of seats to the closest exit, whether the exit is forward or backward, and the importance of taking a moment to understand how to open the exit door. Why is this important and what does it have to do with the hybrid work environment? It is important because it is a clear strategy to survive an emergency event. When the chaos of an emergency situation ensues, it is easy to get caught up in the initial emotional response. The mind and body go into fight or flight mode and parts of our brain stop thinking and simply react. "The fight or flight response is an automatic physiological reaction to an event that is perceived as stressful or frightening. The perception of threat activates the sympathetic nervous system and triggers an acute stress response that prepares the body to fight or flee. These responses are evolutionary adaptations to increase chances of survival in threatening situations. Overly frequent, intense, or inappropriate activation of the fight or flight response is implicated in a range of clinical conditions including most anxiety disorders, (Psychology Tools, 2021)". COVID and the resulting new work / life environment has created this same response in many, resulting in the behavioral disorders mentioned earlier in this chapter.

As a pilot, this author completes pre-flight and other emergency checklists for every flight. These checklists include procedures for various emergencies that can occur at different stages of flight, and outline specific actions that are committed to memory so response is instantaneous so that everyone on-board stays safe during an emergency. Emergencies are never planned, but the response to them should be planned to mitigate risk for all the stakeholders.

What we are witnessing in this new world is that there was no plan to deal with the kind of chaos caused by the pandemic. Companies and employees alike have been caught up in the fog created by the disruption to the normal flow of events, and we froze. No one was ready for it; people, companies and governments went into fight or flight mode and simply reacted - throwing supply chains, economics and personal lives into chaos. We are likely going to face more tumult going forward, with climate change, terrorism, disease, cyber-attacks and other potential economic tumult. Companies, leaders and employees need to have a plan to respond to any of these emergencies going forward. The military develops plans to deal with very complex threat scenarios. The response to those scenarios is practiced until the recognition of the threat and actions to mitigate it are accomplished quickly and precisely to protect people and assets. Perhaps organizations can learn from this example to protect people and business assets.

Circling back to the first sentence in this section, the first action of a leader is to put their oxygen mask on first, meaning that leaders must be certain that they are in an emotionally and mentally healthy place, only then are leaders in a position to help others. In a Harvard Business Review article on *How to Manage a Hybrid Team,* author Rebecca Knight discusses the importance of understanding your biases with regard to how you view your employees. This understanding is an important part of the self-work that will lead to success or failure as a leader. When left alone, employees can easily make assumptions based on whether they feel like their leader is dedicating enough time to them. Favoritism can be assumed and result in disengagement along with high turnover (Knight, 2020). It is vital for the leader to understand themselves and work each day to better understand their employees.

COMPASSION WITH BOUNDARIES

Being compassionate toward your employees does not mean there are no expectations of performance. In this environment however, there must be some degree of flexibility in how those expectations are met (Knight, 2020). The "end of the workday" has become rather nebulous because there are many employees who now work irregular hours. The first question for the leader becomes, how do I care for my people and accomplish organization goals? The second question is, how do I show compassion and support for my people without owning the issues and potentially compromising my own boundaries for emotional and mental health? There is a fine line between empathy and enablement. Empathy will lead to trust; enablement will lead to poor performance.

An effective leader understands their own triggers. Emotional intelligence and self-awareness are key in properly managing the answers to the two questions above. Gaining intelligence regarding your employees based on their emotional responses to the hybrid environment is key to helping them evolve through the process of self-discovery and the leader's example. In John Maxwell's book *The 21 Indispensable Qualities of a Leader,* he discusses the concept of courage. John writes, "Every test you face as a leader begins within you. The test of courage is no different...Courage isn't the absence of fear. It's doing what you are afraid to do. It's having the power to let go of the familiar and forge ahead into new territory", (Maxwell, 1999, p.40).

Courage in this context means being vulnerable and authentic. In the past it was viewed as a weakness for a leader to show vulnerability, emotion and their humanness. Instead, leaders were supposed to be stoic figures who drove people for results to accomplish the mission of the organization. When results were not met by the people they had, they found new people who could achieve the desired goals. Leaders rarely got involved in the day-to-day lives of their employees other than work anniversaries, birthdays or holidays. When most people worked within the four walls of the business, the social aspect of work became one of the reasons employees would stay with a company… even if their job was not particularly satisfying. Today, some have returned to the familiarity of the office while others continue to work remotely, for both sets however, nothing is normal.

What we recognize now is that being vulnerable does not equate to weakness; rather, it demonstrates great strength of character, which is another leadership quality named in Maxwell's book (Maxwell, 1999, p.4). Employees need to see and hear their leader experiencing the same challenges they face. In fact, it is the leader who can show them how to deal with adversity, by first, admitting honestly that they too are experiencing challenges, and how those challenges make them feel. While the specific challenges people are experiencing vary, the common thread is that everyone has experienced something, and being human means that we have a natural emotional response to those experiences. Leaders need to be ok with letting those who are entrusted to them know how they feel, but also be able to explain and demonstrate how they are constructively dealing with it. Modeling of productive and collaborative behavior and being creative and inclusive in the face of adverse conditions will help employees see what good looks like. Employees can then begin to model these behaviors, and develop some of their own to accomplish the work and develop bonds with leadership that promotes individual value.

There is something to the saying "fake it till you make it". Sometimes a leader must make the choice to acknowledge the way they feel, but act in a way that creates a path to a solution. There is actually scientific evidence to support the fact that we can choose how we feel about ourselves or a situation, and that choice repeated over time creates a sort of psychological conditioning, ("Scientific Truth Behind 'Fake It Till You Make It'," 2018). By choosing to respond to adversity in a positive and constructive way, we can become that person over time, which then becomes part of our character. Being of good character earns trust; trust when stewarded by a skilled leader grows into momentum and a shared vision for success. People will follow a visionary leader of great character not because they have too, but because they want to.

CREATING A CULTURE OF SIGNIFICANCE

In 2015 Scott Mautz wrote an article for Entrepreneur Magazine that listed six steps for companies and leaders to follow in order to create a culture of significance. Employees at all levels who feel that they are valued and therefore significant to the team and the greater organization create a culture that is energized with new ideas and becomes resilient.

The six steps Mautz listed are: "Recognition, Respect, Work-Life Harmony, Care for the Person, Be Authentic, and Promote Interdependence and Teamwork, (Mautz, 2015)". Today, these steps are still important but perhaps executed differently than they would have been in 2015. We will briefly examine each to begin to define what it looks like to build a culture of significance in a hybrid work environment.

Before a leader or organization begins the process of culture building, this author believes they must begin with one simple premise… *the people who work for you are a gift; they are to be treasured as such, and cared for. These people have entrusted leaders and their associated organizations with some of the best years of their lives, their livelihoods, their personal and professional growth, the person they have become and the legacy they leave behind.* Human Resources when viewed through this lens should focus on the individuals, the human beings who also chose the leader and the company during the hiring process. The trust they give cannot ever be treated lightly. It is not just a job. People are not replaceable like the AA batteries in the TV remote. Sure, others can do the job, but the person, the whole human being behind the title or job description is not *replaceable* and turnover is costly. This is not to say that there are not times when change is necessary, but do not forget the dignity of the person in the process.

Giving Recognition: This is an important piece of any healthy culture that champions employee significance. The nuance here is understanding how and when people want to be recognized for their contributions. Some are embarrassed by the attention that public recognition brings, while others embrace it. Organizations want to celebrate personal achievement that leads to company success, but caution must be taken to make sure that is not the only time recognition is given. In the hybrid environment a constant-drip recognition strategy can be more effective. Yes, celebrate the big wins, but in a disconnected workforce the little daily wins are just as important. For some, just a simple thank you for doing all they do each day to balance home and work, can have a major impact and create a sustainable culture of significance.

Respect: What does this mean in an environment where you don't have someone in the next office who could overhear a conversation, notice poor body language or disengagement in a meeting? Virtual meetings tend to be talking heads and it is easy to check-out, multi-task, and text or email all while still looking in the general direction of the camera. Often people don't turn their cameras on…is that really showing-up for a meeting? If this was at the office, people would see you. We work in a virtual office now, but the same rules should apply. Respect in the hybrid environment means showing up for work. Know who is going to be in the meeting and present yourself appropriately. If this were in a board room, people would get there early, get comfortable, and be ready to take notes and be engaged. Leaders need to model the behavior first. Show up, start on-time and end on-time. Be fully engaged and be inclusive to encourage participation. Acknowledge ideas and feedback. All feedback and ideas have some value, if not to simply provide insight into how someone thinks, which is valuable for coaching. Individualized coaching helps people become their best selves, which is part of the leader being a good steward of the relationship. Never miss an opportunity to learn something about people by listening to them. In his book "The Coaching Habit", Michael Bungay Stainer writes about approaching coaching opportunities with a sense of curiosity, not just questioning for the sake of questioning, but to unlock under-lying root causes for observed behaviors (Stainer, 2016, p.62).

Work-Life Balance: This is certainly the most challenging in the hybrid environment because it looks different for everyone. Some workers are single, some have families, a spouse who works, hobbies, school, kid's programs, etc. In this environment, leaders must act as life-work coaches to help their people navigate their personal situation to find the balance point. Each situation is unique and leaders must be equipped with training and support to serve in this capacity.

Caring for the Person and Being Authentic: Leaders face many of the same challenges as their people. It is important for the leader to share what they are going through as well. This creates a common bond with employees. Leaders today need to realize that it is acceptable for them to be human and lead by positive example. Open and honest dialog will promote trust and create an environment that says, "I understand it is difficult; we will figure this out and get through it together." In the current environment, many performance gaps that leaders are seeing are caused by underlying personal challenges - scheduling conflicts, and other emotional / behavioral issues that, as discussed earlier, affect almost half of the American workforce (Jernigan, 2021). Care for the person involves helping them get to the root of performance issues and providing the support and resources they need for personal development. The stress created by the pandemic and its after-effects has removed the veil that existed when employees and leaders checked their personal issues at the door and came in to the workplace. Personal challenges and issues were hidden behind the persona of our work personalities. Today, everything is laid bare. What was separate is now together with no clear delineation. Stewardship for the leader is caring for the whole person, but it starts with the leader acknowledging their own challenges in the new environment and modeling methods and behaviors to evolve and adapt.

Promoting Interdependence and Teamwork: This is likely one of the most challenging areas when it comes to creating a culture of significance. People tend to think of teamwork as working or meeting with a group of co-workers in person. Most of the ideas around team-building and interdependence revolve around physically working together on an activity to solve a particular problem. The virtual world brings challenges to this aspect of helping people feel connected and significant at work. Today teamwork looks more like digital cohorts working toward a common goal. The missing piece is the informal meetings after the meeting over coffee or in the hall that led to better understanding, comradery and ideation. The keys to success in the virtual environment include but are not limited to: clear expectations of the work to be done, clear responsibilities based on individual contributor strengths, designated time for ideation and check-ins throughout the project time-line, flexibility to pivot if a better strategy is discovered, intentional inclusion and diversity, and as mentioned earlier a constant-drip of recognition for even the smallest win. Even failure can be turned into a win if the learning is applied to next steps. One of the best examples of not being afraid to fail is Pixar Entertainment.

Peter Sims wrote about an interview with Ed Catmull, co-founder and President of Pixar, (Sims, 2012). Rather than being obsessed with perfection out of the gate, the creative team at Pixar was encouraged to fail first. Catmull and Pixar's directors believe it is "easier to fix problems than to prevent errors." Andrew Stanton, Director of *Finding Nemo* and *WALL-E*, states, "My strategy has always been: be wrong as fast as we can…which basically means, we're gonna screw up, let's just admit that. Let's not be afraid of that."

An approach like this in hybrid organizations would likely speed up the process of success. So much time is spent to not make an error, that great ideas are missed because there is simply no space for them in many strategic plans. If teams know that they have the space and support to fail fast, learn and try again, then perhaps other organizations could produce success after success like Pixar. At the time of the interview, the company had 11 blockbuster hits, not because they tried to be perfect, rather because they were not afraid of new ideas from team members up to and including major re-writes and sometimes, complete do-overs on productions (Sims, 2012).

A CULTURE OF EMPLOYEE SIGNIFICANCE STARTS AT THE TOP

"The buck stops here" is true when it comes to organizational culture. There are many examples of company values, mission and vision statements which are all good. Where they break down is in how those values actually impact the way the work gets done. Stephen Covey offers a natural perspective in his book *Principle Centered Leadership,* (Covey, 1999, p.161-162). He states, "The only thing that endures over time is the law of the farm: I must prepare the ground, put in the seed, cultivate it, weed it, water it, then gradually nurture growth and development to full maturity." He counsels leaders to place these natural laws and principles at the "…center of your relationships, at the center of your management contracts at the center of your entire organization."

These natural principles and laws that Covey describes in his book are indeed at the heart of any thriving, sustainable culture of significance. People are creatures of nature and therefore the law of the farm applies. One can draw parallels to the concepts, strategies and actions required to cultivate a robust harvest with the people and resources entrusted to a leader. CEO's and farmers have much in common. They both must turn resources into a sustainable yield. A farmer must be a good steward of the land, adapt to environmental and economic changes, new regulations, employee turnover. Like the farmer, organizational leaders must be good stewards the resources they have been given to produce a sustainable yield regardless of the challenges. Covey is correct in saying that natural laws prevail, both on the farm and in business.

Culture is not a nebulous statement of what a company should be; rather, culture is what the people doing the work *experience* inside and outside the walls. As leaders, the focus must be on the total employee experience. How the people in the C-Suite treat each other and approach the work trickles down to the middle-management, and finally to the workforce. Any toxicity at the top of the organization will find its way to the bottom. In a hybrid workforce, there are many more back-channel communication methods than in the office. These back-channel communications can impact an organization positively or negatively. Much communication in the remote workforce is written, and much of that is informal via text groups, chats, etc. Careful attention must be paid to how a message may be perceived by the recipient. Communication and actions that do not align with any stated culture proposition immediately erode trust, reduce the significance people feel and manifest in lower engagement and performance gaps. Stated in terms of the law of the farm: The farmer could have great vision for what the crop could be, and start with the right resources, but the crop could fail if the farmer did not approach the work of running the farm with intentionality, and did not address challenges or threats that could impact growth and sustainability.

Seeds are designed by both nature and science to grow; however, inattention will kill them. People are the same. No one ever starts a job wanting to fail. Everyone starts a new job, like a new planting… it is within them both to grow and be fruitful, but poor care by the farmer or the leader can have a negative impact on the results, because the initial vision of what it could be did not align with the way the crops or people were cultivated and cared for. Every seed is important to the farmer because it can produce for many years. Every employee should be just as important to leaders for the same reason.

CONCLUSION

The path to employees feeling significant at work starts with the leader feeling significant. A leader who feels they are not valued will not be able to develop plans or people. "Put your oxygen mask on first" means getting real about feelings, biases and self-worth. Leaders need to ask for help, and find resources and mentors who can guide them to a place of balance, health and clarity. Only then they can help others do the same. Everyone has heard the phrase, "Give someone a fish and you feed them for a day; teach them how to fish and you feed them for a lifetime." Actions have more meaning than words. This authors' recommendation for a change to this old phrase is," Give someone a fish and you feed them for a day; *show someone that you can catch a fish* and they will then let you teach them."

Leaders cannot just talk their employees through some steps to adapt to the new work-life environment. Leaders must first acknowledge their shared challenges, develop a clear plan to overcome them, and be able to show their employees how to work together to achieve their goals. Why are some of the best coaches in the world former players? It is because other players respect their experience and choose to follow them in order to achieve that same success. That coach has worn the cleats, done the drills, won and lost and now stands ready to teach, mentor, and coach a player to shorten their learning curve based on a transference of experience with knowledge. Show someone you can catch a fish, and they will ask you to teach them if they have a need that compels them to learn; just tell someone about it and they are likely to have doubts regardless of their need.

This chapter is about people and the leaders sacred responsibility to be a good steward of the people entrusted to them. Harvard Professor, the late Clayton Christensen, published a paper entitled *How Will You Measure Your Life,* (Christensen, 2010). This paper was written long before the pandemic, but he makes several key points that are applicable to creating a culture of significance. He writes, "Management is the most noble of professions if it's practiced well. No other occupation offers as many ways to help others learn and grow, take responsibility and be recognized for achievement, and contribute to the success of a team. More and more MBA students come to school thinking that a career in business means buying, selling and investing in companies. That's unfortunate. Doing deals doesn't yield the deep rewards that come from building up people."

He also discusses the importance of humility. He writes that one should never assume that only people smarter can teach you something, because that attitude will limit learning and limit the value placed in others. Ultimately it limits the interdependence leaders must foster to build employee significance in a sustainable way. Christensen continues, "Generally, you can be humble only if you feel really good about yourself – and you want to help those around you feel really good about themselves too." A sense of humility is essential to the steward leader. Earlier in the chapter we discussed being vulnerable and authentic. Neither of these is possible without humility.

Success as a leader is not determined by a title or income; rather, success as Christensen notes is measured by the lives that are better because of a leader. The greatest quarterbacks of all time never claim a win for themselves. They praise the team for a winning season. In business it is exciting to discuss Return on Investment, Earnings Per Share and Profit Margins. What creates all of that, however, is people getting the work done, not just for a paycheck, but because they believe in the work they are doing and they want to accomplish it successfully because of those who lead them. Everyone who is called to leadership must shoulder the great responsibility to take good care of precious resources. Those resources are the people who have been placed in their care. If done well, a sustainable culture of employee significance and value will be the result.

REFERENCES

Chamorro-Premuzic, T., & Berg, K. (2021, August 3). Fostering a Culture of Belonging in the Hybrid Workplace. *Harvard Business Review*. Retrieved October 26, 2021, from https://hbr.org/2021/08/fostering-a-culture-of-belonging-in-the-hybrid-workplace

Christensen, C. M. (2010, July 1). How Will You Measure Your Life? *Harvard Business Review*. Retrieved October 29, 2021, from https://hbr.org/2010/07/how-will-you-measure-your-life

Covey, S. R. (1999). *Principle-Centered Leadership*. Free Press.

Jernigan, L. B. (2021, June 5). The mental health crisis: A toolkit for business leaders. *Psychology Today*. https://www.psychologytoday.com/us/blog/license-shine/202106/the-mental-health-crisis-toolkit-business-leaders

Mautz, S. (2015, July 20). 6 Steps for Creating a Culture of Significance from the Ground Up. *Entrepreneur*. Retrieved October 28, 2021, from https://www.entrepreneur.com/article/248626

Maxwell, J. C. (1999). *The 21 Indispensable Qualities of a Leader: Becoming the Person Others Will Want to Follow*. HarperCollins Leadership.

Psychology Tools. (2021, May 31). *Fight Or Flight Response*. Retrieved October 28, 2021, from https://www.psychologytools.com/resource/fight-or-flight-response/

Sims, P. (2012, July 30). *Pixar's Motto: Going From Suck to Nonsuck*. Fast Company. Retrieved October 29, 2021, from https://www.fastcompany.com/1742431/pixars-motto-going-suck-nonsuck

Stanier, M. B. (2016). *The Coaching Habit: Say Less, Ask More & Change the Way You Lead Forever*. Box of Crayons P.

Survey: 40% of Employees Are Thinking of Quitting Their Jobs. (2021). *World Economic Forum*. Retrieved October 20, 2021, from https://www.weforum.org/agenda/2021/06/remote-workers-burnout-covid-microsoft-survey/

The Scientific Truth Behind 'Fake It Till You Make It'. (2018, December 5). *Cognition Today*. Retrieved October 28, 2021, from https://cognitiontoday.com/the-scientific-truth-behind-fake-it-till-you-make-it/

Chapter 8
Adapting on the Run:
The Critical Role Leaders Played in Sports During the COVID-19 Pandemic

Brodie Waters
University of North Florida, USA

ABSTRACT

This chapter examines the impact COVID-19 has had on the world of sports and the critical leadership traits that emerged during this challenging time. Sports leagues around the world were dramatically impacted by the global pandemic, and as they navigated the many "new norms" that were created during this time, certain leadership qualities became extremely important to determining an organization's success. Specifically, the ability of leaders to effectively communicate, be flexible with operational procedures, and to establish a culture of creativity all proved to be instrumental in determining an organization's ability to persevere through the many challenges they faced.

It was March 11, 2020, when everything in the world of sports would change as we had come to know it. The National Basketball Association's (NBA) Utah Jazz were in Oklahoma City to take on the Thunder and the Jazz's All-Star center, Rudy Gobert, was announced to be out of the game due to an illness. Moments before tip-off, with both teams already on the court, the referees brought the coaches of both teams together for a discussion. Several minutes later, each of the team's went back to their locker rooms, while the public address announcer in the arena notified the more than 16,000 fans in attendance that the game was being temporarily delayed and the teams would be back out on the court soon. After conferring more with the

DOI: 10.4018/978-1-6684-3453-6.ch008

NBA league office, the referees notified the announcer that the game was officially being postponed. The announcer relayed the news to the fans who were both confused and irritated at not being able to watch their team play. Little did they know at the time that they were now a part of what many viewed as the seminal moment when the COVID-19 pandemic became global news.

By the time the Jazz and Thunder were set to square off that March evening, COVID-19 was certainly on the radar of many in the medical field and in isolated other parts of the world, especially in China. In fact, earlier that same afternoon, the World Health Organization officially characterized COVID-19 as a pandemic. Dr. Anthony Fauci, head of infectious disease for the National Institute of Health who would soon become a household name, had addressed lawmakers in Washington, D.C. that day advising them against the gathering of large crowds. However, it was when COVID-19 disrupted sports that the global awareness of the virus escalated at a pace few could have anticipated. Gobert received notification shortly before gametime on March 11th that he had tested positive for COVID-19, and when the results were shared with the league office, they officially postponed the game at 8:27pm local time. As they were processing the ramifications of having a player test positive, the NBA quickly realized the enormous potential exposure possibilities their players were facing. Not only had Gobert's teammates all been exposed, but within the previous five nights, the Jazz had competed against the Boston Celtics, Detroit Pistons and Toronto Raptors. Taking into account that all of those players may possibly have been exposed and then expanding that to teams they had each competed against in the nights following their games against the Jazz, and you quickly were talking about more than half of the league having potential exposure to COVID-19.

Less than five minutes after the announcement was made over the public address system in Oklahoma City that the Jazz game was being postponed, reports began surfacing on Twitter that the NBA was suspending the season. The league made it official later that evening in a statement which announced that the league was halting operations following the conclusion of that evening's schedule of games until further notice. They stated that they would use the hiatus to determine next steps for moving forward in regard to the coronavirus pandemic.

Within 24 hours following the NBA's decision, almost every major sports league around the world had cancelled or suspended operations. The NCAA cancelled all remaining winter and spring sports championships, which included the men's and women's March Madness tournaments, which typically generates nearly $1 billion, representing more than 75% of the NCAA's annual revenue (Dosh, 2021). The National Hockey League suspended its season, Major League Baseball cancelled Spring Training and delayed the start of its season, top soccer leagues around the world, including in the United Kingdom, Spain, Italy, Germany and France all announced the suspension of their seasons. The PGA TOUR cancelled its flagship event, The Players Championship, which was taking place that weekend, and the Association of Tennis Professionals (ATP) suspended its tour as did Formula One racing, one of the world's most followed sports.

Immediately, we all experienced the extremely powerful platform that sports maintain in society, as within hours almost every other industry followed suit and closed or significantly altered their operations.

As the realities began to set in among sports as to the various ramifications the cancelling or suspension of play was going to have, the importance of leadership took center stage. Leagues and teams around the world were challenged with creating completely new business models on the fly, focusing on trying to resume competitions while ensuring safe environments for employees and players, delivering compelling content for fans, and ultimately attempting to find ways to salvage critical revenue streams. To accomplish these objectives, a few specific leadership traits emerged as critical to navigating through this "new normal."

COMMUNICATION

To Play or Not to Play

As with other industries, executives in sports are placed in positions of leadership, but a job title or role doesn't automatically make someone a true leader. That designation is earned by gaining the trust and respect of those he or she has been tasked with leading, which understandably can take time to achieve. As the COVID-19 pandemic set upon the world, perhaps no role of a leader was more important than the ability, and willingness to effectively communicate.

By mid-March 2020, almost every sporting organization in the world had suspended or cancelled play. The COVID-19 pandemic was impacting the entire world, and the initial decision to suspend play was an obvious one. Over the next several months though, leaders of teams and leagues were working through the enormous impacts not competing were having, both from a financial standpoint, as well as how the lack of sporting events were impacting society.

The suspension of play had massive impacts on league and team revenues, including lost revenue from ticket sales, concessions and parking, sponsorship dollars being withheld and the impact of reduced or deferred broadcast revenues. Every organization had to either implement or create contingency plans to minimize financial losses as best possible. Initial decisions by organizational leaders often centered around if a postponement was an option, or if a complete cancellation was required.

While most organizations announced a temporary suspension of play, including leagues such as the NBA, National Hockey League (NHL), Major League Baseball (MLB), English Premier League, Formula One Racing and the PGA TOUR to name a few, due to the timing of some seasons and events, a few organizations such as the NCAA were forced to cancel altogether, including the extremely profitable March Madness tournament. Based on the concerns taking place around the world due to the many unknowns at the time of the pandemic, suspending or canceling play were some of the easier decisions leaders of sports organizations would have to make. The real tests of leadership would come in the months following as they navigated if and when to restart operations, and how they would communicate those decisions with the many constituents, ranging from fans and media to health and government officials. But most importantly, how to communicate with their players, balancing the priorities of health and safety with the financial pressures to resume competitions.

As the league that was the first to suspend play, the NBA and its commissioner, Adam Silver, would also find themselves taking the lead in many respects in restarting play. Since becoming commissioner in 2014, Silver quickly was viewed as a difference maker, being both incredibly sharp and future-forward thinking for the NBA, and empathetic to challenges facing many players, including the subject of racism that was at the forefront of many conversations in the United States at the time. One year after taking the helm of commissioner, he was named Executive of the Year by Sports Business Journal, and one of Fortune's 50 Greatest Leaders. The goodwill he had built up over the years would prove critical as he faced perhaps the biggest challenge of his tenure in the COVID-19 pandemic.

Almost immediately after suspending play in March, the NBA worked tirelessly to develop a plan to restart the season. First and foremost, Silver consistently communicated with players and assured them that their safety would be at the forefront of any plan to resume play. Masterfully getting widespread approval from ownership, team executives and the NBA Players Association, in late June Silver was able to announce the league's plan to resume play beginning at the end of July, which would feature 22 of the 30 teams competing in a "bubble" environment in Orlando, Florida in front of no fans (Aschburner, 2020). The plan required rigorous testing of all players, coaches, and support personnel, and required players to live in designated hotels on Disney property while being prohibited from leaving the Disney campus. At a time when there were still many unknowns about COVID-19, and no vaccine was currently available, there were many questions as to if the NBA would be able to pull this off. A big challenge was for the NBA to get the players on-board with not only adhering to strenuous testing policies, but also to agree to moving into the NBA created "bubble", without the ability to be joined by family members.

The trust that Silver had developed with the players over the past several years through consistently following through on promises made served him extremely well when trying to get buy-in on the restart plan. With more than 250 players comprising the 22 teams who would be invited to play, only 10 players opted out of participating, with much of the credit for such a low number due to the compassion Silver showed when taking into account player concerns and the way he effectively communicated with them the plans the NBA was taking to address each concern.

Despite the massive logistical challenges, the NBA was able to complete a reduced season and full-length playoffs, resulting in the Los Angeles Lakers being crowned world champions. Not only was the season, which lasted until early October, completed, but the COVID-19 protocols implemented were deemed to be extremely successful, with zero cases of COVID-19 being detected. The efforts of the NBA to create the "bubble" cost close to a reported $200 million dollars, but the resumption of play recouped an estimated $1.5 billion for the league (Lombardo, 2020). Silver's leadership through the "bubble" season was widely praised, and in many ways has served as a template for guiding an organization through a pandemic. At a time when much of the country were at odds with various safety measures and regulations the government were implementing, the NBA's ability to have so many people exhibit the discipline to follow such comprehensive health and safety protocols shined a light on Silver's unique talent of effectively communicating with a variety of constituents while being empathetic to the various concerns of many.

While Adam Silver was able to leverage the trust he had gained through the years with his players into a widely praised successful execution of completing the season in the "bubble" with no positive tests recorded, Major League Baseball and its commissioner, Rob Manfred, faced a different set of challenges. Manfred had become commissioner in 2015, and during his tenure had struggled to connect with players, fans, and media alike. Challenging situations, including a 2017/2018 cheating scandal involving sign-stealing by World Series Champion Houston Astros, highlighted his time as commissioner prior to 2020, and his handling of that and other situations had been widely criticized. Players around the league were livid at Manfred's decision to ultimately not punish any players on the Astros and allow them to keep the World Series trophy, which he then further compounded by infuriating baseball purists by referring to the trophy as just a "piece of metal."

The day after the NBA suspended its season on March 11th, Manfred announced that Major League Baseball also would be suspending its season indefinitely. The league went to work on developing a plan to conduct the 2020 season, almost immediately running into obstacles ranging from state health restrictions, travel protocols and player salary adjustments. Communication between the league and the Major League Baseball Players Association (MLBPA) appeared rocky to say the least, and the league's first proposal to restart was submitted on May 26th and was quickly dismissed by the MLBPA. Multiple other proposals were submitted back and forth between the groups, with each being denied by the other. On June 23rd, one day after the MLBPA voted down the league's most recent proposal, Manfred imposed a 60-game season with expanded playoffs, despite the objections of the players (Lacques, 2020). Much of the contention between the two sides revolved around the belief of the players that in late March Manfred had committed to pay the players on a prorated basis for a shortened season, and then two months later tried to change the league's position. This broken communication led to further distrust between the players and the league, and nearly kept the season from restarting.

Ultimately, unlike the NBA, who were able to get their players to agree to conduct the season in a "bubble" (as did the National Hockey League, utilizing locations in Toronto and Edmonton), Major League Baseball decided to hold games at stadiums throughout the country, albeit without fans in attendance.

This approach meant that players from teams would be required to travel to away games, making it much more difficult to track and monitor player movements when not at the ballpark. Almost immediately several teams experienced outbreaks of COVID-19, with most of the cases being traced to travel or players not adhering to safety protocols of mask wearing, social distancing or visiting non-designated team facilities. In all, more than forty games were cancelled during the 2020 season, but the league was able to conduct playoffs, ultimately crowning the Los Angeles Dodgers champions, who defeated the Tampa Bay Rays in the World Series, which was held in Arlington, Texas due to COVID-19 restrictions in California. While the season was able to be completed, the lack of trust Manfred had with the players and his inability to effectively communicate the league's position on how to start the season safely and successfully were widely condemned and created more tension for soon to be negotiations with the MLB Players Association over a new Collective Bargaining Agreement.

These two examples illustrate how critical it is for leaders to not just be able to effectively communicate their position, but to also make others feel as though their thoughts and concerns are being considered. As we begin to emerge from the pandemic, leaders at every level now must realize the importance of consistent and honest communication. It is critical that we understand that communication isn't just about the words we say, but also equally important is listening to what others are saying. There continue to be so many uncertainties surrounding the pandemic and how organizations are responding, that leaders must go above and beyond to articulate policies and protocols. Even more so, leaders must display true empathy for how others are feeling through these challenging times. Everyone wants to feel like they have been heard. Policies ultimately may turn out in a way the employee didn't agree with, but if leadership has done a good job of both explaining why decisions have been made, along with taking the time to truly listen and take into consideration the perspectives of others, common ground can likely be found, and organizations can come together to move forward.

And while communication certainly is a key trait for successful leadership, there are other traits that have emerged through the COVID-19 pandemic as extremely important for leaders to possess.

FLEXIBILITY

Seasons start, seasons end, off-seasons occur and then seasons start again. Sports are cyclical in their operations, perhaps more so than most any other industry. Leagues and teams invest enormous amounts of time and resources in developing successful processes for selling tickets, securing and fulfilling sponsorships, executing gameday operations, engaging fans and managing complex budgets. Once these plans and protocols are put into place, it can be easy for leagues and teams to become set in their ways and get comfortable with the status quo. In many circumstances, there is rigidity within an organization, with decisions made and things done because of a "that's the way we do things here" mentality.

Like other industries, plans in sports were widely set when the global pandemic brought the entire world to a sudden halt. Schedules had been finalized, tickets had been sold, sponsorship activation plans were in place and budgets had been completed. But COVID-19 threw everything into a state of chaos, and in many respects, the status quo was no longer relevant. However, in cultures frequently mired in routines, there is little flexibility in altering the way things are done, which led to considerable challenges in dealing with the pandemic. But throughout sports, there were some shining examples of leaders who embraced the need to be flexible, and not only managed to execute during extremely challenging times, but often found their willingness to adapt to the situation led to new processes that will be long-lasting for their organization.

A Search for New Revenue

Less than 24 hours after the NBA announced the suspension of their season, the National Hockey League also announced they were suspending the remainder of the 2019-2020 season. The league had less than a month remaining in their regular season, which was scheduled to conclude on April 4, 2020. The conclusion of the regular season leads right into the NHL Playoffs, which include several months of play, and typically generate significant ratings throughout North America. Upon announcing the suspension of play, Commissioner Gary Bettman indicated that their goal was to resume play as soon as it was appropriate and safe. As did other leagues, the NHL quickly went to work on developing plans for how they could complete the season.

Ultimately the NHL developed a process somewhat similar to the NBA's "bubble" although the NHL version included 24 teams competing in two cities, Edmonton and Toronto. The modified season included qualifying games and round-robin style seeding games, followed by playoffs. The season culminated with the Tampa Bay Lightning defeating the Dallas Stars to win the Stanley Cup. Overall, the NHL was widely applauded for being able to complete their season in a safe manner, but the lost revenue from the modified season being played in front of no fans and significant changes to the broadcast opportunities was substantial.

Heading into the 2020-2021 season, Commissioner Bettman and Deputy Commissioner Bill Daly were keenly focused on the financial challenges facing clubs from the losses of 2020, as well as the continued challenges in front of them for a 2021 season. Like other professional sports leagues, sponsorship dollars at the team level in the NHL are critical to the viability of each organization. Most teams had success maintaining partnerships with corporate sponsors through the pandemic, despite games being cancelled and fans not being allowed to attend. However, a growing challenge each team was facing was finding "new" value to provide to sponsors who stayed with them through these challenges times. Commonly referred to as "make goods", for sponsors to continue supporting teams there were going to have to be additional assets included into existing partnerships.

Teams and leagues constantly walk a tight rope of balancing providing assets of value to corporate partners with maintaining a viewing experience for fans that doesn't become overrun by corporate branding. The most visual components of most competitions are the field, court or ice the games are being played on, as well as the uniforms the players compete in. Beginning in 1980 the NHL has allowed teams to sell signage on the boards around the ice rink, and by the end of that decade every team featured sponsors on their boards (Seide, 2021). By the 1990s the sponsors began having a presence on the ice itself. Technology has allowed the sophistication of the signage to improve dramatically, but through the years the NHL was steadfast on not allowing jersey sponsors.

However, with the unprecedented challenges COVID-19 placed on teams, leadership at the NHL understood that these dire circumstances required that they be flexible with teams looking to find ways to offer make goods to existing sponsors. In December 2020, the NHL announced that for the 2020-2021 season they would grant each team permission to sell a half-dozen new assets to recoup lost revenue during the pandemic, including allowing teams to place sponsor logos on player helmets, providing entirely new assets teams could either sell or provide to existing sponsors. And while studies had shown that fans were strongly against the NHL placing sponsor logos on jerseys, the implementation of logos onto helmets was fairly well received by fans. Almost every team placed a sponsor logo on their helmets, and most were intentional about trying to incorporate the logo in a tasteful manner that didn't significantly alter the overall look of the helmet.

The willingness of the NHL's leadership to be flexible with teams on finding ways to provide additional value to sponsors played an important role in the league's ability to withstand the financial challenges brought on by the pandemic. Furthermore, their openness to adjusting their stance on assets they would make available to sponsors is leading to additional revenue opportunities for teams. Witnessing the general acceptance shown by fans with the allowance of helmet logos, the NHL announced that beginning in the 2022-2023 season they will allow teams to sell jersey sponsorships, which is commonplace in soccer leagues throughout the world, and have even recently been allowed in the NBA.

For a variety of reasons, the NHL had elected through the years to refrain from selling jersey and helmet sponsorships. However, as we have discussed, a critical component of leadership is having empathy for others, which in this situation were the teams struggling with lost revenue and strained sponsor relations. And while having empathy is important, it is also vital that leaders be willing to be flexible at times to find solutions to challenges presented. Leadership at the NHL realized the difficulties their teams were facing and decided to alter the stance they had taken on jersey and helmet sponsorships, and the end result was extremely positive for the teams, sponsors, and even acceptable for fans.

A New Kind of Racing

While in the United States, the NFL, NBA and MLB tend to garner most of the sports media coverage, in other parts of the world Formula One (F1) racing captures one of the largest audiences of any sport. With an average viewing audience of nearly 100 million fans each race, the sport has seen its popularity, which historically has been centered around Europe and Asia, begin taking hold in the United States as well. Spurred by the success of the Netflix original series "Drive to Survive", which debuted in 2019, Formula One has been successful in expanding its audience to extend beyond avid racing fans and has attracted a younger audience, drawn in by the compelling stories of the drivers and teams showcased in the Netflix series.

Formula One features 10 teams (including the likes of Mercedes, Ferrari, McLaren and Red Bull Racing), with each team fielding two cars per race. The teams compete in a season that features approximately 20 races, held at different locations around the world. Given the global nature of the sport, the COVID-19 pandemic obviously had a significant impact on Formula One's ability to conduct the 2020 season. And while being an outdoor sport provided some relief to COVID concerns, Formula One races typically draw enormous crowds, on average in excess of 200,000 spectators per race, which would not be feasible during the pandemic. On March 13, 2020, just two hours before the initial practice race of the season opening Australian Grand Prix was scheduled to begin, Formula One announced that the race was being cancelled due to COVID-19. With races scheduled to take place around the world, it quickly became apparent that the Australian Grand Prix would not be the only race impacted by the pandemic. While Formula One executives rapidly went to work developing plans for how and when to start the 2020 season, they also knew that falling out of the public eye would tremendously jeopardize the great momentum the sport had been experiencing the past several years.

One advantageous development that had taken place in recent years with Formula One was the emergence of its F1 Esports Series, which was launched in 2017. Revolving around F1's official video game, involvement in the Esports Series expanded to include official Formula One racing team's creating their own esports teams to compete in the F1 Esports Series championship. Leadership at Formula One realized that this existing platform could potentially serve as a platform to maintain fan engagement with their fans, but only if they could quickly pivot and create an opportunity for current F1 drivers to compete. Only one week after announcing the cancellation of the season opening Australian Grand Prix, on March 22, 2020, Formula One launched the F1 Esports Virtual Grand Prix (EVGP) series, which would be a first-of-its-kind virtual racing series that involved participation from fans, official F1 drivers, and other various celebrities.

An unimaginable number of hours go into planning and executing all the various elements of a Formula One race, and the task, as is the case in other industries when it comes to primary lines of business, becomes all consuming. However, leadership at Formula One recognized an opportunity in front of them and allowed the staff some flexibility to pursue a virtual program as well. The results were almost immediate and were fantastic for Formula One. The organization successfully secured participation from several Formula One drivers, along with various stars from other sports. The Virtual Grand Prix provided a platform for fans to connect and engage with their favorite drivers in ways unlike ever before. The drivers weren't confined to wearing helmets as they are during real Formula One races and being able to conduct the virtual races from the comfort of their own homes also allowed fans to get a chance to have a more personal interaction with the drivers than was ever previously possible. And the realism of the virtual games also was able to showcase the incredible skill these drivers possess, as they competed on remarkably accurate reproductions of iconic racetracks around the world. All in all, more than 30 million viewers tuned in to watch the F1 Esports Virtual Grand Prix, which streamed live on the official Formula One YouTube, Twitch and Facebook channels, as well as on F1.com (Dixon, 2020).

The easy approach for Formula One during the pandemic would have been to put all available resources into trying to develop restart plans for traditional races, keeping the focus on getting back to the status quo. But because the leadership at

Formula One provided the employees the opportunity to be flexible in pursuing new opportunities during a time of constraints and limitations, they not only provided terrific and highly engaging content for their fans while physical races were unable to be conducted, but they also actually expanded their fan base, bringing in a younger audience who already were participating in virtual gaming.

When the 2020 Formula One season resumed in July of 2020, many fans of the sport found themselves even more connected to their favorite drivers and teams due to the phenomenal access and interaction they had experienced through the F1 Esports Virtual Grand Prix. The willingness to be flexible with exploring new opportunities has positioned Formula One to come out of the pandemic with more momentum and excitement in the sport globally then perhaps ever before.

As unique as the sporting industry is, the necessity for good leaders to be flexible is vital regardless of the type of work or environment. The pandemic brought unprecedented challenges not just to entire industries, but perhaps more importantly, to every individual and their personal lives. Ranging from the loss of a loved one, to the logistical challenges of having to work remote, to becoming a care giver or to the very real emotional toll many experienced through these times, normal routines have been dramatically altered. Through these times, leaders have been provided with an incredible opportunity to listen and take note of what others are going through, and then adapt their operational plans in order to better accommodate the needs of their employees, customers, or shareholders. The ability to be flexible during these challenging times have resulted in outstanding results in many scenarios, several of which will have long-lasting sustainability beyond the pandemic. However, leadership that were unable, or unwilling to adjust with the times have in many cases found themselves with a disgruntled staff, depleted customer base and decreasing and sometimes unsalvageable revenue streams.

CREATIVITY

COVID-19 brought daunting challenges to organizations across all industries, and that certainly was the case with sports. And while we have discussed the critical importance of communication by leadership and their willingness to be flexible in the face of a crisis, there was another very significant leadership trait that emerged through the pandemic. In sports, the inability to hold competitions in front of fans placed an enormous financial burden on leagues and teams, which led leaders of some organizations to display incredible examples of creativity and innovation. At a time when panic set in among many about how the world of sports could survive both the sudden suspension of play, as well as the restrictions imposed once competitions were allowed to resume, leaders of several organizations stood out in their ability to inspire their staffs to think outside of the box and reimagine a "new" fan experience.

A New Idea from One of the Oldest Sports

The Open Championship is the oldest golf tournament in the world, first held in 1860 in Scotland. Frequently referred to in the United States as the British Open, The Open Championship is held annually each July, and is arguably the centerpiece of the global golf calendar. Organized by the Royal & Ancient (R&A), one of golf's governing bodies, The Open attracts the best players in the game and is broadcast around the world. Other than during both World Wars, and once in 1871 when there wasn't a trophy, The Open Championship has been conducted every year without fail. However, with the COVID-19 pandemic effecting areas around the world, it was announced on April 6, 2020, that the tournament to be held in July would be cancelled, and not rescheduled.

Martin Slumbers, Chief Executive of The R&A, said, "Our absolute priority is to protect the health and safety of the fans, players, officials, volunteers and staff involved in The Open. We care deeply about this historic Championship and have made this decision with a heavy heart. We appreciate that this will be disappointing for a great many people around the world, but we have to act responsibly during this pandemic and it is the right thing to do. I can assure everyone that we have explored every option for playing The Open this year but it not going to be possible."

Among the many other competitions around the world that were being either suspended or cancelled, the decision to cancel The Open was understood, but nonetheless left golf fans everywhere extremely disappointed. Almost immediately after the announcement was made, leadership at the R&A began collaborating with various partners in an effort to come up with a unique way to engage with fans in the absence of that year's tournament.

"From conception to delivery we only had 11 weeks," said Malcolm Booth, The R&A's Director of Sales & Marketing, who was instrumental in the development of the program. "We wanted to find something that could fill 'Open Week' maintaining The Open's special place in the sporting calendar despite the cancellation. There was some great innovation starting to happen in lockdown and we wanted to seize the opportunity to do something that would inspire sports fans globally."

Steeped in history, with past champions including golfing greats such as Arnold Palmer, Jack Nicklaus, Gary Player, Tiger Woods and Rory McIlroy to name a few, an idea was developed to utilize cutting edge technology to bring the past and present together in ways never seen before.

The result was an award-winning production called The Open For The Ages, which spliced together 50 years of archived footage from some of the greatest Open Championships, utilizing CGI technology along with advanced analytics to create a fantasy tournament that brought together past champions from as far back as 1954 in an epic competition. Additionally, there was a unique fan engagement component, with fans able to vote on who they thought would win this ultimate championship, with those votes factored into the determination of the winner.

"We really wanted to involve fans as much as possible in The Open For The Ages," said Booth. "We have created a digital membership for The Open, called The One Club, and its mission is to bring fans from all over the world closer to The Open. This project was perfect for engaging that audience and allowing them to be part of its creation."

The Open For The Ages was broadcast internationally over a four-day period, as well as streamed through various outlets during the week the actual tournament was scheduled to have taken place. This new creation allowed golf fans around the world to enjoy a unique Open Championship and generated tremendous levels of engagement with fans on social media channels.

Despite not being able to conduct an actual tournament in 2020, this incredibly creative project provided The R&A with a fantastic opportunity to actually grow their fanbase during a year with no tournament, while also providing opportunities for tournament partners to receive value during what otherwise could have been a tournament week filled with disappointment at the cancellation.

A Different Kind of Fan

Across the pond back in the United States, Major League Baseball's New York Mets were preparing to begin the 2020 season in late July. The league had decided to begin the postponed season with a shortened schedule and with teams playing in their home stadiums, but in front of no fans. With most states implementing restrictions on crowd gatherings, the decision to play in front of no fans was expected, and most of the previous months had been spent trying to create a plan to be able to conduct a season of some sorts. The logistics of testing players and coaches, organizing proper social distancing within locker rooms and during travel and protocols for sanitizing equipment all became fairly standard from one team to the next. However, how teams would address lost revenue and, perhaps more importantly, find ways to remain engaged with their fans, became an enormous topic that each team addressed differently.

Lou DePaoli, who was Executive Vice President & Chief Revenue Officer for the New York Mets at the time, worked tirelessly with his staff to address both of those concerns. Extreme efforts went into accommodating existing sponsors as best as possible, finding "make goods" where they could, to provide value to their sponsors. The losses in ticket revenue, concessions and parking were inevitable and something every team was going to suffer from. But DePaoli, and other executives around the league, understood that in addition to trying to find ways to offset the lost revenue with cost containment measures, they were going to have to get creative to find ways to maintain engagement with fans at a time when the in-stadium experience was no longer an option.

One of the more unique ideas that surfaced initially started with German soccer club Borussia Monchengladback, and quickly was adopted by other leagues and teams around the world (Gregory, S.). DePaoli and his staff saw that the German club had created cardboard cutouts which were placed in the stands in substitute of real fans. Visually from a television standpoint, it helped to minimize the visual oddity of playing in front of an empty stadium, while also providing a source of revenue for the club. For the Mets and DePaoli though, the concept of cardboard cutouts provided a great opportunity to engage with their fans and make them feel a part of home games, even when they couldn't attend. Furthermore, while sales from the cardboard cutouts could help during a time when revenues were suffering, the Mets determined that funds generated from this program should go towards charitable efforts related to the COVID-19 pandemic.

The Mets implemented the cardboard cutout program beginning with their home opener, offering free printouts for fans who renewed their season tickets for the 2021 season. They allowed fans to customize their cutouts with an image of their choosing, and the response was fantastic. Demand and interest were so high in fact, that quickly the program was expanded to allow any fan the opportunity to have a cutout created.

"Every day we took a look at the number of orders, and we were amazed at how successful the program became." DePaoli said. "During a time when everyone was separated due to the pandemic, it served as a fun opportunity to bring our fans back together."

Throughout Major League Baseball, several other teams followed the Mets, and the images of cardboard cutouts filling the seats of what otherwise would have been empty stadiums became one of the lasting memories of how sports adapted through a global pandemic. What began as a program focused on season ticket holders and family members of the players, rapidly became an initiative that was utilized in a variety of ways. Viewers of broadcasts occasionally would see a famous cardboard "fan" in the stands, such as actor Tom Hanks, whose cardboard persona was displayed at the stadium of the Oakland A's, where Hanks had worked as a peanut vendor as a teenager. Other fans used the cardboard cutouts to bring family together who had been unable to see each other due to quarantine restrictions, and cardboard grandparents and grandchildren were often seen sitting side by side at a ballgame. And some used the program to honor lost family members with a great seat at their favorite ballpark.

The Mets and other organizations throughout Major League Baseball realized that the cardboard cutout program provided a unique way for fans to still feel like they were part of the team, even when they weren't able to attend in person.

For DePaoli, he also saw an additional, unexpected value the program brought.

"Creating this program not only generated some great revenue for charities we aligned with, but it also really brought our staff together." DePaoli said. "At a time when departments had their normal responsibilities drastically altered, we had staff from all sorts of departments working together on this to get the cutouts placed on seats. From finding the right vendors to figuring out solutions for how to mount the cutouts onto the chairs, the entire staff worked together to pull this together, and it created a sense of camaraderie during a really tough time."

The pandemic placed a massive burden on teams in all sports to address lost revenue in seasons that were either cancelled or that resumed play before limited or no crowds. Furthermore, and perhaps even more problematic, they faced the risk of significant future losses if engagement with fans was severed. Many leaders realized that just doing business as usual was no longer going to be a recipe for success, and those that had created a culture where innovation and creative thinking were encouraged fared much better than those organizations where employees felt as though good ideas could only come from the top. In fact, successful leaders realize that occasionally the best ideas may come from someone completely outside of the organization. In the case of cardboard fan cutouts, Borussia Monchengladback, the first team to use the cutouts, got the idea from a passionate fan, who approached the team with the concept. The willingness of the team to embrace the idea of someone from outside of the organization and then effectively execute the program speaks volumes about the leadership present within the organization.

As society adjusts to a myriad of new "norms" as we emerge from the global pandemic, organizations across industries are discovering that consumer behaviors and expectations have changed in a variety of ways. Whether it is expectations with regards to health and safety measures at places of business, to newfound efficiencies discovered through technologies that became essential, common approaches that have been taken for decades may no longer resonate with customers or clients. More than ever, there is an onus on leaders to not only bring creative minds to the decision-making process, but even more so, for organizations to survive post-pandemic, leadership must foster an environment that encourages and facilitates creativity from every employee at every level.

The global pandemic caused a massive shift in how business is conducted for organizations around the world. And that certainly was the case in sports, which holds such a unique position in society. For generations, sports have served as a vehicle to bring people together and often to provide a platform for fans to temporarily escape from the rigors of everyday life. When it came to COVID-19, the rapid response to the pandemic of leagues with global followings such as the NBA, Major League Baseball, Formula One and the English Premier League, emphasized the seriousness of the pandemic to the entire world. And due to the important role sports occupies in society, leaders within these organizations were evaluated on how they navigated through these challenging times. And perhaps never was there more of a need for leadership. Across all sectors, organizations often found that their success or failure largely depended on the ability of their leadership to guide their organizations through these unprecedented challenges. But as has been the case throughout history, adversity often reveals the true colors of a leader. And throughout sports, there were shining examples of leaders who excelled in the areas of communication, flexibility, and creativity, and have positioned themselves and their organizations for tremendous success post-pandemic.

REFERENCES

Aschburner, S. (2020). *Silver, NBA Players seek 'new normal' in return to play amid pandemic*. https://www.nba.com/news/adam-silver-social-unrest-return-play-inside-nba

Dixon, E. (2020, June 19). *F1 Virtual Grand Prix pulls in 30m total viewers*. https://www.sportspromedia.com/news/f1-virtual-grands-prix-total-viewers-audience-tv-digital-social-esports/

Dosh, K. (2021). NCAA Has Confirmed Its Basketball Revenue Distribution Plan for 2021, But Impact of 2020 Will Linger. *Forbes*. https://www.forbes.com/sites/kristidosh/2021/02/28/ncaa-has-confirmed-its-basketball-revenue-distribution-plan-for-2021-but-impact-of-2020-will-last/?sh=104a721f391a

Gregory, S. (2020, April 29). German Soccer Fans are Putting Cardboard Cutouts of Themselves in the Stands to Avoid Games in 'Empty' Stadiums. *Time*. https://time.com/5828699/soccer-cardboard-cutouts/

Lacques, G. (2020, June 23). Major League Baseball implements 60-game 2020 season as players agree on safety protocols. *USA Today*. https://www.usatoday.com/story/sports/mlb/2020/06/23/mlb-implements-60-game-schedule-beginning-around-july-24/5308390002/

Lombardo, J. (2020, October 19). NBA preserved $1.5B in revenue at Disney, but losses are steep. *Sports Business Journal*. https://www.sportsbusinessjournal.com/Journal/Issues/2020/10/19/Leagues-and-Governing-Bodies/NBA-bubble.aspx

Seide, J. (2021, August 1). *A Brief History of Rinkside Advertising*. https://thehockeywriters.com/a-brief-history-of-rinkside-advertising/

KEY TERMS AND DEFINITIONS

Collective Bargaining Agreement: Agreements typically negotiated between professional sports leagues and its players, covering subjects such as minimum and maximum salaries, benefits, health & safety protocols, revenue sharing, roster sizes, etc.

Esports: Name given to organized electronic sports, typically in the form of organized video game competitions. Over the past several years the global Esports market has grown to generate in excess of $1 billion annually.

Formula One Racing: One of the most popular sports in the world, Formula One Racing, commonly referred to as F1, is the premier level of open-wheel racing cars, with events taking place around the world. Its popularity is highest in Europe and South America, with rapidly growing audiences in North America and Asia.

Major Championships: In men's professional golf, The Open Championship, The Masters, United States Open and PGA Championship are considered golf's major championships. In women's professional golf, the major championships are Chevron Championships (sometimes referred to as the Dinah Shore), United States Women's Open, Women's PGA Championship, The Evian Championship and the Women's British Open.

Make Goods: Term used in sports marketing referring to situations when teams, leagues or athletes are unable to fulfill certain obligations of a sponsorship agreement, and provide "make good" provisions to the sponsor to account for lost sponsorship opportunities.

Playoffs: Following the completion of a regular season, the highest performing teams compete in an elimination style tournament, ultimately culminating in a champion. Leagues vary on how they determine how many teams qualify for the playoffs, and the format of the tournament.

Sports Sponsorship: Critical component of professional sports, where brands pay money to leagues, teams and/or athletes in exchange for recognition, promotion and/or hospitality. Common forms of sponsorships include venue naming rights, logo placement on jerseys or fields, player endorsements and media rights.

Section 3
Leading in the Digital Age

Chapter 9
Accelerated Digital Transformation:
A Framework for Leading Digital Innovation and Change

Deepak Arora
Crowley, USA

Breann Alexus Waiters
University of North Florida, USA

Lakshmi Goel
University of North Florida, USA

ABSTRACT

The pandemic has accelerated the need for organizations to embrace digital strategies for processes that are both internally as well as externally facing. The demand for innovation in how a firm serves customers, supports teams, and empowers employees has necessitated the adoption of digital solutions. In this chapter, the authors provide a framework for how organizational leaders can envision digital transformation in a way that is in alignment with business strategy. Digital innovation, while left to the IT enterprise in the past, is now elevated to the level of organizational strategy and can be instrumental to business competitiveness and continuity. Strategic digital transformation can help organizations build agility and resilience, capabilities that have proven to be essential in the face of unpredictable forces, such as those experienced during the COVID-19 pandemic.

DOI: 10.4018/978-1-6684-3453-6.ch009

1. INTRODUCTION

In simple terms, digital transformation is the adoption of digital technology by a company. Digital transformation is implemented by companies for various reasons, ranging from competitive necessity, to serve as a driver for better operational performance (Hess et al., 2016). When successful, digital transformation can yield manifold benefits, such as increases in sales or productivity, innovations in value creation, as well as novel forms of interaction with customers, and other stakeholders (Matt et al., 2015).

Technology is reshaping the way we work faster than ever. Even before Covid-19, the digital landscape was disrupting the workplaces to adopt smarter ways of collaborating and engaging within the organization. The pandemic only accelerated the adoption and scaling of the technologies in every dimension of our modern workplaces. It fundamentally changed the way we engage with the stakeholders both internally and externally. Advancing digital transformation can spur organizational growth and overall economic development, and is now accelerating even faster. The pandemic caused the organizations to (re)-work their digital transformation blueprints as the topmost priority. Digital transformation has thus become the most essential pillar for building a future-proof organization. The nature, intensity and pace of digital transformation varies by industry, organization, and operations, as some areas require a more transformative approach than others.

Given this variability, how should leadership teams rebuild their organizations to ensure a workplace that is conducive for providing a superior customer experience and an exceptional employee experience, while ensuring sustainable growth and profitability? How should companies redefine their innovation strategy to create differentiating value through their business models ensuring their operating models are digitally enabled to capture and deliver the new value to their stakeholders? While balancing the disruption and change cascading at each level of the organization, how can organizations continue to embrace their values and protect the culture that has been enabling the organization for decades?

We address the questions raised above by linking digital transformation to organizational strategy. We provide a "digital blueprint" that identifies multiple dimensions of digital transformation and provide examples of companies that have led successful charges in doing so. The intent of this chapter is to provide a framework for innovation and change that can serve as a blueprint for organizations in the process of digital transformation.

2. A FRAMEWORK FOR DIGITAL INNOVATION AND CHANGE

2.1 Literature Review

Digital Transformation is using digital technology in all areas of business that enables an organization to lead with better decisions through data analytics, implement effective processes, and deliver superior value to our customers and employees. Prior literature indicates that there are certain elements in common in digital transformation strategies that are independent of the industry or firm (Matt et al., 2015). There are some models for digital transformation that exist in prior research. Figure 1 below represents one such simple model of digital transformation along the dimensions of operational and functional strategies.

Similarly, financial aspects have been considered critical in value creation and structural changes enabled by the use of technologies for digital transformation.

While these models provide a starting point to link digital transformation to business strategy considerations, they fall short in describing the nature of digital transformation itself, often simplifying all transformation efforts as the use of technologies.

Figure 1.
Matt, C., Hess, T., & Benlian, A. (2015). Digital transformation strategies. Business & information systems engineering, 57(5), 339-343.

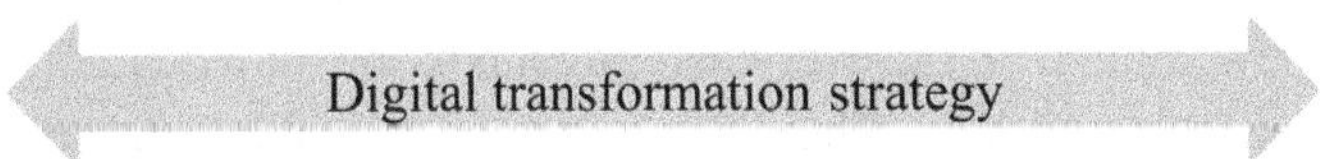

Figure 2.
Matt, C., Hess, T., & Benlian, A. (2015). Digital transformation strategies. Business & information systems engineering, 57(5), 339-343.

We build on this prior literature to provide a digital blueprint that is more encompassing of various factors within the dimensions of digital transformation. Our blueprint is substantiated by examples from the industry.

2.2 The Digital Blueprint

We propose that the digital blueprint of an organization can be articulated in two dimensions – the primary axis describing *what* we are transforming and the secondary axis describing *how* we are transforming. The "what" of the transformation are the business model, operating model and the experience for customers and employees with an organization, and the "how" of the transformation are digitization, digitalization, and data analytics.

Specifics of each of these elements would require to be defined in the context of the organization. SImilarly, the timeframe and roadmap to accelerate the adoption and scaling at all levels of the organization needs to be defined within the context of organizational capabilities. However, we provide pointers and signposts of how transformation can be achieved for each aspect within organizational strategy.

2.2.1 *Business Model*

The business model of an organization defines the value proposition to the customer. Digital transformation entails redefining the proposition to arrive at new values. Hence, business model transformation is about the incremental value that can be offered to the customers digitally. It should be aimed to be agile to consistently innovate the new value with the ever-changing landscape of technology and unmet future needs of the customers. The digital disruption enables and repositions the business strategically and, in a way, offers more sustainable growth and profitability if executed right. It is highly critical to define the business strategy first before the

Figure 3.

How are we transforming?	What are we transforming?		
	Business Model (Digital & Platform Enhancements)	**Operating Model** (Processes & ways of working)	**Customer & Employee Experience**
Digitization (Information to data)	Real time access to quality business data in the cloud platform – Single source of truth and trust	Real time access to quality processes data in the cloud platform – Single source of truth and trust	Customers and Employee empowerment through quality data that can be used for decision making
Digitalization (use of technology to transform process, business model etc..)	Business transformation through digital enhancements and digital platforms	Operations and process transformation through digital automation improving ways of working	Digital enterprise design for better engagement and superior experience for our customers and employees
Data Analytics (Data-driven leadership & decision making)	Creating & Capturing busines value through advanced analytics	Operations and process improvement through advanced analytics	Using predictive and prescriptive analytics to improve customer and employee experience

digital strategy. Digital is an enabler and not the end; it enables the products or services to be offered digitally. Digital technology can radically change how the value is created, captured, and delivered to the customers. It can empower businesses to shift the value chains and competitive landscape altogether.

With the rise of retail e-commerce, one area that has witnessed exponential growth is the supply chain. Over the last two decades, the supply chain industry has evolved from barely modern logistics operations to managing complex end-to-end supply chains. Supply Chain Management is the management of the flow of goods and services and includes all processes that transform raw materials into final products. Supply chains are becoming increasingly globalized and more complex. Innovative technologies such as artificial intelligence, machine learning using advanced analytics, IoT, 3D printing (3DP), and Robotic Process Automation (RPA) can potentially and significantly disrupt the management of supply chains that exist today.

Thus, in considering digital transformation across their business model, firms can think about ways to digitize, digitalize, or incorporate data analytics into supply chain management. Business model transformation is centered around the customer and an outside-in strategy to digital innovation.

2.2.2 *Operating Model*

While the business model focuses on an outside-in strategy, the foundation of the operating model is centered around the people, processes, design, and an inside-out strategy to the digital innovation. While business models offer value through new value proposition, an operating model enacts the digital factory to offer that new value proposition. Without transforming the operating model, the business transformation is incomplete. People, processes, and design transformation are much more difficult than building a new digital product or service. The organizational inertia and incumbent processes can slow down the whole transformation and thus equally critical to be disrupted parallelly. Organizations must consider the digital center of operations excellence to steer the disruptive change and support employees to navigate smoothly. The digital technologies are to be adopted and cascaded at all levels of the organization to achieve operational efficiencies, accelerate growth, and mature analytics capability to make data-driven decisions.

Digital transformation of the operating model requires a strong commitment from the senior leadership to not only make investments but also embrace the new ways of working and digital culture. The digital factory presents an incredible opportunity for businesses to become more agile and nimble by adopting an organizational design that will promote the adoption of big-data (predictive & prescriptive analytics), automated processes (RPA, iBPMS), and a culture that promotes and embraces continual innovation in the sectors that it serves. The shared digital center of excellence will enable learning across the organization and support integrating the services pyramid to not only achieve economy of scale and scope but also faster adoption of digital technology to meet customer and employee needs.

Digital transformation of the operating model iis less about technology and more about talent and leadership. As the organizations undertake the transformative journey, it is paramount to invest in upskilling the talent to adapt to new ways of working. A programmatic approach to roll out talent development and training for the digital skills must be emphasized enough in the digital blueprint. The employees must be equipped with the new skills to offer future-ready digital services and reengineer its foundations on technology, processes, and culture.

2.2.3 *Customer and Employee Experience*

Customer-centricity is the key to digital business models. Organizations must embrace the opportunity to achieve the new dynamics of technology-led innovation and alignment to the future needs of customers and employees. The digital service models must strive to be more flexible and agile to adapt to the dynamics of the technology. The network structure, as opposed to a single hierarchical structure, will enable more collaborative working both within and between teams. The three dimensions of people, processes, and technology must move synchronously for the overall design and development of digital products and services. The reliability, integrity, and suitability of the data is the key to achieving data-driven leadership through the deployment of modern machine learning and artificial intelligence algorithms to achieve excellence in services that organizations provide to the customers. The modular yet integrated data platforms will empower the employees to service the needs of customers and address challenges proactively.

3. APPLICATION TO INDUSTRY

In order to provide specific examples along the dimensions of the business model, operating model, and customer and employee experience, we discuss how Amazon, Best Buy and Netflix created value through digital transformation.

3.1 Amazon's Business Model Transformation

Amazon, which started as an online bookseller in Jeff Bezos's garage, has flourished into a multinational technology company focusing on e-commerce, cloud computing, digital streaming, and artificial intelligence. Amazon is taking a unique approach in the way of digital transformation by transitioning from an exclusively online platform to opening brick and mortar stores.

This shift in Amazon's business model has required the improvement and implementation of technologies that connect the online platforms to the physical stores. For instance, Amazon 4-star stores are physical stores that are curated with popular Amazon products that have received an average rating of 4.4 stars. Through digitization and data analytics, the 4-star stores are pulling reviews and most purchased products from Amazon's website database to then determine which products will be placed in stores. Digital price tags display on each item, allowing customers to see real-time prices that are also directly taken from Amazon's website. Along the lines of reducing human labor emerges the even more innovative 'Amazon Go' cashier-less convenience and grocery stores. Through the use of an app and a combination of sensors and cameras, an Internet of things (IoT) shopping experience is provided to the customer. After the initial scan into the store, Amazon has enabled customers to shop freely and more quickly through the omittance of the typical checkout experience. The digitalization of these brick and mortar stores is what deems them to be a great example of digital transformation.

Amazon executives believe that with the emergence of Amazon brick and mortar stores, better engagement with customers will arise, as well as, giving consumers a chance to see and handle products in person. With this network of physical stores, the discovery of insightful customer data and new shopping experiences for customers become available.

3. 2 Best Buy's 'Renew Blue' Operating Model Transformation

In the summer of 2012, the iconic retailer, Best Buy, was just coming off a $1 billion-plus loss. In an effort to salvage the company, executive chairman, Hubert Joly, was brought in. Through research and an outside-in analysis of the company, Joly discovered that the company still possessed great strengths and most of its problems were self-inflicted. The 'Renew Blue' transformation would change Best Buy's operating model through digitalization, emphasizing store operations and employee leadership.

As discussed previously, when transforming a company's operation model, senior leadership is vital to properly execute the change. During store visits, Joly discovered that Best Buy's search engine did not work properly. By enhancing the online platform, they could better serve customers and remain competitive in a space that was shifting online. It was also discovered that many customers spent a lot of time in the store but still left empty-handed as a result of a lower online price. This is where the idea of online price matching came from. In-store operations changed as well. Much of the stores were filled with CDs, movies, and video games, which didn't make much sense in a world that was transitioning digitally. To make the physical stores more useful, Best Buy began opening Samsung and Apple stores within Best Buy stores, giving consumers the ability to compare products with an expert. This partnership was extended to Microsoft, Sony, LG, Google, and Amazon. By partnering with Amazon, Best Buy received the exclusive rights to the Fire TV platform to be embedded in smart TVs.

After just one year of the 'Renew Blue' transformation, Best Buy experienced a 20% increase in domestic online sales, re-launched their loyalty program, improved both strength of management teams and employee engagement, and exceeded multi-year costs reduction targets. As the transformation continued, Best Buy was able to return $1.5 billion of cash to stakeholders and continue the growth of both online domestic revenue and cost savings. (Waldorf, n.d.)

To withstand the ever-approaching digital takeover, Best Buy has begun making plans to shrink stores and use more store space to fill online orders and curbside pickup orders. COVID-19 has also accelerated the need to transform the company's operations. As a part of the company's strategy to persist, employees are being trained to work in different zones of the store, as well as, completing virtual sales and remote customer support.

3.3 Netflix's Impact on the Customer and Employee Experience

Netflix's recommender systems have led it to be the leading video streaming service in the industry. When transitioning from DVD rentals to an online streaming service, Netflix wanted to answer one question, "How can we personalize Netflix as much as possible to a user?" For this digital transformation to work, Netflix would rely heavily on data analytics and digitization. Through doing this, it allows them to use predictive analysis to suggest which titles a customer would like to watch. Not only does Netflix use this system to recommend titles to customers, but they also use it in the decision-making process of the business, varying from personalized thumbnails and promotional content to which projects to move forward with.

A large amount of data is collected and analyzed to provide the best experience to the customer. Data sources for the recommender systems include stream-related data, metadata related to a title, search-related text information, as well as external data such as reviews from critics and box office information. In addition to that data, demographics, culture, language, and other temporal data are used in their predictive models. (Chong 2020.) In their attempt to improve the user experience, many data analysts and data engineers were brought on to the project. Through digitalization, the inclusion of specific algorithms such as Personalized Video Ranking (PVR), Trending Now Ranker, Continue Watching ranker, and Video-Video Similarity Ranker contributes to the accuracy of the recommendation engine. (Mixon 2021.) Netflix faced many challenges in trying to enhance the recommendations provided to customers. A few being, the creation of different models to predict a single output, implementing instant search, and allowing different indexing schemes and metrics to further optimize the user experience. (Chong 2020.)

By investing so heavily in data science to implement and enhance the recommender systems, Netflix saves $1 billion a year, cancellation rates are lower while streaming rates have increased, and overall member satisfaction has increased as well.

4. BUSINESS IMPLICATIONS AND CONCLUSION

There is no universal framework that may fit all sizes. Each organization would require building its own digital blueprint based on its capabilities, talent, and maturity. What is common among organizations seeking digital transformation are the fundamental questions that the leadership teams should be answering as they engineer their digital blueprints.

"To tackle our biggest societal challenges, we need an innovation pipeline that delivers every drop." -- MIT President Rafael Reif, 2015

In some industries, the need to digitally transform is immediate. For example, the logistics and transportation industry is undergoing a massive change of connectivity through platforms. The subject change will be more profound than the 3PL and 4PL change the industry witnessed a few decades ago. With increasing digitization, platform-based business models will connect new players, and wash away inefficient old ones, and harness the cloud. The shipping industry itself is secondary and has a strong dependency on the disruptions at both ends. To that point, both ends are evolving to platform-based models and the ship management can't truly escape that disruption. It is now time that we drive the change before the change drives us as a company. The controlled maneuver is any day better than the free-fall. Logistics hubs now coordinate with multiple stakeholders, involving containers, finance, fuel, transport, regulatory approval, and more. Multi-party coordination of the asset-intensive industry is round the corner.

It is vital for companies in all industries to keep a close eye on innovations that may disrupt their industry. Although such technologies may be on the horizon, or at a nascent stage, there may be solutions that have emerged in the early stages of development in parallel to interest building by established players in the industry. As most organizations seek to exploit the benefits of these emerging technologies, few companies may realize the need to jump the S-curve sooner.

Figure 4. Business models can leverage the next S-Curve with emergent technology

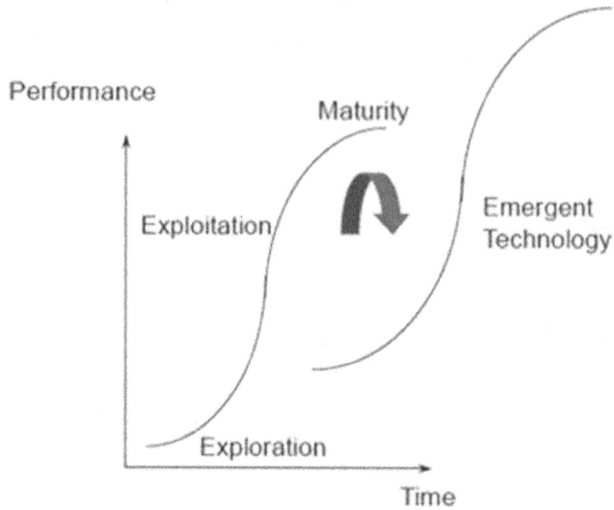

Figure 5. Role of technology in unmet needs of the customers

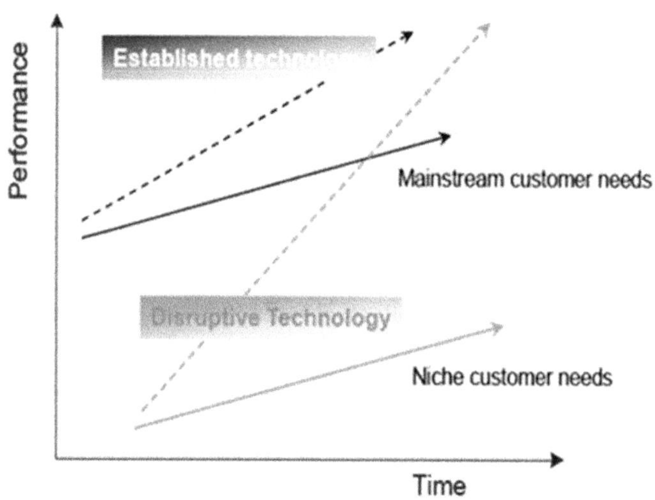

One of the breakthrough innovations that will change the warehouse management as it is big run today,

An example is the technology of Robotic Process Automation a.k.a. RPA. The disruption is not the use of programmed mechanized robots but Autonomous Mobile Robots (AMR). According to McKinsey & Co, the transportation and logistics industry stands to gain 89% incremental value over time through AI adoption. Retail could see 87% incremental value over time. Traditionally the distribution centers and fulfillment centers are run mechanically with the use of manual labor in their control processes whether it is inventory management, replenishment chain, reverse logistics, or dispatch processes. A very few established players such as Amazon and Walmart have invested in the infrastructure to manage these warehouse management processes by use of modern robots. The AMR's are programmed using the most advanced artificial intelligence capabilities to make decisions on optimization and forecasting of different functions of warehouse management to integrate robotic process automation (RPA). AMR's have sophisticated algorithms built-in based on millions of data points to improve efficiency in almost all operational processes of warehouse management. By adding intelligence, guidance, and sensory awareness, robotics has evolved from "dumb" automated guided vehicles to "intelligent and aware" autonomous mobile robots.

Robots may soon become the newest coworkers in the warehouse. The labor costs can be cut by 70% and operate during the day and night with the same costs. The vast majority of warehouse operations have relied solely on people-executed processes, but next-generation autonomous mobile robots are transforming warehouse operations. While traditional industrial robots were stuck with simple tasks, autonomous mobile robots are intelligent and can follow humans through a complex warehouse as the employee selects items for an order and can also be used to deliver goods to and from people. These collaborative robots support, not replace humans. Those investing and innovating will ensure their enterprises remain competitive in the future. Gartner supply chain predictions highlight the importance of emerging technologies and where supply chain leaders are finding value (Panetta et al.,, 2018).

By 2023, over 30% of operational warehouse workers will be supplemented, not replaced, by collaborative robots.

Modern organizations especially those in the e-commerce and retail industry will compete through advanced supply chain management. In fact, how an organization manages its supply chain performance will become a source of differentiation. In a fast-paced life, the consumer expects faster and faster delivery. Even Amazon's 'Prime Now' same-day delivery commitment has surpassed consumers' expectations. Keeping that in mind, the organizations must evolve their existing supply chain mechanism to be more robust yet agile. The companies are expected to jump S-curves of the innovation faster than ever.

According to an independent survey carried out by SDCEXEC (Askew, 2018) only half (50.6 percent) of executives polled indicated that they are investing in warehouse robotics in any capacity and only ***5.8 percent have reached full adoption***. In terms of implementation, the main challenges companies faced were understanding where to start (35 percent), finding the right robotics supplier (11 percent), and interruption to current services (10 percent). In terms of implementation, the main challenges companies faced were understanding where to start (35 percent), finding the right robotics supplier (11 percent), and interruption to current services (10 percent).

With the statistics enumerated above, many companies will benefit from the evolvement of the technology. The technology already exists however to commercialize and offer the service at a sustainable growth price is still a challenge. A few start-up companies that are disrupting warehouse automation include GreyOrange[1], Seegrid[2], 6RiverSystems[3], Commonsense Robotics, Exotech, and Magazino. GreyOrange is a global distribution automation software and robotics company that helps organizations leverage flexible automation capabilities to optimize distribution and fulfillment speed, accuracy, and costs. The company's GreyMatter software uses Artificial Intelligence, Machine Learning, and other advanced capabilities to ensure superior performance in fast-moving distributed environments that require maximum uptime, accuracy, and efficiency. The main barriers to robotics are the cost and the logistics of implementation. Some artificial intelligence systems are cloud-based and priced based on volume, allowing the price to scale with company demands. Warehouse robotics, however, require a larger upfront investment. Therefore a few established companies will fall behind from not jumping the s-curve at the right time.

Amazon is one such company that jumped the S-curve at the right time back in 2012 and acquired Kiva Systems later known as Amazon Robotics[4]. On the other hand, there are organizations that have been in the logistics and supply chain business for years and haven't recognized the potential to invest in modern technology such as AMR. The organizational inertia and lack of timely investment in R & D can cause severe damage to growth and profitability.

As a starting point, the digital blueprint we have provided in this chapter can serve as a starting point for organizations to think about where new technologies may fit along the dimensions of what is to be transformed, and how.

REFERENCES

Askew, S. (2018, Oct. 31). *The Future of Innovation in the Supply Chain Industry.* Supply and Demand Chain Executive. https://www.sdcexec.com/software-technology/blog/21025509/the-future-of-innovation-in-the-supply-chain-industry

Chong, D. (2020, April 20). *Deep Dive into Netflix's Recommender System.* Towards Data Science. https://towardsdatascience.com/deep-dive-into-netflixs-recommender-system-341806ae3b48

Herrera, S., Fung, E., & Kapner, S. (2021, August 19). Amazon plans to open large retail locations akin to Department Stores. *The Wall Street Journal.* https://www.wsj.com/articles/amazon-retail-department-stores-11629330842

Hess, T., Matt, C., Benlian, A., & Wiesböck, F. (2016). Options for formulating a digital transformation strategy. *MIS Quarterly Executive, 15*(2).

Kasula, C. (2020, June 28). *Netflix Recommender System — A Big Data Case Study.* Towards data science. https://towardsdatascience.com/netflix-recommender-system-a-big-data-case-study-19cfa6d56ff5

Matt, C., Hess, T., & Benlian, A. (2015). Digital transformation strategies. *Business & Information Systems Engineering, 57*(5), 339–343. doi:10.100712599-015-0401-5

Mixon, E. (2021, Mar. 20). *Data Science at Netflix: How Advanced Data & Analytics Helps Netflix Generate Billions.* AI Data & Analytics Network. https://www.aidataanalytics.network/data-science-ai/articles/data-science-at-netflix-how-advanced-data-analytics-helped-netflix-generate-billions

Nassauer, S. (2021, Feb. 25). Best Buy Steps Up Digital Overhaul as Slowdown Looms. *The Wall Street Journal.* https://www.wsj.com/articles/best-buy-workers-powered-through-covid-19-pandemic-then-they-lost-their-jobs-11614256495

Panetta, K. (2018, Dec. 18). *Gartner Predicts 2019 for Supply Chain Operations.* Gartner. https://www.gartner.com/smarterwithgartner/gartner-predicts-2019-for-supply-chain-operations

Waldorf, T. (n.d.). *Renew blue: Best buy's turnaround.* https://www.tjwaldorf.com/renew-blue-best-buys-turnaround/

ENDNOTES

1 https://www.greyorange.com/
2 https://seegrid.com/
3 https://6river.com/
4 https://www.amazon.jobs/en/teams/amazon-robotics

Chapter 10
Digital Leadership:
How to Thrive in the 21st Century

Greg Gutkowski
University of North Florida, USA

ABSTRACT

Every company, regardless of size and industry, is in the digital technology business—whether they realize it or not. The authors define digital leadership as having practical skills to lead or guide other individuals, teams, or entire organizations. The main point they are making is that such leadership is impossible without a basic technical understanding of the impact of digital technologies on the business. This does not mean that digital leaders should be software developers, system integrators, or advanced data analysts. However, they should know what is technically feasible to shape and communicate their vision.

INTRODUCTION

Today, humanity as a whole doubles our knowledge base every year. This is happening as digital technologies continue to get cheaper, faster, easier to use, and even more omnipresent. Worldwide, there are already more smartphones than toothbrushes or toilets. Each smartphone has more computing power than the computers that took us to the first Moon landing.

Knowledge is defined here as all the data, text files, audio, videos, and images created by all humans globally. However, defined this way, knowledge does not imply effective use of it all. Knowledge by itself, without translating it into wise action with a new product, application, or service, is just useless digits rusting away on some remote hard drive.

DOI: 10.4018/978-1-6684-3453-6.ch010

It is very unlikely that we are going to slow the trend toward generating more knowledge. At the same time, the average human IQ and/or capacity to process knowledge is not likely to expand anytime soon. Actually, most of our cerebrums are already showing symptoms of overheating from information overload.

So how do we close this serious gap? How can humans thrive with such constantly expanding amounts of data, information, and knowledge?

We don't have all the answers, but we have a lot of experience dealing with data, information, and knowledge in most industries and companies of all sizes. Over the last 25 years, we have helped numerous Fortune Global 500 as well as mom-and-pop small businesses. This allows us to share our experiences on what has worked in the past in these areas. It also provides us with a unique perspective to formulate a vision of what may work in the future.

In a nutshell, you have the choice to ride the wave of the digital tsunami or to be swept away by it. To thrive in the 21st century, you will need a good 'digital surfboard' made of a combination of the right skills, aptitudes, and attitudes. The trick will be to develop an ideal combination of individual skills based on individual aptitudes. This will have to be coupled with the right attitude toward lifetime learning as well as cooperation utilizing superior communication skills.

For such a vision to materialize on an individual level, at least three things will have to happen:

- Easy access to easily digestible knowledge about what is out there digitally, presented as instructional, motivational, and inspirational, especially for young students
- Self-assessment of aptitudes in the context of that knowledge
- Subsequent skills development based on such assessment

On a community level, we will have to provide much better matching of educational, professional, employment, and other economic opportunities. Today, most of the matching happens with respect to traditional jobs based on rigid resumes and inflexible job and task descriptions. Future jobs will change faster than current job descriptions are being updated now!

We need to improve this inefficient process and also expand it to support aptitudes, talents, attitudes, apprenticeships, internships, entrepreneurship, and continuous education beyond K-12 and college. New digital technologies can be highly relevant here by connecting all members of the community and facilitating seamless matching based on complex multidisciplinary criteria beyond simplistic and rigid job descriptions.

It is worth noting that 70% of the U.S. population has no college degree. This is similar to most developed countries. But even a college degree is not enough for one to thrive in the 21st century. However, the future belongs to individuals who, regardless of their official educational attainment, will treat learning as a key lifetime activity. Such an attitude toward education will allow people to continually reassess their own aptitudes and skills in the context of never-ending change.

For this to happen, we need to create easy access to a top-quality education that demonstrates the impact of never-ending digital transformation on our careers, lives, and society as a whole. Digital technologies can play a great role here providing omnichannel online education to support a variety of learning styles.

Economic progress and development cannot be effectively managed by a central authority. It can be influenced by central tax and regulation policies, but it will not happen without a superior, sustainable, and community-based coordination of local talents, skills, education, and economic opportunities.

Every company, regardless of size and industry, is in the digital technology business—whether they realize it or not.

On one end of the scale are e-commerce companies that are totally dependent on internet technologies. All their business interactions are driven by software and all transactions are digital. They live and die by social media and online advertising supported by sophisticated real-time analytics. This includes tracking physical shipments as well.

On the other end of the scale are companies that consider themselves traditional operations: construction, manufacturing, logistics and transportation, retail, food production, healthcare, or various home-related services such as HVAC, roofing, plumbing, pest control, or landscaping. Their core operations will always be physical in nature. After all, we can agree, there will be no digital dinners, digital roofs, or digital coffee anytime soon.

Nevertheless, with inadequate digital tools to manage their business, these traditional, physical businesses will lose to more productive competitors. Today, traditional companies depend too heavily on many manual, error-prone, ill-timed processes and poor communication about the status of these processes. It is unlikely that they can extend a superior customer experience with such a fragmented approach. And their customers judge them by their experience with the ease of 1-click ordering via Amazon.

The best example in this category is a traditional company where many clerical people are involved in many disjointed processes, even if they use various software packages to perform individual steps. For example, digital marketing software does not pass leads to the customer relationship management (CRM) software, CRM does not communicate with dispatch, and invoices are issued with considerable delays and errors due to the lack of integration between warehouse management and accounting. Thus, a basic product may be physical, such as home construction, yet due to many manual disjointed steps spread over time, space, and multiple vendors, the whole process and communication are very inefficient.

Therefore, regardless of the industry and size of the business, the success of any enterprise depends more and more on digital leadership.

We define digital leadership as having practical skills encompassing the ability of an individual to lead or guide other individuals, teams, or entire organizations. The main point we are making is that such leadership is impossible without a basic technical understanding of the impact of digital technologies on the business. This does not mean that digital leaders should be software developers, system integrators, or advanced data analysts. However, they should know what is technically feasible to shape and communicate their vision.

The best example is Sam Walton who built Walmart to be the largest company in the world (in terms of employees) by leveraging the best technologies in logistics, transportation, and analytics. Yet, Sam Walton was not an IT genius. He was just very skilled in understanding and communicating how technology can help his business. By the way, if he were alive today, his fortune would have exceeded the fortune of Bill Gates by a factor of 3 or 4. Thus, one can argue that there is more value in applying technology than in building it.

This is truer today than ever before. In business software, the technology cost itself is not a barrier anymore. The prices of technology went down 10,000 times in the last twenty years and even a small mom-and-pop shop can have a very sophisticated cloud-based business system for $100 per month.

We see the same trend regarding digital marketing/marketing automation, CRM, enterprise resource planning (ERP), and accounting software. Thus, a bottleneck to productivity is not the lack of software, or its cost, but a good understanding of its value and leading your organization to leverage them. Just like Sam Walton did.

In general, as a society, we are continually challenged to understand and keep up with what is technically feasible and inexpensive. This is mainly due to the very rapid progress in digital technologies.

There are three major drivers of change in business today.

1. The first is the very rapid progress in digital technologies. It is both a problem and an opportunity. A great opportunity for those who can leverage it and a great problem for those who cannot keep up.
2. Also, developed societies are experiencing a generational changeover with baby boomers retiring and taking their business process knowledge with them.
3. The third driver is increased global competition. Many countries do a better job of educating their K-12 students in the STEM disciplines. The United States may have a strong position in developing software, but that software is available worldwide. The bottleneck is not in the software itself, but in failing to understand how to use it to make a profit.

The resulting problem is six-fold:

1. We do not have enough educators ready to teach the newest technologies, creating a digital education gap.
2. Subsequently, there are not enough students who have mastered digital skills, creating a digital skills gap.
3. Since more and more jobs depend on digital skills, we are experiencing a shortage of workers who have the right mix of traditional and digital skills, which has led to a labor shortage.
4. There is a lot of anxiety in society over the fear of being replaced by robots driven by artificial intelligence. Whether these fears are warranted or not is irrelevant, as perception is reality.
5. Businesses themselves are very well aware that they have to be agile; i.e., be able to react quickly to technology changes. Yet, how to accomplish that is very challenging, given the shortage of digital skills at the upper management levels of most traditional companies.
6. Last but not least, executives are paralyzed with too many technology choices, and the marketing hype coming from powerful technology vendors does not make the decision about process improvement any easier.

In light of the above, the most logical solution is to enhance the knowledge level among the business community concerning what is feasible as well as regarding the best practices to execute a common-sense implementation of digital technologies. Thus, there is a need to create a comprehensive Digital Leadership program for business professionals.

The program should be made up of two components:

1. Executive Digital Leadership
2. Managerial Digital Leadership

First, we should address the single most important component, which is a common understanding of the current state of technologies among c-suite executives. With so many technical terms and so much hype generated by Silicon Valley and the press, it is hard to have a common understanding of basic terms. Today, if one gathers ten executives in one room, there will be ten different understandings of what artificial intelligence, big data, the internet of things, or cloud computing are all about. Yet, without a common understanding of the foundation, it is almost impossible to extend consistent leadership down the ranks.

Following Executive Digital Leadership is Managerial Digital Leadership education. This one focuses more on practical case studies of the best implementation of various business software for marketing, sales, operations, customer service, and accounting and billing. We often see that each of these functions is done with the help of software packages, yet many of these software packages do not communicate with each other, thereby preventing the automation of an effective workflow. In traditional industries, there is a lot of potential for productivity improvement by getting much better real-time visibility of the process to be able to spot any problems immediately.

Both programs should be made up of online courses supplemented with periodic live seminars led by experienced subject matter experts. It is our experience that blending online education with live instruction is the most effective way to teach digital technologies.

Both programs should give users unlimited access to online educational courses that can be taken and retaken at any time. Both programs should be supported by an online social learning community whereby each of the course participants can discuss topics of interest with other participants as well as an instructor. All the programs should be supplemented with optional books to support various learning styles.

Most companies are interested in their staff learning more about:

- Digital Transformation
- Digital Marketing
- Digital Selling
- Customer Experience, and
- Real-time Business Analytics

In the following section, we will define digital disruption or how the digital revolution forces impacted existing companies and their traditional business models.

"I came, I saw, I digitized" - there is some truth to this paraphrase of Julius Caesar's famous quote, "I came, I saw, I conquered." Yes, some of the new digital companies conquered whole industries in a very short time

DIGITAL VICTORS

· Digital photography > Kodak
· Netflix > Blockbuster
· Amazon > Retail
· Uber > Taxis
· Airbnb > Hotels
· Social media > Print Media
· YouTube > TV
· iTunes > Music Business

· Online ads > Print Ads
· Hard drive manufacturers > Dropbox
· Camera producers > Cameras in smartphones
· Wikipedia > Encyclopedia Britannica

Some companies and entire industries either vanished or were marginalized by this digital tsunami. Kodak completely missed the switch to digital photography and Blockbuster to streaming videos. Retailers keep losing business to Amazon, taxis to Uber, hotels to Airbnb, traditional media to social media, TV to YouTube, music recording studios to iTunes, and last but not least, print and TV advertising to online ads.

Hard drive manufacturers got surprised by DropBox and fancy digital camera producers by cameras built into smartphones. Encyclopedia Britannica stopped printing after 244 years, replaced by Wikipedia and the World Wide Web.

NEW BUSINESS MODELS

- Netflix > Blockbuster
- 1 digital song > 1 CD with many songs
- Streaming anywhere > Record player
- 1 digital pic > 36 paper pictures

The disruption was not just technological, either. Digital technology enables completely new business models. The best example is Netflix vs. Blockbuster. The new model is a monthly subscription of unlimited movies for less than $10 without ever having to leave home. The Blockbuster model called for driving to a store to rent a single movie for $3 and having to drive back to return it or pay penalties if one forgot to drop it off.

In the past, we all had to buy a physical album or CD for over $12 with about 10 songs, even if we liked only 3 or 4. With vinyl albums, we were limited to playing it only on a record player—not all of which were portable. Now we can buy any single song digitally and play it on any Wi-Fi or Bluetooth-enabled device anywhere in the world.

We faced a similar situation with developing rolls of film and getting pictures printed. You took a roll of film to a photo shop and got back 36 prints, which, to your dismay, included 30 pictures of very poor quality. This was due to your own steep learning curve on how to master a traditional 35mm camera. Now, we point and shoot with our smartphones without hesitation, check the picture quality, retake immediately if necessary, and post the pic on social media. We very seldom print anymore.

Think about it "Uber, the world's largest taxi company owns no vehicles. Facebook, the world's most popular media owner, creates no content. Alibaba, the most valuable retailer, has no inventory. And Airbnb, the world's largest accommodation provider, owns no real estate. Something interesting is happening." (Tom Goodwin, 2015)

This quote makes a very good point that some of the new business models do not even require ownership of physical assets. In all of these cases, the new value provided by these digital companies is in connecting customers with service providers online.

NOTHING NEW

For a perspective on digital disruption, it is worth mentioning that it's not such a new phenomenon. Walmart became the largest retailer in the world by leveraging telecommunication and by digitizing its supply chain capabilities.

Sam Walton started with one store in Arkansas in 1969, at a time when Sears and Kmart completely dominated retail in the U.S. In about twenty years, it was Walton's turn to dominate the American retail landscape. Kmart is no longer independent, and its parent company, Sears, is not doing very well either. Walmart invested heavily in digital technologies to optimize warehousing, shipping, and pricing. Sears and Kmart missed that trend and paid a very high price for it.

Today, Walmart has over 11 thousand stores in 28 countries and it is the world's largest company by revenue and the world's largest private employer with 2.2 million employees worldwide. (Statista, 2022)

Walmart is not resting on its laurels. It seems to have found a good answer to competition from Amazon. Right now, you can order online anything that Walmart carries and pick it up at the nearest store with no shipping charges. This is especially appealing when purchasing heavy and large items for which Amazon would have to charge considerable shipping fees. Given the vast and very efficient logistics of Walmart, the marginal cost of shipping additional items to any of their stores is near zero.

AGRICULTURE PRECEDENCE

There is a lot of fear that digital transformation will result in a lot of job losses and increased unemployment. I could not agree less. Here is why:

In 1900, 40% of the total labor force in the United States was employed in agriculture. One hundred years later this number has shrunk to 2%. At the same time, the total population of the United States increased from 76 million to 282 million— almost tripled. (World Bank, 2021)

Yet the price of food has gone down so much that even the poor face obesity problems today. How did that happen? Simply put, there was a tremendous increase in farmworker productivity due to mechanization and automation. One good Harvester combine replaced many expensive horses and many expensive workers, and the savings were passed down to consumers. This is how the wealth of the nation was and is being built; i.e., by increased productivity.

MILITARY PRECEDENCE

The U.S. military is probably the largest and the most sophisticated digital organization in the world. Even Visa, Walmart, or Facebook cannot come close.

Constant technological inventions force this large institution to adapt to changes all the time. The stakes are very high—it's the freedom of the country in the context of nefarious activities of rogue dictators around the world who do not have democratic processes to stop them from military mischief.

Let's imagine what kind of pressure the invention of an airplane, or a tank, or a missile, or the radio put on our military. They have to keep adapting very fast to develop new weapons, train soldiers, and deploy and reorganize command and control protocols in light of new weapons and communication capabilities.

They have done a great job at that, as the U.S. military put a stop to two world wars in a row in the last century. And today, no other military even comes close to matching U.S. overall global deployment and communication capabilities. If an organization as large as the U.S. military can do it, so should most businesses as well.

However, most businesses think that they do not face a mortal threat. Unless they are about to be disrupted by the digital transformation. Just ask Kodak, Blockbuster, or Encyclopedia Britannica.

AUTOMATION FEARS OVER THE YEARS

Following are several telling quotes regarding the fear of automation over the last 200 years:

"The rapid industrialization of the English economy cost many craft workers their jobs. Many such unemployed workers, weavers, and others turned their animosity towards the machines that had taken their jobs and began destroying factories and machinery. These attackers became known as Luddites, supposedly followers of Ned Ludd, a folklore figure. The first attacks of the Luddite movement began in 1811. The Luddites rapidly gained popularity, and the British government took drastic measures, using the militia or army to protect the industry. Those rioters who were caught were tried and hanged or jailed for life. Unrest continued in other sectors, such as with agricultural laborers in the 1830s when large parts of southern Britain were affected by the Captain Swing disturbances. Threshing machines were a particular target, and hayrick burning was a popular activity." (Wikipedia, n.d.)

"We are being afflicted with a new disease of which some readers may not yet have heard the name, but of which they will hear a great deal in the years to come—namely, technological unemployment. This means unemployment due to our discovery of means of economizing the use of labor outrunning the pace at which we can find new uses for labor." (Keynes, 1930)

"The rise in unemployment has raised some new alarms around an old scare word: automation. How much has the rapid spread of technological change contributed to the current high of 5,400,000 out of work? ... While no one has yet sorted out the jobs lost because of the overall drop in business from those lost through automation and other technological changes, many a labor expert tends to put much of the blame on automation. ... Dr. Russell Ackoff, a Case Institute expert on business problems, feels that automation is reaching into so many fields so fast that it has become "the nation's second most important problem". The number of jobs lost to more efficient machines is only part of the problem. What worries many job experts more is that automation may prevent the economy from creating enough new jobs. ... Throughout the industry, the trend has been to bigger production with a smaller workforce. ... Many of the losses in factory jobs have been countered by an increase in the service industries or in office jobs. But automation is beginning to move in and eliminate office jobs too. ... In the past, new industries hired far more people than those they put out of business. But this is not true of many of today's new industries. ... Today's new industries have comparatively few jobs for the unskilled or semiskilled, just the class of workers whose jobs are being eliminated by automation." (TIME Magazine, 1961)

"I am therefore transmitting to the Congress a new Manpower and Training Development program to train or retrain several hundred thousand workers, particularly in those areas where we have seen chronic unemployment as a result of technological factors and new occupational skills over a four-year period, in order to replace those skills made obsolete by automation and industrial change with the new skills which the new processes demand." (Kennedy, May 25, 1961)

"Technology is creating both new opportunities and new obligations for us—an opportunity for greater productivity and progress—obligation to be sure that no workingman, no family must pay an unjust price for progress.

Automation is not our enemy. Our enemies are ignorance, indifference, and inertia. Automation can be the ally of our prosperity if we will just look ahead, if we will understand what is to come, and if we will set our course wisely after proper planning for the future.

That is the purpose of this commission. I hope and I expect that its work will benefit the workingman and benefit the businessman, and serve the interests of the farmer and the professionals and all of our people in America." (Johnson, 1964)

In 1978, the historian Ian Turner predicted, that the world was about to enter a period as significant as the Neolithic or Industrial revolutions. He predicted that, by 1988, at least a quarter of the Australian workforce would be made redundant by technological change…

"In the 1980s, new technologies can decimate the labor force in the goods-producing sectors of the economy…" (Jones, 1982)

However, none of the fears documented above have materialized and, in the meantime, the whole world got richer, healthier, better educated, and enjoying freedoms like never before.

FROM 1820 TILL TODAY

· The percentage of people living in extreme poverty decreased from over 90% to 10%
· Illiteracy has shrunk from 90% to 17%
· Child mortality declined from 45% to 4%
· The percentage of people living in democracies increased from 1% to 55%

https://ourworldindata.org/a-history-of-global-living-conditions-in-5-charts/

All these impressive numbers were made possible ONLY due to the progress in technologies; that is, automation. It is also worth adding that in the meantime cars, airplanes, telephones, movies, the radio, TV, cameras, electricity for homes, air conditioning, refrigerators, computers, the Internet, antibiotics, vaccines, social security, and running water in your tap had been invented.

The way automation and new technologies generate wealth are pretty simple:

1. New technology saves time, hence labor, hence cost
2. The price of a given product goes down
3. More people have more money to spend
4. Since people love to spend when they can afford it, they create demand for more products and services—often luxuries or near-luxuries
5. New products and services are introduced
6. New technologies impact these new products and the original ones as well
7. Back to #1, times the number of new products, which gives us a multiplier of wealth creation

As long as individuals are free to benefit from inventions in a free market, humans will find creative ways to adapt to most circumstances, increasing their own wealth and that of society as a whole.

We should welcome these changes, not fear them. Technology plays a major role not only in wealth creation, but also in eliminating a lot of mundane, boring, tedious, and expensive tasks, leaving time for more value-added activities such as thinking, designing, or spending more time doing the things we love.

Dropping off and picking up dry-cleaning, filling out paper forms, retyping numbers between various systems (and then getting yelled at for making mistakes), looking for missing paperwork, translating, answering phones from unhappy customers, constant scheduling and rescheduling meetings, sending and answering emails and matching them with text or voice messages, printing invoices, posting content on social media, ordering office supplies, basic cooking, balancing checkbooks, cleaning, lifting, moving, lubricating, fixing, making trip reservations, paying bills, reordering basic cleaning supplies, unnecessary driving, unnecessary meetings, and unnecessary flying (with the associated security delays), retrieving and cleansing data by hand, analyzing spreadsheets by hand, being put on hold by your service provider—all of these tasks can be automated and/or eliminated so we can do something more fun and productive.

Today, most businesses large and small spend at least 50% of their time on the manual tasks described above. (Manyika, et al., 2017). Think about the potential for our economy if we significantly decrease this number!

REFERENCES

Goodwin, T. (2015). *The Battle Is For The Customer Interface*. TechCrunch. Retrieved from https://techcrunch.com/2015/03/03/in-the-age-of-disintermediation -the- battle -is-all- for-the- customer - interface/ ?guccounter = 1&gucc _ referrer = aHR0 cHM6 Ly93 d3cu Z29v Z2xl LmNv bS8& guce _ referrer _sig= AQAA AGO _ UNXd PwqBj Uyp8 vEIc HkeK HJ _ Kdsr oYtu KzO0 pP4N klYm P8xCX _ 3WA _ qT2Q X8qP zpEEAf _ Vh77 qQ36 wXdF zfB2 DPV3 etgA QwDU 1bjN zbpy ka2J NEiy nIKW nyNt 2z5d Qmmf wO0B MVAb avXK r4fg WDkj joy8 iF96 0xUV XkJF FnM

Jones, B. (1982). *Sleepers, Wake*. Oxford University Press.

Keynes. (1930). Economic Possibilities for our Grandchildren. In *Essays in Persuasion*. New York: Harcourt Brace.

Manyika, L., Chui, B., & Woetzel, B. Ko, & Sanghvi. (2017). *Jobs lost, jobs gained: What the future of work will mean for jobs, skills, and wages.* McKinsey Global Institute. Retrieved from https://www.mckinsey.com/featured-insights/future-of-work/jobs-lost-jobs-gained-what-the-future-of-work-will-mean-for-jobs-skills-and-wages

Statista Research Department. (2022). *Walmart – Statistic & Facts.* Retrieved from https://www.statista.com/topics/1451/walmart/#topicHeader__wrapper

The World Bank. (2021). *Employment in agriculture (% of total employment).* Retrieved from https://data.worldbank.org/indicator/SL.AGR.EMPL.ZS

Time Magazine. (1961). *The Automation Jobless.* Retrieved from https://content.time.com/time/subscriber/article/0,33009,828815,00.html

Wikipedia. (n.d.). *Industrial Revolution.* Retrieved from https://en.wikipedia.org/wiki/Industrial_Revolution

Chapter 11
Building Organizational DNA: Leading With Agility in the Digital Age

Jill M. Callinan
Raeveology, USA

Michelle Broadbent
M. Broadbent Design, USA

ABSTRACT

To stay relevant in a world set on fast forward, organizations need to ensure they have all the critical components in place to stay relevant. More than just great products and services, organizations need to ensure they have the right mix of strategy, culture, leadership, and agility: the modern building blocks required for today's business continuity. This chapter will address how these components are interdependent and all contribute to creating an environment where people are connected and inspired.

Figure 1.

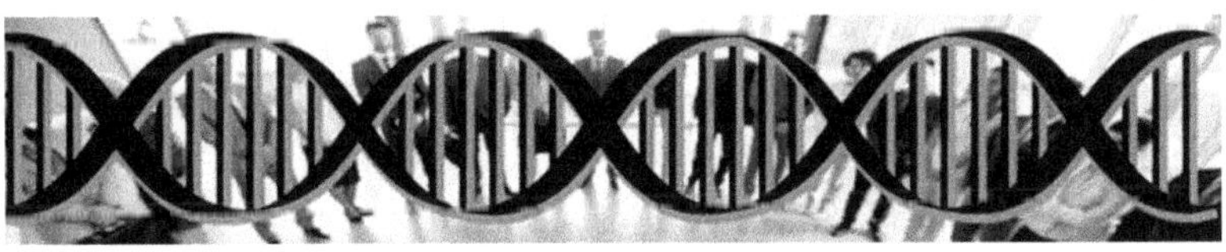

Evolution is constant. Relevance in this digital age requires more than just great products and differentiated market share. Corporations must invigorate and reinvent their organizational DNA (oDNA), or they will quickly get eaten by the competition. Let us assume for this chapter that oDNA is the backbone, consisting of culture and

DOI: 10.4018/978-1-6684-3453-6.ch011

Figure 2.

strategy coiling around each other interdependently. The primary glue in this oDNA structure, keeping these coils aligned and connected, include leadership and agility. Altogether, these components are building blocks critical for business continuity in today's rapidly changing world.

Strategy has always had the leading role in the path toward success, as it keeps the wheels in motion. Culture, however, has recently emerged as an equal, if not slightly more important asset, especially as organizations become more and more decentralized. To ensure organizations are moving toward having a solid oDNA with an inspirational strategy and a people centric culture, today's leaders require new and different skill sets, much different from traditional management.

LEADERSHIP, EMERGED

"If your actions inspire others to dream more, learn more, do more and become more, you are a leader"-anonymous

Leadership, in the modern sense, consists mainly of mindsets and behaviors, while agility is the ability to move quickly and easily. Organizations need both to be successful. One of the hottest corporate trends today: organizations are shifting toward leadership's ability to build a culture of agility, inspire the people and ensure everyone is focusing on the same vision, all in a remote world.

The recognition and need for this emerging skillset is so prevalent that many Colleges and Universities are offering accredited programs dedicated to its study. (Thomas, n.d.) Leadership embraces emotional connections and wields emotional intelligence to drive the organization toward the same vision. Leaders start with themselves as a role model. They change the way they show up and how they interact with others. Leaders build leaders. Their focus is on motivating the people and building a culture in which people feel safe, connected, autonomous and inspired. When people are passionate about their work, anything becomes a possibility.

For too long traditional 'command and control' management saw emotions as noise- not helpful to their operations. Outdated styles like blame and shame are being replaced by more emotionally intelligent, modern leadership styles favoring empowerment, self organization and learning. Organizations are quickly realizing the benefits of cultivating leaders who can be both strategic and inspirational in their thinking and behavior.

As you look to the future and think about what it is going to take to lead and challenge the minds of our geographically dispersed, multi-sensory, multitasking generation, organizations will need to continuously upgrade their oDNA to support it. Self-employment is rising in America because people want more freedom. Freedom to be mobile, to choose clients and work they enjoy and freedom to be happy and not feel trapped or dispensable. Understanding these and other trends will be critical to building a culture that will attract the talent of the future who can essentially operate from anywhere. "Gone are the days of traditional leadership in which bosses give instructions and expect their subordinates to follow blindly. Authoritarian administration like that…" (Olito, 2020) could only thrive in the industrial age, when change was not a constant, and corporations did not need thinkers, they needed doers.

Since people did not become this advanced overnight, it's important to understand exactly how society got here. By re-visiting some of the key economic and world events that defined corporate trends over the decades, one can easily identify emerging trends that will be required for sustaining and thriving in the future. Additionally it serves as a reminder to remember why it is important to keep going forward.

A LOOK BACK

Beginning with the roaring 20s of the 1900s right into the roaring 20s of today, you can follow how history's economic and world events impacted the mindsets and behaviors of management and organizational leaders over this last century. In parallel, as you follow that same timeline, the introduction of various technologies and other innovative tools, coupled with these same economic and world events, also tells us a story about "change" in the employees. Not simply changes in what they can do and how fast they can do it; changes in where people choose to work. Let us take a brief journey through time.

After the first World War, our country took drastic steps into a more modern consumer-based world. As indoor plumbing, radios, automobiles, televisions, motion pictures and other amenities went from desirable to attainable, people moved from the farms (self-employed) to the cities (gainful employment). There was money to be spent and people felt a sense of security. Welcome the beginning of "the Greatest Generation''. Characterized by their perseverance, hard work, and desire to serve, at a minimum. This generation would face the Great Depression and then a decade later, they would engage in America's role in World War II. The drafting of men into the war led to a shortage of available workers, the result of which is another key shift in history- women were brought into the workforce in astounding numbers.

The devastation, bloodshed and change resulting from these historic events did not break this spirited generation. They survived, they thrived and when the war was over, they celebrated. They celebrated so well that beginning in 1946 the country had record breaking numbers of births, a trend continuing until 1964. Welcome "the Baby Boomers' '. On the foundation of a vastly growing industry, the Greatest Generation continued to sacrifice and work hard to secure stability and opportunity for their children (the Boomers) to experience the American Dream- which, at the time, was synonymous for a better life. This hard working generation was the backbone of their organizations. People dedicated their lives to working for 1 company. Loyalty was everything. For a while this worked because in turn, organizations were loyal to their people.

The Boomers, raised in times of rising affluence and prosperity are also characterized as loyal but also extremely hard working, competitive, confident, and career focused. As you get into the late 1960s and early 1970s the Boomers started finishing college and entering the workforce. This highly competitive generation was no stranger to the hard work and grind of the generation before, however as industries started to grow and expand, so did competition for position and power. The result, questionable business practices and the unfortunate rise of the command and control management style. The closer a person was to the information and the power, the safer they would be. Service to others from the greatest generation was slowly changing to service to self with the rising boomers. For employees, there was no room for agility, originality, autonomy or thinking. The best employees did what they were told, and were often rewarded for it by positions, power and money.

Then, in 1981, Ronald Regan made an executive decision as POTUS, to fire 11,000 air traffic controllers that were on strike. Although the intent was centered around keeping our commercial air travel industry afloat, an indirect theme emerged that was not necessarily intended: CEOs interpreted this act as permission to do the same. 'Layoffs' became a common aggressive business decision to balance the books and guard against short term economic impacts. Employees went from irreplaceable to re-alignable. Safety was off the table; loyalty no longer worked both ways, and therefore no longer worked. Authoritative, counter productive management continued to thrive. How could this madness ever stop? Welcome Gen Xers to the party and welcome to the birth of the digital age.

At the onset of the 1990s and early 2000s, Gen Xers entered a new kind of workforce and a major shift from industrial production work to knowledge work began. This is the first generation of the digital age. From Atari to Tesla, this generation had a front row seat in life's digital transformation. This is the first generation to capitalize upon modern concepts like "work life balance". Unfortunately, they still had experienced many leftover' boomers' and even some of the 'greatest', in key managerial, decision making positions who had very clear ideas of what managing people was about. Note: although some of the behaviors and mindsets displayed by the Boomers in positions of authority left much to be desired, this generation was not all bad! Their knowledge, work ethic and dedication is what makes them priceless.

Gen Xers, classified by self-reliance, diversity, practicality, flexibility and a work hard- play hard mentality, may be most noted for their role in the birth of the internet. They welcomed, expanded, learned and built businesses (dot.com boom) with ease. As the internet grew, new industries were born, tech companies popped up everywhere and for the first time in history, information was instantaneously available at the tips of everyone's fingers. Enter, the remote employee, who can do anything from anywhere. In addition, we welcome the Millenials whose very presence demanded change.

Thanks to technology, remote employment became the symbol, for many, of the ultimate work-life balance. Organizations that did not offer this type of flexibility became undesirable. Top talent started to move toward these flexible roles, leaving the older larger organizations slow to change and maybe? eager to catch up. Smaller startups and growth organizations have naturally adopted the more modern ways of working, ensuring they would attract the best talent and secure their future in the digital age. Retaining this talent, however, will require cutting edge mindsets and behaviors that have not previously prevailed; trust, psychological safety, relationships and teamwork are just a few.

In 2001, a much smaller event took place that would open the hearts and minds of organizations toward adopting better ways of working. This event would not even be a blip on the grand historical radar, however the outcome would drastically change the game for organizations by introducing a modern way of approaching work. A group of technologists and successful business folks who saw the increasing need for change in how teams approached work and delivery gathered together in Snowbird, Utah. From this event, the 'Agile manifesto' was born, outlining a non prescriptive, philosophical approach to work based on a set of guiding values and principals. The manifesto, originally intended for software development teams, took off like wildfire in Silicon Valley, as it helped organizations overcome many of the archaic policies and practices and positioned them to be more aggressive in the newly booming digital world. The philosophy, however, applies to more than just technology teams. Any kind of team can adopt the same mindsets and approach work in a similar way.

Over the next two decades, the proof of success of adopting this new way of working would set sail across the nation changing the dynamics of teams, work management, customer centricity, learning and product delivery in organizations. Terms like 'Scrum' and 'Kanban' are starting to become common vernacular, however not every organization is ready to transform into this modern way of working, but they will if they are to survive.

Most recently, in 2019, Covid-19, hijacked the driver's seat in the game of business continuity. This epidemic virtually shut down the nation and some of the world for an extended period of time. Almost all non essential employers were required to close their doors, forcing even the most rigid resisters of the work from home model to yield. The long term impacts of this time are still to be discovered and understood. The short term result- similar to our forefathers of the greatest generation, we survived, we thrived, and we proved we could do it without having to be in an office everyday. Welcome the 'hybrid-work' model - forever saying goodbye to the 9-5 daily grind.

Post epidemic, the digital world is still intact, and still moving at a phenomenal speed. Relevance is everything. People seek organizations with inspirational visions and missions that speak to their values. Thanks to social media, transparency is our default setting in life, corporations need to also adopt this setting and ensure their leaders are transparent with their strategic goals and objectives which ensures people feel their work is connected to the overall picture. The future is about having strong oDNA- where culture is foundational to strategy. The rest of this chapter will focus on the concept of leadership and how leaders are the primary drivers of Organizational DNA.

MANAGING VS. LEADING TODAY

Often used interchangeably, the words "management" and "leadership" are two very different beasts. Managers are members of organizations responsible for execution of work, typically hired or promoted into these positions. Leaders, on the other hand, are about setting the vision and leading and the people. Leaders may or may not have a 'title' but they are continuously focused on motivating people, ensuring the organization is rich with communications, influencing and coaching. We would like to think that all managers are also good leaders, this is not always the case. Inspiration and Influence separate the two. (Duggal, 2022) (Diffen, n.d.)

Figure 3.

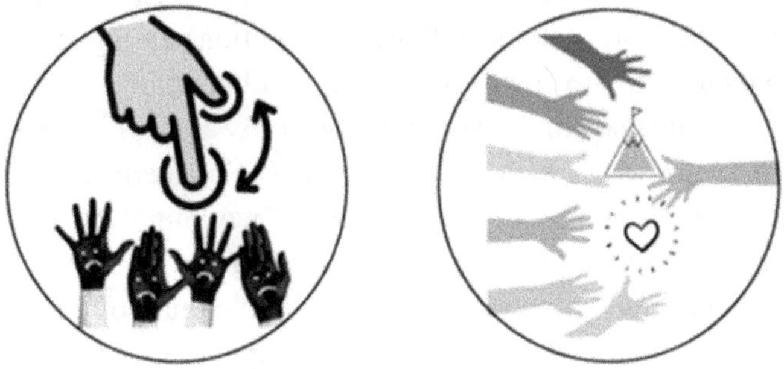

"Management" is about executing functions and giving direction.

"Leadership" is about inspiring and motivating the people.

Power in management comes from a title, power in leadership comes from within. Although subtle and invisible, mindset, attention, thoughts and behaviors make up the power and energy required to empower and rally the people toward the organization's vision.

With the emergence of the digital era, jobs have become more complex, more knowledge based and more self driven- all direct challenges to traditional management. "*We may be approaching the time in our history when the word "management" is tossed onto the linguistic trash heap.....this era doesn't call for management, it calls for a renaissance of self direction*". (Pink, 2011) Organizations will need leaders in key roles to build an environment of trust, accountability, safety, feedback, and motivation so that teams can be self organized and self managed.

AGILITY AND LEADERSHIP

As mentioned above, the Agile Manifesto introduced a new way of approaching work by outlining some of the key mindsets and behaviors leaders must embrace in today's organizations. For example, the Manifesto suggests higher value is placed on face-to-face communication over written communication. It does not mean that written communication is no longer important, rather it implies that having interpersonal relationships and face to face discussions tend to bring resolution and value to teams faster and we value those a little bit more. Other practical shifts agile leaders must embrace include autonomy, self-organizing teams, empowerment, flexibility in approach, and frequent short iterations.

So, what is agile leadership? It is not a button you can press, or something that can transform overnight. Rather, it's about having the right leadership behaviors and mindsets along with a solid understanding and execution of an agile way of working. In addition to their ability to create and sustain a culture of agility, the best agilists are extremely socially and emotionally intelligent. Awareness is their super power, it allows them to empathize with people and also helps them create ripple effects throughout the organization.. They are capable of working with the entire system and influencing the whole organization and its culture.

Agile leadership is about creating a team centric culture of empowerment and autonomy while removing roadblocks so that employees can be more effective and productive. How do you know if teams are working in agile? Find out where the decision making is. Two of the key oDNA traits include autonomy and self-organization. These depend entirely on agile leadership's ability to move decision making processes from traditional managers directly to the teams and the people closest to the work. Agile teams are cross functional- in that they have all of the skills and competencies required to complete the work at hand. The combination of the right skills, autonomy, and self-organization has proven to the world that agile teams work together better.

Along with the mindsets discussed above, there are also a number of tenets specific to an agile way of working that agile leaders implement across organizations: transparency, working in small batches, limiting work in progress and ensuring feedback loops are happening frequently, at the right time, with the right people.

TRANSPARENCY

Transparency in the workplace creates openness for all employees. Whether it be communication of strategic objectives at the executive level or real time feedback at the team delivery level- transparency, a zero cost practice, leads to better employee engagement, improved trust and lower job stress. When employees' see leadership being actively open and inclusive in their organization, they will feel encouraged to share.

Agile leadership ensures teams have the autonomy and ability to be transparent by ensuring teams have the right tools and processes in place to visualize their work, as this visualization is key to the team having the right conversations to reach their goals. Historically, it was not strange for team members to 'hide their cards' and not share what they are working on. Agile teams work a bit differently, as all of their work (both current and future) is tangibly laid out. Now the team sees everything, nothing is hidden, there is less opportunity for confusion and a much better chance of team alignment. Laying out all of the work makes it possible for team discussions,

Figure 4.

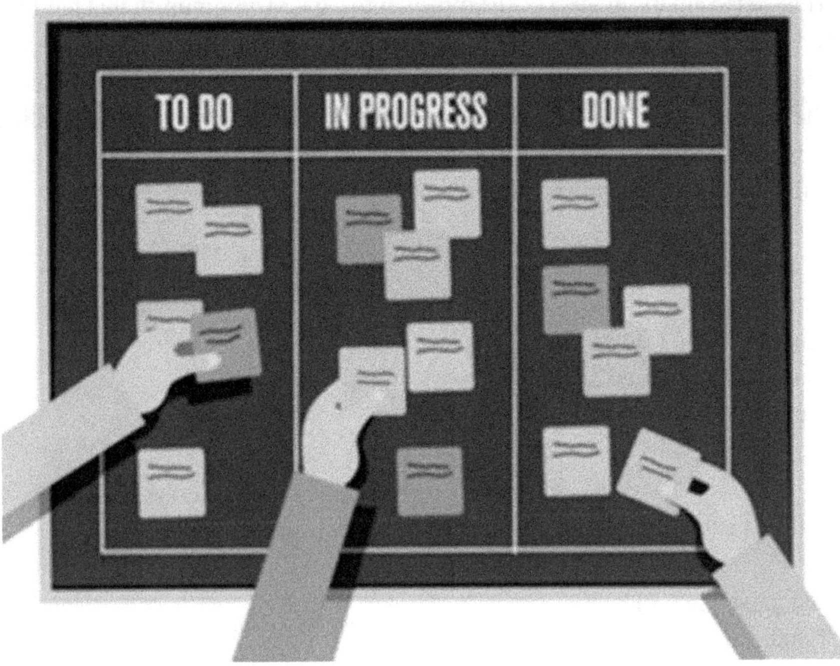

sharing of ideas and views, identifying key blockers and alignment of thinking on the team, critical elements of a sustaining culture! Ultimately, transparency increases both understanding and collaboration. Introducing the Kanban board. Kanban, a Japanese word, is loosely translated as "card you can see".

Kanban and other workflow tools provide the tangible visibility that teams need to collaborate and align on their prioritized work. Tools show what work is in progress- what has not started and needs to be worked and what is complete. This type of visibility allows teams to see patterns (items in progress for too long, too many items not started, etc) that allow for innovative dialogue, recognizing bottlenecks early and opportunities to pivot on how work is being completed.

WORK IN SMALL BATCHES

One of the key practices of an agile team is working in small batches as it reduces cycle time and gets quicker feedback. Breaking work down into smaller increments also improves efficiency, visibility, and control. To prevent wasting large amounts of time, agile teams explicitly break down work into smaller more manageable sized chunks that are less intimidating to approach and easier to estimate.

A simple example:

Jeff needs to cut his grass. He just moved into a gated community that has bylaws related to the length of his green fibers. Given the size of his property, the task seems daunting, and at first, he does not see a possibility in which he can complete this over the weekend and have any time for himself. Feeling defeated, he applies an agile approach to this situation. First, he breaks down all the required tasks needed to get his lawn to an appropriate length:

1) Purchase lawn mower
2) Purchase gas
3) Cut Left Side Lawn
4) Cut Right Side Lawn
5) Cut Front Lawn
6) Cut Back Lawn

Next, Jeff estimates how long each of these tasks may take:

1) Purchase lawn mower- 1 hour
2) Purchase gas- 15 mins
3) Cut Left Side Lawn- 1 hour
4) Cut Right Side Lawn- 1 hour
5) Cut Front Lawn- 2 hours
6) Cut Back Lawn- 1 hour

Now, Jeff makes a realistic plan that he can accomplish and do so over the weekend:

Friday Night: Purchase mower and gas (1.15 hours)

Saturday: Cut Front and Back Lawns (3 hours)

Sunday: Cut Side lawns (2 hours)

Not only can Jeff complete his mowing within the time frame, but he also identifies that he has plenty of time for himself, much more than he initially thought!

Breaking down work is not always easy, and there is no single way to approach this science. Agile leaders understand the importance of this approach and promote taking the time to break work down for teams to provide better estimates for delivery.

A tool/exercise for prioritization:

"Moscow" (Must have/do, Should have/do, Could have/do, Won't have/do) is an agile tool, developed by Dai Clegg for helping teams with prioritization of work when you are short on time. After teams have made work visible, they then collaborate and decide which work is priority. Tools like this are simple and create healthy dialogues for teams to align.

LIMIT WORK IN PROGRESS (WIP)

Now that you have broken our work down, made it visible and gave it some estimations, it's time to put together a plan. Planning work in agile also requires considering a few team performance indicators that traditional plans do not: estimations, capacity, and velocity. Estimations are predictions of how long we think the work will take to complete. Capacity is the realistic amount of time team resources have available to work. i.e If a person works a 40-hour week, 30 hours of which is available for work (10 are in meetings, etc.) you cannot assign them more than 30 hours' worth of work and expect them to be effective, inspired, happy or able to finish. Finally, velocity is the measurement of how much work a team typically delivers in an iteration (a specified period of working time).

Limiting work in progress ultimately prevents multitasking demons and increases focus. Traditionally, everyone thinks they have all been great multi-taskers! Multitasking was looked at as a strength. Because people were so certain of their ability to multitask, plans incorporated work and due dates that were completely unattainable, and teams would more than likely be too far down the road to easily pivot, resulting in negative ripple effects. As we have learned, our multi-tasking colleagues are great at starting several tasks. Completing work, on the other hand, is a different story. When there are too many balls in the air, prioritization and focus become unclear, teams get out of sync and collaboration goes out the door.

To solve for focus and clarity, agile teams limit the amount of work in progress at a given time. Putting a more personal spin on this- let's consider a Saturday morning. You wake up and make a list of chores that need to be completed. These may include laundry, dishes, walking the dog and going to the bank. Now, it's possible that you start laundry and do dishes in parallel. Can you really walk the dog and go to the bank at the same time? No. So only one of these two tasks would be in progress. Here is where prioritization is important. If your dog is barking because he just ate a huge roast beef off of your table, do you take him for a walk first or go to the bank? If you choose yes to prioritization of banking over bowels- you will surely be surprised.

There are several activities and experiments to prove that there is a price to context switching. By focusing on separate unrelated tasks, up to 20% productivity is lost for each task. For example: When working on a single task, we are at 100% productivity. When adding another task (2 tasks), we drop to 80% productivity; at three tasks, we drop to 60% etc. In the new digital world, there is no credit for incomplete work or work in progress. Agile leaders need to remove the wrongly glorified assumption that multitasking makes teams more effective. A culture of focus, collaboration and finished work is what today's leaders need to embody.

The cost of context switching combined with the benefits of estimation, capacity and velocity makes limiting work in progress critical. Agile leaders limit the amount of work that is planned to be completed in an iteration. Limiting work in progress allows teams to focus on the same thing and also forces the discipline to say no and abandon archaic expectations of getting it done now or off with your head!

INSPECT AND ADAPT

Feedback is one of the most underrated assets an agile team can receive. This, too, is free and can be solicited by anyone at any time. Traditionally, feedback generated fear, perceived as negative, it was not welcome or exciting. When approaching work with an agile mindset, teams adopt the right processes to inspect their work on a frequent basis and welcome this feedback. This information helps the teams quickly make decisions on whether to continue or pivot in a new direction. Agile leaders understand the criticality of these processes and ensure they are executed regularly so that they can be actioned on by the teams.

The process of inspecting and adapting promotes a culture of learning. In the past, mistakes would be hidden and not shared, resulting in repeated efforts and wasted time. In an agile way of working, these 'mistakes' are critical to team learning, not occasions for critique or to assess individual performance. When working in agile, the focus is on team delivery, and therefore the feedback is for the team.

LEADERSHIP AGILITY AND ORGANIZATIONAL DNA

As mentioned above, strategy and culture (oDNA) along with leadership and agility are the building blocks to sustainability. Now that we are aligned on what agile leadership is and the key tenets necessary for an agile way of working, we can look at how these similar mindsets and behaviors can positively impact oDNA- and influence both strategy and culture.

When trying to inspire and align an organization, a good strategy must start with leadership creating a shared vision that provides a sense of purpose and establishes the reason for existence. A vision should serve as a 'north star', reflecting where the organization wants to go. At the simplest level, a shared vision is a picture that everyone in the company carries in their heads and hearts, converting 'the' company into 'our company'. It creates a sense of commonality and gives coherence to organization-wide activities. A shared vision allows everyone to see the big picture and allow teams to plan and focus on work that aligns the appropriate priorities. "When everything is a priority then, nothing is a priority". Finally, this gives the team power to say "no' to work that does not align with the overall vision.

While strategy orients people around the organization's vision, culture is about the organization's ethics, people, behaviors and work environment. A company's culture is what defines them, impacting everything from employee retention to public image. When employees feel integrated with the corporate culture, they feel a sense of ownership and want to contribute in a meaningful way. Good corporate culture will positively impact employees' well being, corporate commitment, motivation and ultimately, the bottom line.

Strategy and culture are interdependent. oDNA cannot have 1 without the other. Leadership's role in connecting the people and implementing agility in the organization are critical for keeping strategy and culture in sync and building employee ownership. If organizations want their customers to love them, they need to create an environment that their employees love first.

What an amazing thought to love what you do and feel safe and empowered to do it at work. When companies begin by caring, they will understand the voice of the employees and ultimately be able to foster the right kind of culture to suit them. If culture was a seed, leadership would be responsible for nurturing that seed until it sprouted, at which point it would be germinated by employees. The beauty comes when people feel empowered, motivated, safe, trusted and connected.

IMPLICATIONS OF NOT CHANGING DNA

An example from early in the digital evolution, Blockbuster is the pinnacle story of a giant moguls in the United States meeting a sad ending due to their refusal to evolve their oDNA. Before Netflix was born, people drove to a store (Blockbuster) to rent DVDs and VHS tapes to see movies. For two decades, Blockbuster reigned as the leading video-rental chain in the United States. At the time, these stores were the only way that people could watch movies that had left the theater without having to buy the content themselves. As their market share was massive, their management team was so sure of their strategy they quickly dismissed the newest player in the industry, Netflix. In 2000, Blockbuster had the opportunity to merge with Netflix and step into the future of content delivery. Management declined. (Olito, 2020)

The world of content delivery was on fast forward. People's ability to get content faster was increasing as Netflix and other smaller players jumped into the market. From 2003 to 2005 Blockbuster lost 75% of its market value. Ultimately, their decision to keep their strategy stagnant and not change would cost them everything including relevance and bankruptcy.

Not long after Netflix became the content provider of choice, the industry exploded. Streaming became part of everyday vocabulary. As the race for market share heated up, Netflix had to reinvent their oDNA. New players on the scene, including Prime, HBO Max, HULU, etc emerged with an edge. They all were able to differentiate by delivering original content. In response, Netflix expanded their content catalog to begin offering new original content as well, including movies, series and documentaries. Hello Joe Exotic, perfectly timed for the Covid-19 shut down.

If organizations are not prepared to respond to the changing market demands and/or get out ahead, competition will eat them alive. The hottest, newest players will steal the best people and ultimately, market share. Without strategy, there is no Vision. Without Vision, there is no clear strategy. without good employees- no good product and differentiation People won't feel challenged and do bare minimum, high turnover, no org loyalty, job changing will be the norm. Ultimately impacts bottom line

THE FUTURE WORKER, UNLEASHED

As the world sees increasing numbers of boomers retiring, while the number of Millenials is rising, companies are experiencing shifts in the skill sets and aspirations of their employees. This new generation, far more tech savvy than its predecessors, has a new set of demands that organizations must recognize when building a culture that can retain and support these resources.

The future is extremely unpredictable, and one can never truly know every detail and always get them right. We do know one thing, however, a traditional top-down leadership hierarchy, which limits decision making, direction setting, participation, and ownership, is one of the key reasons that Millennials may have gained a reputation for disloyalty. They continue to bounce from job to job in search of a place that will offer them what they seek: the chance to build new skill sets, take ownership, and lead, regardless of title or role

This is the big shift organizations need to embrace. As more and more Millennials come into the workforce, organizations must face the reality that they are dealing with a generation of individuals who are highly competent, intelligent and used to having information at the tips of their fingers instantaneously. This is not a group who has much interest in being controlled, or having their creativity stifled. As technology advances, and automation appears in every corner, the future worker will be about creativity and differentiation.

To embrace the future workers, Leaders have no choice but to focus on rebuilding their oDNA. Employees, especially in a remote world, regardless of their identified generation need to feel connected and safe at work.

REFERENCES

Diffen. (n.d.). *Leadership vs. Management*. Retrieved from https://www.diffen.com/difference/Leadership_vs_Management#:~:text=%20Leadership%20vs.%20Management%20%201%20Summary.%20Managing,Often%20the%20same%20people%20play%20wear...%20More%20

Duggal. N. (2022). *Leadership vs Management: Understanding the Key Difference*. Simplilearn. Retrieved from https://www.simplilearn.com/leadership-vs-management-difference-article

Olito, F. (2020). Rise and Fall of Blockbuster. *Business Insider*. Retrieved from https://www.businessinsider.com/rise-and-fall-of-blockbuster

Pink, D. (2011). *Drive*. Riverhead Harcover.

Thomas, G. (n.d.). What is Modern Effective Leadership. *weLead*. Retrieved from https://www.leadingtoday.org/what-is-effective-modern-leadership/

ADDITIONAL READING

Blog, C. (n.d.). Strategic Alignment: What Is Strategic Alignment and How to Achieve It. https://creately.com/blog/business/how-to-achieve-strategic-alignment/

Bresiger, G. (2018). Self-Employment is a Rising Trend in the American Workforce. https://nypost.com/2018/03/25/self-employment-is-a-rising-trend-in-the-american-workforce/

Glassdoor Team. (2021). Transparency in the Workplace: Why It Matters and How to Practice It - Glassdoor for Employers. https://www.glassdoor.com/employers/blog/transparency-in-the-workplace/

Indeed Editorial Team. (2021). Corporate Culture: Definition and Examples. https://www.indeed.com/career-advice/finding-a-job/what-is-corporate-culture

Msander. (2013). The Benefits of Working with small Batches – *The Techwriting Engineer*. http://techwritingengineer.com/the-benefits-of-working-with-small-batches/

KEY TERMS AND DEFINITIONS

Agile Manifesto: non prescriptive declaration introducing a more philosophical approach to work based on a set of guiding values and principals. The philosophy, however, applies to more than just technology teams. Any kind of team can adopt the same mindsets and approach work in a similar way.

Agility: Behaviors and mindsets required to ensure teams can pivot and adapt to a continuously changing world, in other words, part of a modern way of working.

Command and Control: An outdated style of management. Typically found where trust is not. Employees are told what to do without regard for their input.

Kanban: Japanese term, loosely translated as sign board. Also a tool for allowing teams to be transparent and manage/pull prioritized work in for completion.

oDNA: oDNA is the "backbone" of an organization, consisting of culture and strategy coiling around each other interdependently. The primary glue in this oDNA structure that keeps these coils aligned and connected, include leadership and agility.

POTUS: President of The United States.

Psychological Safety: Ideas are embraced, voices are heard, failures are opportunities to learn and people feel safe to be their best.

Scrum: Agile Framework providing guardrails to teams, ensuring they focus on the same goals and move chunks of work together, in shorter iterations (typically 2-4 weeks).

Chapter 12
Hybrid Leadership Styles Then and Now:
Identifying Different Patterns

Cynthia Maria Montaudon- Tomas
https://orcid.org/0000-0002-2595-6960
UPAEP Universidad, Mexico

Ingrid N. Pinto-López
https://orcid.org/0000-0002-1580-1375
UPAEP Universidad, Mexico

Anna Amsler
https://orcid.org/0000-0003-3183-0878
Independent Researcher, Mexico

ABSTRACT

Although there are classical and modern leadership styles, from a historical perspective, hybrid leadership practices have been the norm. It is essential to state that the idea of hybrid leadership is not new, nor has it resulted from hybrid working conditions. This chapter analyzes hybrid leadership from different perspectives, tracing its origins, the start of publications in the field, and its evolution. A short bibliometric analysis is included to provide a general background about how the study of hybrid leadership has evolved. The different leadership styles and models connected to hybrid leadership will be analyzed, as well as its main characteristics. The goal is to present an overview of hybrid leadership and how it has been applied in different contexts.

DOI: 10.4018/978-1-6684-3453-6.ch012

INTRODUCTION

Hybridity denotes the combination of two or more concepts or activities (Townsend, 2015) and explains heterogeneous arrangements in which elements of different origins are mixed (Brandsen, Van de Donk & Putters, 2005). As a concept, hybrid leadership has been used to depict a leadership that integrates different forms or characteristics, for instance, mixed leadership patterns (Leithwood, Mascall, & Strauss, 2009). It can also be put into practice through a combination of transactional and transformational leadership (Jones & Hunter, 2016), a reflective hybrid approach to connecting leadership style and stakeholder perspective, a blending of gender leadership strengths in a more impactful and effective manner (Bourgeois, 2004), and even androgynous leadership (Park, 1997; Blake-Beard, Shapiro, & Ingols, 2020).

Hybrid leadership has been connected to distributive leadership, which is top-down, bottom-up, and horizontal, bringing the decision-making capabilities to those near the problem (Turner, Thurlow, & Rivera, 2020). It is also related to quantum leadership based on the interconnectedness of leadership behaviors; (Malloch & Porter-O'Grady, 2003); and as an interactional field in which leadership-follower relationships are the asset (Erçetin & Kamaci, 2008).

From a cultural perspective, hybrid leadership is described as a constant, fluxional, and dynamic blending of the global and local, traits and behaviors, personal and contextual, and the past and the present (Tian, 2013). Based on the trait theory, hybrid leadership is a blend of instrumental and expressive traits, as well as reactive and proactive traits of leaders (Bolden, 2011), resulting in a mix of qualities and abilities to lead and of follower and leadership characteristics (Snelling, Exworthy & Ghezelayagh, 2020). Hybrid leadership can be associated with chameleon leadership, which is triggered by the situations at hand; leaders shuffle, mold, add, cast off old styles, and develop new ones (Buchen, 2012).

Some leadership styles are more visible in hybrid leadership analysis, such as autocratic-transformational or democratic-transactional leadership styles. Leaders employ a hybrid of several styles based on their contextual situation since real-world leadership application uses a hybridization of the various forms of leadership (Vann, Coleman & Simpson, 2014). Hybrid leadership is visible in adopting alternative leadership styles, including visionary, transformational, and democratic leadership commonly integrated with transactional leadership, while other styles are adopted occasionally, especially authoritative and delegative leadership. This new style helps explain the multidimensional leader who can vary the nature of their relationship to the follower to respond to a community's evolving local political, social, economic, and cultural elements (Eti-Tofinga, Douglas, & Singh, 2017).

BACKGROUND

The use of binary categories of leadership has been a tradition in different areas of work and life in which one or another style is preferred but not both. Strides have been made to move towards leadership as a hybrid activity which entails a range of approaches inspired by varying ideas arising from a reconsideration of distributed leadership (Gronn, 2009).

Leadership styles, although different, sometimes overlap due to similarities in traits, skill applications, and other characteristics attaining a blended or hybrid quality. Additionally, over time, leaders evolve, and so does their style, creating hybrid leadership brands that become unique (Buchen, 2011).

As an emerging leadership model, hybrid leadership is based on a cultural model that constantly shifts and blends with additional cultures. Leadership cannot be separated from culture; therefore, culture produces hybrid leadership (Tian, 2013). Hybrid leadership cultures imply a mix of discursive influences from various sources, as well as changes in meaning and the way in which some cultural aspects that are less visible are as important (Crevani, Eckman, Lindgren, Packendrorff, 2015).

Hybrid leadership has been present in different areas, such as higher education, to refer to the leadership performed in hybrid educational models (Tonini, Burbules & Gunsalus, 2016) and as a response to globalization (Tian, 2020). In nursing, hybrid leadership gives leaders a conceptual framework for leadership that allows for the intricacies of the current and future follower issues and accommodates for the pressure points of the context (Matson, 2014). In medical areas, hybrid leadership has been analyzed from the perspective of a mix of managerial and clinical roles applied to medical leaders and a mix of trainees and medical leaders in the profession (Snelling, Exworthy & Ghezelayagh, 2020).

In the military, hybrid leadership is used as a form of dual leadership (Gronn, in Leithwood, Mascall & Strauss, 2009), and in politics, as an aid in developing fair negotiations and diplomacy (Pugliese, 2017). At the country level, hybrid leadership has been used in transitions and transformations (Rugerinyange, 2016) and policymaking to promote transparency and governance through hybrid leadership councils (Ba, Ellerby, Green, Kinderman, Kauffman, Weinert, & Ali, S, 2019).

Hybrid leadership rejects the idea that one form of leadership is universally applicable and that the notion of each culture is unique, recognizing a flow of knowledge and experience through interconnectedness across international boundaries (Tian, 2013). The hybrid leadership framework expands the understanding of leadership work as a positional and distributed leadership, opening a new conceptual space to help understand how leaders recognize and contextualize their actions (Hognestad & Boe, 2015). Leadership is not a one-dimensional concept; for example, responsible leadership integrates both ethics and strategy, including stakeholder theory and corporate sustainability (Agarwal & Bha, 2020).

In order to understand the state of hybrid leadership in scientific literature, a bibliometric analysis was carried out using databases from the Web of Science. This will help identify trends in the interest and study of hybrid leadership and its evolution throughout the years. Data was collected on September 8th, 2021. The search yielded 21 results from 2006 to September 2021, considering articles, book chapters, editorial materials, early access, and review articles, of which seven are reported as open access. Table 1 shows the number of publications per year, considering the previously mentioned time frame.

As can be observed in Table 1, there are few publications on the subject of hybrid leadership, being 2017 the most productive year with only five documents. This fact shows that this is still a new line of study with great opportunities for research.

The countries with the most publications are listed below in table 2.

Table 2 demonstrates two leading countries in which publications related to hybrid leadership have originated, Australia and the UK. The main research areas for hybrid leadership are presented in table 3.

Table 1. Number of publications on the subject of hybrid leadership

Year	Number of articles
2006	1
2007	0
2008	0
2009	1
2010	0
2011	0
2012	0
2013	0
2014	2
2015	4
2016	0
2017	5
2018	1
2019	4
2020	2
2021	1

Source: Developed by the authors with information from the Web of Science, 2021.

Table 2. Countries with the most publications on the subject

Country	Number of articles
Australia	4
United Kingdom	4
Denmark	2
Netherlands	2
Norway	2
Scotland	2
United States	2
Brazil	1
Fiji	1
India	1
Israel	1
Russia	1
Singapore	1
South Korea	1
Sweden	1

Source: Developed by the authors with information from the Web of Science, 2021.

It is not a surprise that one of the main areas of research in the field of hybrid leadership is business economics, while the second is education and educational research.

The main publishers are shown in table 4.

Sage and Taylor & Francis are the leading publishers, closely followed by Springer Nature.

MAIN FOCUS OF THE CHAPTER

This chapter aims to analyze hybrid leadership from different perspectives through a literature review that focuses on the diverse approaches to leadership and the styles that have emanated from them. A bibliometric analysis is included to trace the origin of the conceptualization of hybrid leadership and its evolution.

The leadership perspectives that categorize leaders according to variables such as culture, gender, age, position, style, and relationship to the followers are explained to provide a better understanding of how hybridization occurs when there are mixed characteristics.

Table 3. Areas of research for hybrid leadership according to the number of published articles

Research areas	Number of articles
Business Economics	6
Education/Educational Research	6
Public Administration	3
Social Sciences	3
Psychology	2
Religion	2
Area Studies	1
Biomedical Social Sciences	1
Government Law	1
Health Care Sciences Services	1
International Relations	1
Philosophy	1
Public Environmental Occupation	1
Sociology	1

Source: Developed by the authors with information from the Web of Science, 2021.

Table 4. Main publishers for hybrid leadership

Main publishers	Number of articles
Sage	5
Taylor & Francis	5
Springer Nature	4
Centro Univ Senac	3
Elsevier	1
IGI Global	1
Wiley	1

Source: Developed by the authors with information from the Web of Science, 2021.

Understanding Hybrids and Hybridization

The notion of hybrid and hybridization can be defined as an offspring of two animals or plants or even different subspecies, varieties, or genera; something that is heterogeneous in origin or composition, that has different types of components. At the personal level, it is used to describe a person whose background is a blend of two or more diverse cultures and traditions (Merriam-Webster, 2021).

The concept emerged in the area of biology, and it was in the 1990s that the use of the word expanded to numerous areas as a way to understand liquid and fluid times (Bauman 2006). It was extensively used in postcolonial theory (Kraidy, 2005) and became a prominent theme in cultural studies (Pieterse, 2001). In social sciences, hybridity became a buzzword in modern times to describe mixtures of cultures, races, languages, systems, and even paradigms. "In cultural studies, hybridity denotes a wide register of multiple identities, cross-over, pick-'n'-mix, boundary-crossing experiences and styles, matching a world of growing migration and diaspora lives, intensive intercultural communication, everyday multiculturalism and erosion of boundaries" (Pieterse, 2001).

In terms of culture, hybridization is the process whereby cultures inevitably mix and mingle, creating new, unexpected, and hybrid cultural forms, artifacts, and identities. As people travel and cultures meet, they do not only clash; they also inevitably mingle and combine to create new and often strange forms. Kraidy (2005) argues that the hybridity that results from this recombinant creation of new cultural forms amounts to nothing less than the cultural logic of globalization. Nevertheless, hybridity also has a negative connotation, as it has been argued as "inauthentic, without roots, for the elite only, does not reflect social realities on the ground. It is multiculturalism lite, highlights superficial confetti culture and glosses over deep cleavages that exist on the ground" (Pieterse, 2001).

According to Pieterse (2001), the process of hybridization is as old as history, but the pace of mixing accelerates, and its scope widens when significant changes occur, such as the introduction of new technologies that enable new levels of intercultural contact. Hybridity is a modern, fluid conceptualization, useful to describe and analyze marginal phenomena and non-hegemonic productions of meaning, not only in terms of identity or culture but also as a form of social and singular imaginary significations (Sayeg, 2008). In this sense, hybrids are considered as a challenge to habitual categories (Latour, 1993).

Hybridity is common in interdisciplinary areas, and its use has become so frequent and overused that it is often taken for granted (Kraidy, 2005). In areas of technology, a postmodern hybrid can be known as cyborgs, something that is at once human and machine, and simultaneously natural and artificial (Hatch, 2013).

According to Gronn (2011), hybridity has figured rarely, if at all, in contemporary leadership research because it has typically centered around well-rehearsed binaries, such as leader-follower. Hybridity in leadership is connected to the notion of diversity in contemporary organizations; it includes different aspects of culture, gender, and age (Bassett, 2020).

The inherent nature of leadership is continuously redefined in contemporary society (Basset, 2020). However, even in hybrid leadership models, the fundamental leadership principles remain the same. Hybrid leadership is considered a rebirth of the essence of leadership; it is protean in nature, adapting to changing demands (Montaudon & Pinto, 2021), switching shape and is mutable and adaptable.

The context has been forcing enterprises to respond in a more flexible way "to survive and prosper in a competitive and unpredictable environment by responding quickly and effectively to any kind of change" (Nejatian, Zarel, Nejati & Zanjrichi, 2018; Montaudon & Pinto, 2021). The global executive's leadership style will have to be able to change from situation to situation (Schindler, 2021).

Different Perspectives about Hybrid Leadership

Multiple leadership theories and models have been developed in the last few decades; some of the most used include traits theory, behavioral theory, skills approach, transformational theory, distributive theory, and situational/contingency (Tian, 2013). "Leadership has changed, is changing and will continue to change" (Hudson RPO, 2015), which inherently involves transformations in the theoretical frameworks and approaches to describe, study it, and even practice it.

In this context, innovations in defining and categorizing leadership have led to more comprehensive perspectives, some of which are based on the notion that leadership differs from situation to situation and is greatly influenced by the context and other external variables. These variables include the maturity and commitment level of the followers (Tian, 2013), the number of followers, certain pressing situations, the pressure level of certain tasks, and crises, among others.

Other approaches have focused on how different styles, traits, and attitudes can intertwine, creating a very diverse set of leadership types, allowing to view the multiple dimensions of leadership (Tian, 2013). Through time, different outlooks about hybrid leadership have emerged, being associated with a composite profile or an evolving process in which leaders become unique through change and adaptation to the conditions at hand (Buchen, 2011).

The following sections present some of the approaches to leadership that allow thinking about hybridization.

The Gender-Based Perspective

Leadership is not gender-specific and depends on a variety of factors such as education, experience, culture, and personality (Górska, 2016). According to Eagly & Johannensen Schmidt (2001), it is not clear to what extent leaders can be influenced by gender and other factors. Yet, certain studies suggest that leaders tend to adapt to social expectations regarding gender perceptions, and leadership from a gender perspective has been analyzed in management and its effects on productivity (Nikulina, Khomenko, Sediakina, & Kanov, 2016); however, it is important to acknowledge that differences are mainly attributed to cultural constructs (Chamorro-Premuzic, 2019).

Nevertheless, some theories on gender and leadership point out that masculine characteristics are related to instrumentality and agency, while female traits are those in the interpersonal and expressive domains (Korabik, 1990). Male leadership tends to be task-oriented, and the predominant style is autocratic (Faizan, Nair & Haque2018). It is commonly associated with strength, intelligence, power, and competitiveness (Chamorro-Premuzic, 2019). Other characteristics are aggressiveness, dominance, and the propensity to take risks (Blake-Beard et al., 2020). Male communication tends to be more monological, hierarchical, aimed at precise objectives, and focused on maintaining a particular image of power (Maiorescu, 2016); confidence and optimism prevail (Górska, 2016).

On the other hand, feminine leadership styles do not seek to find enemies but achieve compromises through collaboration. It is based on honesty, prudence, and decency. Women leaders tend to have a clear orientation towards people and a participatory style (Faizan, Nair & Haque, 2018). Their leadership focuses on the social aspects and emotional needs of a group and places a particular value on human life and well-being, and they seek to respond adequately to the needs of the organization, institution, or country they serve, so a humane, empathetic, and emotional approach may prevail (Appelbaum, Audet, & Miller, 2003). Relationships are valued, there is dialogic communication, and decisions are usually based on the principles of cooperation, interaction, and equality (Maiorescu, 2016).

The gender-based perspective also includes androgynous leadership (Blake-Beard, Shapiro & Ingols, 2020). Most successful leaders have a balance of gender traits; female and male traits are equally important. Most relevant traits include gregariousness assertion, social skills, trustworthiness, and the ability to inspire, persuade, and motivate (Tully, 2007). Androgyny in leadership means integration (Tully, 2007) and is an archetype that represents the coming together of maleness and femaleness (Blanchard & Sargent, 1984). It is a mix of male and female leadership traits; a fusion of qualities and abilities of masculine and feminine leadership (Shabbir, Ishtiaq, & Zia-ud-Din, 2017) that includes male leadership traits and values the strength of female leaders, meaning that it is a leadership that is high in instrumentality and expressiveness with greater sensitivity.

The androgynous leadership style has been supported by the ideas of Bem (1974), who suggested that masculinity and femineity are not completely opposed to leadership perspectives and that the term androgynous can be used to refer to individuals who portray both feminine and masculine psychological characteristics. Androgeny as a leadership style has been incorporated into the conceptualization of gender on leadership, referring to leadership that mixes feminine and masculine characteristics through integration rather than polarization (Blake-Beard, Shapiro

& Ingols, 2020). People who possess masculine and feminine traits have been categorized as a new breed of leaders (Burgeois, 2004).

In 1984, Blanchard & Sargent proposed a series of guidelines for men and women in terms of andragogy in leadership. In the case of men, guidelines included understanding the value of women, expressing feelings, personalizing experiences, building support systems, learning to fail, viewing work as personal fulfillment, as well as practicing emphatic and active listening. The guidelines for women included being powerful, having a clear and visible impact, being entrepreneurial, stating their needs, intellectualizing and generalizing ideas, dealing directly with feelings, owning their leadership, taking more risks, and becoming empowered.

Velumyan (2020) proposed seven steps to balance masculine and feminine leadership. These steps are based on the acceptance that a person has both feminine and masculine features that are applied to leadership; the expansion of one's perception regardless of gender; the focus on dominant qualities; awareness of the context; visualization of the desired outcome; exploration of effective models of behavior; and finally, the implementation of new habits.

The Culture-Based Perspective

"In the 1980s, scholars began to consider the impact of national cultures on leadership behaviors" (Tian, 2013), which led to a consensus regarding the absence of universality in terms of leadership values and characteristics. "Culture includes the way people interact with each other, how they solve problems, and how they justify themselves" (Duncan, 2018). Lewis (2006) established three basic types of cultures: linear-actives who plan, schedule, organize, pursue action chains, and do one thing at a time; multi-actives who do many things at once, planning according to the relative importance that each appointment brings; and reactives who prioritize courtesy and respect, reacting carefully to the other side's proposals.

Increasing globalization processes have made hybrids out of contemporary cultures. Although specific values and traditions remain, cultures have gravitated towards constant growth and transformation as they coexist with different ideas, knowledge, and changing contexts (Tian, 2013). Since leadership is intertwined with culture, to a certain extent, hybrid cultures create a form of hybrid leadership (Tian, 2013).

Lewis (2006) suggested that there are combinations among the different types of cultures and that a leader can be a hybrid to some degree because personality and context have an important effect, and in any place or time a leader is subjected to a contextual influence involving background personal life and personality preferences.

A study conducted by Falayi (2016) suggests that hybrid leaders use culture intentionally, situationally, and often intuitively; they display strong cultural affinity in interactions and show awareness and emotional intelligence. A hybrid leadership in terms of culture tends to be context-sensitive (Eti-Tofinga, Douglas, Singh, 2017). In this sense, hybrid leaders could be bicultural or multicultural individuals with regards to their country of origin, family background, and even the company culture of where they work.

The Generation-Based Perspective

In recent years, interesting changes have occurred in the workforce, creating space for up to five different generations who collaborate and need to be led. Through adequate leadership, different generations can work together effectively, and hybrid leadership helps bridge the gap, leveraging the strengths for the different generations. This requires managing challenges within culture, ideals, values, and practices, understanding that all generations have something to contribute and that it is vital to understand intergenerational diversity to create intergenerational equity, which will help prevent or reduce discrimination based on age (Aydogmus 2019).

Leadership competencies are not changing, but methods are. How generations approach authority, leadership, and loyalty is essential. Leadership needs to be transparent and responsible, providing excellent working experiences for all (Salopek, 2006). A one-size-fits-all approach to leading amid a great generational diversity no longer works (McNally, 2017). It is important to develop meaningful engagement between leaders across generations by being aware of the generational differences and the particular contributions of each generation.

Generations create unique challenges for both leaders and organizations. Leaders from different generations will have particular styles and traits, but the employees from other generations will have distinct expectations concerning the leader. Millennials, for instance, will lead by laying out the vision and welcoming those who are willing participants; they want to inspire others and lead by example. For their part, generation X leaders will seek inclusion, and they are able to communicate with different generations as they are considered diplomats. Boomers will lead using their power and influence over others; they are decisive strategic thinkers who share, teach, and mentor (Keene & Handrich, 2015).

The various expectations about communication practices, approaches to work, and assumptions held by different generations can no longer be ignored. Through the generation-based perspective, hybrid leadership is a mix of skills and traits from different generations and the ability to lead in multigeneration environments. It helps connect with people from different backgrounds. Multigenerational leaders need to acknowledge the differences in order to harness diverse talents to operate productively and facilitate cooperation (Salopek, 2006).

The Technology and Work-Based Perspective

Although hybrid leadership can encompass the merging of different attitudes, traits, behaviors, profiles, and characteristics, it is often understood as a mix of virtual and face-to-face leadership skills, mainly due to the exponential growth in the practice of hybrid work. The hybrid work paradox is supported by the flexibility of remote work and the inspiration and ease of in-person work (Spataro, 2021), which might seem like a contradiction in itself but can bring numerous benefits to organizations if managed and practiced correctly. In this sense, hybrid leadership from the technology and work-based perspective is related to the ability to lead both online and offline, leading from the distance and on-site.

Hybrid work models involve managing on-premise and remote teams in synchronous and asynchronous manners. This often leads to working in isolation and with less supervision, which requires increased levels of trust in employees. The hybrid workforce is a learning environment in which loyalty becomes essential (Aydogmus, 2019). Leaders need to share values and show respect, be trustworthy and communicate change. Additionally, workplace hybridization can entail leading geographically dispersed teams, which can become a challenge.

Gartner (2021) has proposed four types of hybrid workforce leaders based on the openness and closeness of their mindset and the maturity of their skillset, which relate to drive performance, champion development, effective communication, contribution, inclusive team climates, trust and psychological safety, and team culture and norms. Hybrid strivers are leaders who have the right mindset but lack the right skill set to lead a hybrid workforce; hybrid laggards are leaders who lack both the right mindset and the required skills to lead a hybrid workforce; hybrid resistors are leaders who have the right skill set but have a closed mind towards a hybrid workforce; and finally, hybrid champions are the leaders with the right mindset and skills to lead a hybrid workforce.

The success of a hybrid workplace is highly dependent on effective leadership, which involves setting expectations and communicating them clearly, keeping team members connected, and promoting a cohesive culture (Crestcom, 2021). Some top skills that hybrid workplace leaders should have are managing transitions, adaptability, building trust and credibility, empathy to the needs of the employees, and commitment (CoreAxis, 2021).

The Leader-Follower Perspective or Distributed Leadership

There is a consensus surrounding the definition of leadership as the "process by which a person influences others to accomplish an objective" (Foster, 2010), which inherently implies that there must be someone to influence; that person is referred to as the follower. Followers are commonly defined by their behavior towards the leader and the established goals, but they can also be defined according to their rank, which generally entails less power and influence than the leader and has led to followers being categorized as subordinates (Kellerman, 2007).

However, even subordinates do not follow all the time; more and more followers think of themselves as free agents and act accordingly, sometimes falling into leader behaviors (Kellerman, 2007). Good followership entails being proactive in the pursuit of organizational goals, which sometimes requires working independently, taking ownership of necessary tasks, and being accountable for one's actions (Wigston, 2019).

Several theories have been developed to describe the relationship between leaders and followers and the definition of each of their roles, traits, and characteristics; hybridity in these conceptualizations combines them. A leader-follower, for example, is when "leaders assume followers' roles and followers assume leadership roles" (Foster, 2010), creating a type of system where there is more collaboration.

This approach sees followers working for a purpose and not a person, pushing followership beyond the idea of subordination and obedience and towards the creation of spaces for innovation and growth. (Foster, 2010). In terms of leadership, leader-follower theory has been linked to servant leadership styles where the leader's focus is not on power or authority but on their followers (Tait, 2020). Distributed leadership is also a hybrid form of leadership in terms of the leader's relationship with their followers. It involves engaging followers through a collaborative attitude "that embraces diversity and good governance while recognizing the complexities of informed and effective decision-making" (Chatwani, 2018).

The Leadership Styles Perspective

Lewin, Lippitt, and White researched the influence of three main leadership styles: autocratic or authoritarian, democratic or participative, and *laissez-faire* or delegative (1939). More styles, such as charismatic and servant leadership, were later added and continued to grow through time. A quick search on the internet yielded one hundred different styles, most of which are combinations of the basic ones. The list is not exhaustive, and many additional styles could have certainly been left out. Table 5 is just an example of the variety in possible combinations of leadership styles.

Leadership styles are often divided into positive and negative, traditional or modern, and even specific classifications such as transformational and transactional. Some of the characteristics of transformational leadership are individual influence, spiritual encouragement, and intellectual stimulation, creating an open culture of trust (Nanjundeswaraswamy & Swamy, 2014). This entails a more balanced leader-follower dynamic where leaders aim to align their followers' values and motivations

Table 5. Leadership styles

Leadership Styles			
Abrasive Leadership	Directing Leadership	Intellectual Leadership	Self-Leadership
Adaptive Leadership	Discursive Leadership	*Laissez-Faire* Leadership	Self-Protective Leadership
Advisory Leadership	Disruptive Leadership	Malevolent Leadership	Servant Leadership
Affiliative Leadership	Dynamic Leadership	Meaningful Leadership	Shared Leadership
Agile Leadership	Emergent Leadership	Military Leadership	Situational Leadership
Authentic Leadership	Emotional Leadership	Moral/ Ethical Leadership	Social Justice Leadership
Anticipative Leadership	Entrepreneurial Leadership	Motivational Leadership	Social/Social Change Leadership
Autocratic Leadership	Exemplary Leadership	Narcissistic Leadership	Socially Responsible Leadership
Autonomous Leadership	Exploitative Leadership	Natural Leadership	Spiritual Leadership
Benevolent Leadership	Exploratory Leadership	Negative Leadership	Strategic Leadership
Bureaucratic Leadership	Facilitative Leadership	Orchestrator Leadership	Supporting Leadership
Charismatic Leadership	Fluid Leadership	Pacesetter Leadership	Sustainable Leadership
Civic Leadership	Formal Leadership	Participative Leadership	Task-Focused Leadership
Coaching Leadership	Functional Leadership	Passive-Aggressive Leadership	Team Leadership
Collaborative Leadership	Global Leadership	Paternal & Maternal Leadership	Team-Oriented Leadership
Commanding Leadership	Hands-Off Leadership	Persuasive Leadership	Title-Less Leadership
Common-Good Leadership	Humane Oriented Leadership	Positive Leadership	Top-Down and Bottom-Up Leadership
Compassionate Leadership	Humanistic Leadership	Primal Leadership	Transactional Leader
Contingent Leadership	Hybrid Leadership	Prosocial Leadership	Transcendent Leadership
Consultative Leadership	Impulsive Leadership	Pseudo Transformational Leadership	Transformational Leader
Cross-Cultural Leadership	Inclusive Leadership	Reactive Leadership	True Leadership
Delegative Leadership	Informal Leadership	Regenerative Leadership	Value-Based Leadership
Democratic Leadership	Innovative Leadership	Relational Leadership	Virtual Leadership
Destructive Leadership	Instrumental Leadership	Resonance Leadership	Virtuous Leadership
Dictatorial Leadership	Integrative Leadership	Responsible Leadership	Visionary Leadership

Source: Developed by the authors with information from Google search engine, 2021.

in the process of attaining organizational goals (Tian, 2013). On the other hand, transactional leadership has a contractual view of the relationship between the leader and the followers, where the organizational goal and individual responsibilities to attain it are the priority (Nanjundeswaraswamy & Swamy, 2014). It occurs when the leader takes the initiative to communicate objectives and tasks to the followers, expecting that they will do their part to get things done (Tian, 2013).

Within the leadership styles perspective, an interesting example is that of the full range leadership model (FRLM), which includes a mix of laissez-faire, transactional, and transformational leadership styles. It is considered an adaptive approach to leadership and not a continuum; it is a mix of behaviors that leaders can apply in different situations. It includes a hands-off leadership approach, management by exception, contingent reward, individual consideration, intellectual stimulation, inspirational motivation, and idealized influence (Stafford, 2010), changing the style to suit every situation.

The leadership styles perspective views hybridization as a mix of different leadership styles and traits. It rejects the idea that one form of leadership is universally applicable and establishes that the key to successful leadership lies in the adaptability to move from one leadership style to another based on changing needs.

Different factors can help determine which type of leadership style is most effective or when a combination of leadership styles is better, such as the number of members in an organization, the degree of interaction and communication, personalities in the workforce, and decision-making processes, among others.

Behavioral Perspective: Constructive and Destructive Profiles

Destructive leadership behaviors refer to certain influencing methods that followers can perceive as a display of hostility (Chénard-Poirier, Morin, Boudrias, & Gillet, 2021). There is a series of concepts that fall within the domain of destructive leadership, such as "abusive supervisors", "petty tyrants", "bullies", "derailed leaders", "intolerable bosses", "toxic leaders", and "harassing leaders" (Einarsen, Aasland & Skogstad, 2007).

More specifically, destructive leadership has also been defined as "the systematic and repeated behavior by a leader, supervisor, or manager that violates the legitimate interest of the organization by undermining or sabotaging the organization's goals, tasks, resources, and effectiveness and the motivation, well-being, or job satisfaction of subordinates" (Einarsen, Aasland & Skogstad, 2007). Exposure to destructive leadership can influence performance and commitment, as well as stress levels and turnover intentions (Chénard-Poirier, Morin, Boudrias, & Gillet, 2021).

According to Balwant (2021), there are two primary manifestations of destructive leadership. One can be leading followers toward goals that contradict the organization's objectives or general interests, and the other can be using hostile behaviors in the process of leading. Leaders sometimes rationalize the use of destructive leadership behaviors as a necessary means to achieve specific ends (Balwant, 2021).

For its part, constructive leadership behaviors refer to attitudes and actions aimed at achieving organizational goals while at the same time improving motivation, promoting well-being, and boosting satisfaction among employees (Chénard-Poirier, Morin, Boudrias, & Gillet, 2021). As a term, constructive leadership is used to describe a positive behavior of leaders towards both their organization and followers; these leaders tend to make optimal use of resources to pursue the interests and strategies of the organization (Arasli, Arici & Kole, 2020).

Considering destructive and constructive leadership approaches, it is generally implied that leaders tend to have behavior patterns that are either good or bad (Chénard-Poirier, Morin, Boudrias, & Gillet, 2021). However, context is very important when analyzing leadership, and there can be profiles that present an amalgamation of constructive and destructive behaviors.

The Direction-Based Leadership

As previously discussed, leadership has often been associated with a superior hierarchical position, usually related to management or supervision jobs. Although leadership and management are two different concepts linked to specific outlooks, skills, and behaviors, they are similar in some aspects; "good managers should strive to be good leaders, and good leaders need management skills to be effective" (Wajdi, 2016).

From a managerial standpoint, leadership can be exercised through different methods such as top-down, bottom-up, horizontal, and even shared leadership. Top-down approaches can be effective if applied in moderation; otherwise, they tend to lean towards bureaucratic, autocratic, and authoritarian styles, confusing positional authority with leadership. In a top-down leadership style, the leader defines decisions and directions and communicates to the followers, with little to no input, who are expected to carry out tasks according to instructions or guidelines (Martinich, 2016).

Bottom-up leadership approaches resemble visionary, democratic, and laissez-faire leadership styles more. Typically, leaders communicate broad goals and let the followers set their own milestones for them (Martinich, 2016). The methods for carrying out tasks are up to the followers, which promotes creativity and engagement. However, neither top-down nor bottom-up leadership styles can be efficient in all types of contexts, which is why a combination of the two has been deemed more appropriate (Martinich, 2016), resulting in hybrid leadership regarding direction.

In this context, one-way hybridization can occur is through agile leadership practices. This involves leaders extending and transcending the competencies that made them successful in the past, as well as developing new capabilities such as transforming themselves to evolve in their mindsets and behaviors and building agility into the design and culture (De Smet, Lurie & St. George, 2018) of the organization by giving their followers a certain level of autonomy to execute goals while also maintaining them aligned with the organization's interests.

Another form of leadership hybridity in the direction-based approach is shared leadership. Studies have been conducted on the matter yielding interesting results; teams with a shared leadership structure tend to do better than those with a traditional vertical leadership structure because when team members are collaborating and working towards common goals, the team's overall performance improves (Martin, Cormican, Sampaio & Wu, 2018). This model is based on the idea that leadership is not only an individual trait but is also an organizational trait, defining shared leadership as a dynamic and interactive process among individuals that aims to achieve group or organizational goals through a mix of peer, lateral, upward, and downward influence (Kocolowski, 2010).

Quantum Leadership

The complexity and uncertainty of this era have led to what has been described as quantum society. In a context of exponential change and the growth of interconnectedness, it becomes important to question current management practices when it comes to people and organizations and the leadership styles that support them (Hanine & Nita 2019). As a result of these transformations, quantum leadership theory was introduced in the 1990s to incorporate principles of quantum physics into leadership (Şenses & Temoçin, 2018).

Quantum leadership is a multidimensional concept that integrates cognitive, relational, ethical, and spiritual dimensions (Hanine & Nita 2019) and is considered a synergistic result of logical and associative thinking (Lazaridou & Fris, 2008). It links the ideas of quantum mechanics, chaos theory, and complexity theory to give another perspective to the organizational challenges faced by leaders worldwide and help rethink the organization's way of operating (Hanine & Nita 2019). This type of leadership is particularly useful when certain contingencies exist, such as the volatile, chaotic, and complex organizational setting or external context (Lazaridou & Fris, 2008).

Some of the main characteristics of quantum leadership include fluidity, flexibility, mobility, and working from the whole (Malloch & Porter-O'Grady, 2009). It involves a particular set of skills that stimulates innovation, promotes effective self-management, facilitates a deep connection between team members, and strives for development and growth, unleashing the full potential of individuals (Hanine & Nita 2019). These characteristics lead to authentic collaboration, compassion, and opportunities to learn and evolve (Nigri & Agulini, 2019).

Issues, Controversies, Problems

Throughout the years, different theories to analyze and categorize leadership have been developed. Through diverse lenses, leadership has been put into boxes that aim to define specific traits and characteristics of leaders according to variables that relate to the person, their behavior, or the context in which they exercise their leadership. However, this seems problematic as cases that fit into a particular category are rare, if not completely absent from the real world.

Identifying all the possibilities of hybrid leadership would be an impossible task, as hybridization entails a combination or mix of various things. For instance, one might find a leader with a combination of servant, democratic, ethical, and authentic leadership that uses androgynous communication patterns while leading in a virtual environment. Combinations are limitless, which makes it difficult to portray a specific supporting theory.

The variety of perspectives from which to analyze hybrid leadership has sometimes led to confusion, creating additional controversies and problems. Additionally, there seems to be a gap in the literature that analyzes hybrid leadership as all the possible combinations that might occur instead of particular mixes inside a pre-established category. As a result, empirical studies that analyze specific hybrid leadership models are also lacking.

SOLUTIONS AND RECOMMENDATIONS

The variety of combinations of leadership characteristics demonstrates that leadership is an ever-changing, adapting concept that is dynamic and fluid. The multiple existing styles are proof of this; it is quite possible that more and more leadership styles will be developed from previous combinations and new additions. Changes in society, technology, economics, and even politics will also yield additional leadership styles and more hybridization between them.

Leadership today requires flexibility, adaptability, and even experimentation. Hybrid leadership provides a pallet of different options to choose from to create effective leadership strategies. Understanding leadership as an infinite continuum of mix and matches can provide a new framework for leadership theories and applications.

FUTURE RESEARCH DIRECTIONS

The gap in literature allows to re-imagine leadership and hybridity and develop new, more comprehensive models supported by empirical studies. Combinations of leadership characteristics have been underexplored, opening interesting opportunities for research. Additional hybrids in leadership can also be identified and analyzed.

To further understand the inherent hybridity in relation to leadership, future research could focus on particular examples from leaders around the world and their personal characteristics and traits while leading, which will help get clarity on how the styles, approaches, and theories presented in this chapter interact and merge in real life.

CONCLUSION

This brief chapter showed the most relevant hybrid models in leadership. However, these are not the only available, and, quite certainly, more hybrid and fluid models will be developed over time. Hybrid leadership is all about being effective, adapting, and changing according to the needs of the followers and those of the organization.

It is almost impossible to force a particular leadership style onto an individual or group because every person searches for specific traits and values in the leader. Additionally, the leadership environment is constantly shifting; it is volatile, uncertain, complex, and ambiguous; furthermore, it is a turbulent, seismic, and explosive context in which leaders adapt, or they fail. By creating hybrid patterns, leaders are able to rise to the challenge.

Hybrid leadership can include different levels of context such as international, national, and local; it mixes different traits and characteristics emanating from culture, education, social norms, and personality, as well as external factors and environments. Hybrid leadership brings concepts and ideas from different areas to help develop a leadership combination to solve problems as they emerge. Every element, characteristic, trait, and style can be combined and recombined without any constraints.

Amid all the uncertainty, one thing is certain: leadership will continue to evolve and change, becoming more complex to analyze from a single perspective. Theories and approaches to leadership will have to evolve as well and adapt to ever-changing contexts and needs in the field, new developments, and emerging trends to allow a more comprehensive view of what leadership is, how it is exercised, and the outcomes each form of hybrid leadership is able to achieve in specific environments.

REFERENCES

Agarwal, S., & Bhal, K. T. (2020). A multidimensional measure of responsible leadership: Integrating strategy and ethics. *Group & Organization Management, 45*(5), 637–673. doi:10.1177/1059601120930140

Appelbaum, S. H., Audet, L., & Miller, J. (2003). Gender and leadership. *Leadership and Organization Development Journal, 24*(1), 43–51. doi:10.1108/01437730310457320

Arasli, H., Arici, H. E., & Kole, E. (2020). Constructive Leadership and Employee Innovative Behaviors: A Serial Mediation Model. *Sustainability, 12*(2592), 2592. doi:10.3390u12072592

Aydogmus, C. (2019). Globally responsible intergenerational leadership. In Intergenerational Governance and Leadership in the Corporate World: Emerging Research and Opportunities (pp. 123-152). IGI Global. doi:10.4018/978-1-5225-8003-4.ch007

Ba, A., Ellerby, K., Green, D., Kinderman, D., Kauffman, S., Weinert, M., & Ali, S. H. (2019). Hybrid leadership councils: Envisioning inclusive and resilient governance. *European Journal of Futures Research, 7*(1), 1–10. doi:10.118640309-019-0155-2

Balwant, P. T. (2021). Is There a Bright Side to Destructive Leadership? How Gordon Ramsay Leads Change in Nightmare Kitchens. *The Journal of Leadership Studies, 14*(4), 81–88. doi:10.1002/jls.21723

Bassett, P. (2020). Leadership: A Protean Institution of the Mind and of Civilization. *The Journal of Student Leadership, 3*(2), 15-21.

Bauman, Z. (2006). *Liquid Times: Living in an Age of Uncertainty*. Polity.

Bem, S. L. (1974). The measurement of psychological androgyny. *Journal of Consulting and Clinical Psychology, 42*(2), 155–162. doi:10.1037/h0036215 PMID:4823550

Blake-Beard, S., Shapiro, M., & Ingols, C. (2020). Feminine? Masculine? Androgynous leadership as a necessity in COVID-19. *Gender in Management: An International Journal.*

Blanchard, K. H., & Sargent, A. G. (1984). The one-minute manager is an androgynous manager. *Training and Development Journal.*

Bolden, R. (2011). *Distributed Leadership in Organizations: A Review of Theory and Research.* Academic Press.

Bourgeois, T. (2013). *The hybrid leader: Blending the best of the male and female leadership styles*. Oakhill Press.

Brandsen, T., Van de Donk, W., & Putters, K. (2005). Griffins or chameleons? Hybridity as a permanent and inevitable characteristic of the third sector. *International Journal of Public Administration, 28*(9-10), 749–765. doi:10.1081/PAD-200067320

Bryman, A., Collinson, D., Grintr, K., Jackson B., & Uhl Bien, M. (Eds.). (2011). The SAGE handbook of leadership. Sage Publications.

Buchen, I. H. (2011). *The Hybrid Leader: Evolving, Adaptable, Unfinished*. Rowman & Littlefield Education.

Buchen, I. H. (2012). Hybrid Futures Intelligence: Circular, Cyclical, and Convergent. *World Futures Review, 4*(3), 33–38. doi:10.1177/194675671200400307

Chamorro-Premuzic, T. (2019). *Why do so many incompetent men become leaders?: (And how to fix it)*. Harvard Business Press.

Chatwani, N. (2018). *Distributed Leadership: The Dynamics of Balancing Leadership with Followership*. Spinger International Publishing. doi:10.1007/978-3-319-59581-8

Chénard-Poirier, L. A., Morin, A. J. S., Boudrias, J.-S., & Gillet, N. (2021). The combined effects of destructive and constructive leadership on thriving at work and behavioral empowerment. *Journal of Business and Psychology*. Advance online publication. doi:10.100710869-021-09734-7

CoreAxis. (2021). *Top Skills Checklist for Nurturing Hybrid Leadership*. https://coreaxis.com/wp-content/uploads/2021/06/CoreAxis-White-Paper-Nurturing-Hybrid-Leadership.pdf

Crestcom. (2021). *Leading in the Hybrid Workplace*. https://crestcom.com/wp-content/uploads/2021/06/Crestcom_Leading-in-the-Hyrbid-Workplace.pdf

Crevani, L., Ekman, M., Lindgren, M., & Packendorff, J. (2015). Leadership cultures and discursive hybridisation: On the cultural production of leadership in higher education reforms. *International Journal of Public Leadership, 11*(3/4), 147–165. doi:10.1108/IJPL-08-2015-0019

De Smet, A., Lurie, M., & St. George, A. (2018). *Leading agile transformation: The new capabilities leaders need to build 21st-century organizations*. McKinsey. https://www.mckinsey.com/business-functions/people-and-organizational-performance/our-insights/leading-agile-transformation-the-new-capabilities-leaders-need-to-build-21st-century-organizations

Duncan, R. D. (2018). Culture, Leadership, Performance: How Are They Linked? *Forbes*. https://www.forbes.com/sites/rodgerdeanduncan/2018/10/30/culture-leadership-performance-how-are-they-linked/?sh=4ddb55c85e44

Eagly, A. H., Johannesen-Schmidt, M. C., & Van Engen, M. L. (2003). Transformational, transactional, and laissez-faire leadership styles: A meta-analysis comparing women and men. *Psychological Bulletin*, *129*(4), 569–591. doi:10.1037/0033-2909.129.4.569 PMID:12848221

Einarsen, S, Aasland, M. S., & Skogstad, A. (2007). *Destructive leadership behaviour: A definition and conceptual model.* doi:10.1016/j.leaqua.2007.03.002

Erçetin, Ş. Ş., & Kamacı, M. C. (2008). Quantum leadership paradigm. *World Applied Sciences Journal*, *3*(6), 865–868.

Eti-Tofinga, B., Douglas, H., & Singh, G. (2017). Influence of evolving culture on leadership: A study of Fijian cooperatives. *European Business Review*, *29*(5), 534–550. doi:10.1108/EBR-10-2015-0122

Faizan, R., Nair, S. L. S., & Haque, A. U. (2018). The effectiveness of feminine and masculine leadership styles in relation to contrasting gender's performances. *Polish Journal of Management Studies, 17.*

Falayi, O. (2016). *American Nigerian Leadership: An Exploration into Hybrid Leadership* (Doctoral dissertation). The Chicago School of Professional Psychology. https://www.proquest.com/openview/27540781abcb80b439cf380f543ac149/1?pq-origsite=gscholar&cbl=18750

Foster, P. A. (2010). *Leader-Follower Theory for the Learning Organization.* http://followership2.pbworks.com/f/Leader-Follower+Theory+for+the+Learning+Organization.pdf

Gartner. (2021). *Are you a hybrid workforce champion or a laggard?* https://www.gartner.com/smarterwithgartner/are-you-a-hybrid-workforce-champion-or-a-laggard

Górska, A. (2016). Gender differences in leadership. *Studia i Materiały, 1*(20), 136-144.

Gronn, P. (2009). *Hybrid leadership.* Routledge.

Hanine, S., & Nita, M. A. (2019). The paradigm of quantum leadership: Ontology, praxis and application to management. *Revue Internationale des Sciences de Gestion*, *2*(2), 837–858.

Hatch, M. J. (2013). *Organization theory: Modern, symbolic, and postmodern perspectives*. Oxford University Press.

Hognestad, K., & Boe, M. (2015). Leading site-based knowledge development: A mission impossible? Insights from a study from Norway. *Thinking and learning about leadership. Early childhood research from Australia, Finland, and Norway*, 210-228.

Hudson, R. P. O. (2015). *The great generational shift*. https://eu.hudsonrpo.com/insights/thinking/the-great-generational-shift/

Jones, H., & Hunter, K. O. (2016). A reflective hybrid approach to connecting leadership style and stakeholder perspective. *Challenging Organizations and Society.*, *5*(2), 950–1006.

Keene, D. L., & Handrich, R. R. (2015). Loyalty, longevity and leadership: A multigenerational workforce update. *Journal of Expertise*, *27*, 34.

Kellerman, B. (2007). What Every Leader Needs to Know About Followers. *Harvard Business Review*. https://hbr.org/2007/12/what-every-leader-needs-to-know-about-followers

Kocolowski, M. D. (2010). Shared Leadership: Is it Time for a Change? *Emerging Leadership Journeys*, *3*(1), 22–32.

Korabik, K. (1990). Androgyny and leadership style. *Journal of Business Ethics*, *9*(4), 283–292. doi:10.1007/BF00380328

Kraidy, M. (2005). *Hybridity, or the Cultural Logic of Globalization*. Temple University. Press.

Latour, B. (1993). *We have never been modern*. Harvard University Press.

Lazaridou, A., & Fris, J. (n.d.). *Slipping the Yoke of the Heroic Paradigm: Looking for Quantum Leadership*. Education Resources Information Center. https://files.eric.ed.gov/fulltext/EJ940819.pdf

Leithwood, K., Mascall, B., & Strauss, T. (Eds.). (2009). *Distributed leadership according to the evidence*. Routledge. doi:10.4324/9780203868539

Lewin, K., Lippitt, R., & White, R. K. (1939). Patterns of aggressive behavior in experimentally created social climates. *The Journal of Social Psychology*, *10*(2), 271–301. doi:10.1080/00224545.1939.9713366

Lewis, R. D. (2006). *When cultures collide: Leading across cultures*. Nicholas Brealey.

Maiorescu, R. D. (2016). Crisis management at General Motors and Toyota: An analysis of gender-specific communication and media coverage. *Public Relations Review*, *42*(4), 556–563. doi:10.1016/j.pubrev.2016.03.011

Malloch, K., & Porter-O'Grady, T. (2009). *The quantum leader: Applications for the new world of work*. Jones & Bartlett Learning.

Martin, J., Cormican, K., Sampaio, S., & Wu, Q. (2018). Shared leadership and team performance: An analysis of moderating factors. *Procedia Computer Science*, *138*, 671–679. doi:10.1016/j.procs.2018.10.089

Martinich, L. (2016). Excellent execution: Balancing top-down and bottom-up management. *IEEE Engineering Management Review*, *44*(2), 20–23. doi:10.1109/EMR.2016.2568720

Matson, K. M. (2014). Revisiting the past, revamping the future: The leadership edition. *Nursing Management*, *45*(8), 47–51. doi:10.1097/01.NUMA.0000452001.49343.29 PMID:25058534

McNally, K. (2017). Leading a Multigenerational Workforce. *Healthcare Executive*, *32*(1), 58–61. PMID:30280532

Merriam-Webster. (2021). *Hybrid*. https://www.merriam-webster.com/dictionary/hybrid

Montaudon-Tomás, C. M., & Pinto-López, I. N. (2021). Developing a Metaphor for Self-Managed Organizations. In *Handbook of Research on International Business and Models for Global Purpose-Driven Companies* (pp. 65–85). IGI Global. doi:10.4018/978-1-7998-4909-4.ch004

Nanjundeswaraswamy T. S., & Swamy D. R. (2014). Leadership styles. *Advances in Management, 7*(2), 57-72.

Nejatian, M., Zarei, M. H., Nejati, M., & Zanjirchi, S. M. (2018). A hybrid approach to achieve organizational agility. *Benchmarking*, *25*(1), 201–234. doi:10.1108/BIJ-09-2016-0147

Nigri, G., & Agulini, A. (2019). *Culture and consciousness toward quantum leadership*. Cultural Perspectives on Creativity, Innovation and Risk-Taking track IACCM-IÉSEG 2019 Congress, Paris, France.

Nikulina, I. E., Khomenko, I. V., Sediakina, A., & Kanov, V. (2016). A feminine style of management in the contemporary business world. In *SHS Web of Conferences. Vol. 28: Research Paradigms Transformation in Social Sciences (RPTSS 2015). Les Ulis, 2016* (*Vol. 282015*, p. 1153). EDP Sciences. 10.1051hsconf/20162801153

Park, D. (1997). Androgynous leadership style: An integration rather than a polarization. *Leadership and Organization Development Journal*, *18*(3), 166–171. doi:10.1108/01437739710168643

Pieterse, J. N. (2001). Hybridity, so what? *Theory, Culture & Society*, *18*(2-3), 219–245. doi:10.1177/026327640101800211

Pugliese, G. (2017). Kantei diplomacy? Japan's hybrid leadership in foreign and security policy. *The Pacific Review*, *30*(2), 152–168. doi:10.1080/09512748.2016.1201131

Rugerinyange, N. (2016). *Traditional and hybrid leadership styles in Rwanda: examining the common leadership styles, influencing factors, and culture in post-genocide Rwanda* (Doctoral dissertation).

Salopeck, J. (2006). *Leadership for a New Age.* Trends. https://www.ngenperformance.com/pdf/articles/TandD.pdf

Sayegh, P. Y. (2008). *Cultural hybridity and modern binaries: Overcoming the opposition between identity and otherness?* Academic Press.

Schindler, J. (2021). Don't Underestimate The "Culture" In Corporate Cultures. *Forbes Magazine*. https://www.forbes.com/sites/forbescoachescouncil/2021/10/14/dont-underestimate-the-culture-in-corporate-culture/?sh=20657dd06f20

Şenses, B., & Temoçin, P. (2016, October). An Interdisciplinary Study: *Quantum Leadership and Hybrid Leadership. In International Symposium on Chaos, Complexity, and Leadership* (pp. 547-559). Springer.

Shabbir, M. A., Ishtiaq, Z., & Zia-ud-Din, M. (2017). The Impact of Hybrid leadership on Employee performance in Textile Sector of Pakistan. *International Journal of Academic Research in Business & Social Sciences*, *7*(4), 359–374. doi:10.6007/IJARBSS/v7-i4/2815

Snelling, I., Exworthy, M., & Ghezelayagh, S. (2020). The chief registrar role in the UK: Leadership capacity and development of hybrid leaders. *Journal of Health Organization and Management*, *34*(1), 1–15. doi:10.1108/JHOM-08-2019-0229 PMID:32018338

Spataro, J. (2021). *Hybrid work is here. Are you ready?* Microsoft. https://www.microsoft.com/en-us/microsoft-365/blog/2021/03/02/hybrid-work-is-here-are-you-ready/

Stafford, M. (2010). *The full-range leadership model: A brief primer.* Instructor Training Material, Squadron Officer School. https://www3.nd.edu/~jthomp19/AS300/1_Fall%20Semester/27%20Sep/Full_Range_Leadership_V1.pdf

Tait, B. (2020). Traditional Leadership Vs. Servant Leadership. *Forbes*. https://www.forbes.com/sites/forbescoachescouncil/2020/03/11/traditional-leadership-vs-servant-leadership/?sh=2cfe67f6451e

Tian, Q. (2013). *Hybrid leadership: a study of the leadership (roles and characteristics) of nine Chinese university presidents with US experiences*. University of Illinois at Urbana-Champaign. https://www.ideals.illinois.edu/bitstream/handle/2142/44354/Qingyan_Tian.pdf?sequence=1&isAllowed=y

Tian, Q. (2020). *Glocalization and the Development of a Hybrid Leadership Model: A Study of Chinese University Presidency*. Routledge. doi:10.4324/9780429284960

Tonini, D. C., Burbules, N. C., & Gunsalus, C. K. (2016). New Models of Hybrid Leadership in Global Higher Education. *Educational Considerations*, *43*(3), 37–46. doi:10.4148/0146-9282.1019

Townsend, A. (2015). Leading school networks: Hybrid leadership in action? *Educational Management Administration & Leadership*, *43*(5), 719–737. doi:10.1177/1741143214543205

Tully, S. (2007). What barriers hold women back. *The Chronicle of Higher Education*. https://www.chronicle.com/article/what-barriers-hold-women-back/

Turner, J. R., Thurlow, N., & Rivera, B. (2020). The Flow System: Practitioner Tools for Navigating Complexity. In Cases on Performance Improvement Innovation (pp. 248-273). IGI Global.

Vann, B. A., Coleman, A. N., & Simpson, J. A. (2014). Development of the Vannsimpco leadership survey: A delineation of hybrid leadership styles. *Swiss Business School Journal of Applied Business Research*, *3*(1), 28–38.

Velumyan, N. (2020). Androgyny: An emerging trend in leadership. *Forbes Magazine*. https://www.forbes.com/sites/forbescoachescouncil/2020/10/28/androgyny-an-emerging-trend-in-leadership/?sh=3d2098095777

Wajdi, B. N. (2017). The Differences Between Management and Leadership. *Sinergi*, *7*(2), 75–84.

Web of Science. (2021). *Hybrid Leadership*. https://www-webofscience-com.e-revistas.ugto.mx/wos?app=wos&Init=Yes&SrcApp=CR&locale=en-US&SID=7DMk6ld5yhZFbHZ8ncM

Wigston, S. (2019). *Followership in Leadership: The Role It Plays*. Eagle's Flight. https://www.eaglesflight.com/blog/the-critical-role-of-followership-in-leadership

ADDITIONAL READING

Duymedjian, R., & Ruling, C. C. (2010). Towards a foundation of bricolage in organization and management theory. *Organization Studies*, *31*(2), 133–151. doi:10.1177/0170840609347051

Harvey, P. (1996). *Hybrids of Modernity: Anthropology, the Nation State and the Universal Exhibition*. Routledge.

Jorgensen, N. (2021). Blurred Lines In A Multigenerational, Hybrid Workforce. *Forbes Magazine*. https://www.forbes.com/sites/forbeshumanresourcescouncil/2021/10/15/blurred-lines-in-a-multigenerational-hybrid-workforce/?sh=6238704f8b68

Oliver, A., & Montgomery, K. (2000). Creating a Hybrid Organizational Form from Parental Blueprints: The Emergence and Evolution of Knowledge Firms. *Human Relations*, *53*(1), 33–56. doi:10.1177/0018726700531003

Papastergiadis, N. (1997). Tracing Hybridity in Theory. In P. Werbner & T. Modood (Eds.), *Debating Cultural Hybridity* (pp. 257–281). Zed.

Powell, M., & Castelli, M. (2017). Strange animals: Hybrid organizations in health care. *Journal of Health Organization and Management*, *31*(7/8), 746–762. doi:10.1108/JHOM-04-2017-0068 PMID:29187080

Rogers, M. (2012). Contextualizing theories and practices of bricolage research. *Qualitative Report*, *17*, 7.

KEY TERMS AND DEFINITIONS

Attitudes: The way people see the world and others and act on it.

Bricolage: A mix and match of different elements.

Fluidity: A state of changeability.

Hybridity: A state of blended of characteristics.

Liquid Times: An era characterized by volatility and uncertainty.

Organizational Goals: Particular objectives aligned with the organization's mission and vision.

Traits: Particular qualities of people.

Chapter 13
Paradigm Shift:
Knowledge Workers as Digital Nodes on a Network

Bruce Kavan
University of North Florida, USA

Lakshmi Goel
University of North Florida, USA

ABSTRACT

The pandemic has accelerated the rate of change for knowledge workers from the traditional office work environment to a more remote or digital environment. In the "resignation era," more than money, people are looking for more flexibility and control over their lives. All these factors seem to suggest a trend towards a hybrid model or virtualization in the workforce. This suggests that we need to view knowledge workers as nodes on a network, capable of accomplishing appropriate outcomes from virtually anywhere. This requires different recruitment, management, and leadership styles to better utilize the power of networking. This networked approach to knowledge work transcends geo-political boundaries which will shift employment into a more global ecosystem not just with business processing organizations (BPOs) but also into individual entrepreneurs. This extension of the ecosystem thus provides access or expands the pool of skilled knowledge workers without regard to the source of talent, relocation expense, or immigration quotas.

DOI: 10.4018/978-1-6684-3453-6.ch013

THE CONCEPT OF "GOING TO" IS WORK CHANGING

People have been working from home for many decades (Olson & Primps, 1984). For example, if you were ill, you took work or office mates brought your work to you. In 1992, AT&T formalized their internal policies on Telecommuting and proclaimed the much heralded first "Telecommuting Day" (Associated Press, 1994). They encouraged workers to simulate working at home from the office by only using those resources that would be available in the home workplace. AT&T touted the many benefits from clearer air to less stressed employees. Despite much hype and promise, telecommuting never established a strong foothold. Why not? Managers are a key ingredient to program success, and many were never comfortable with the concept of workers being "out of sight" (Dingel & Neiman, 2020). After all, the industrial revolution took about 100 years to move us from primarily an agricultural environment to a manufacturing one. The pandemic compressed this transitional time period to months.

Forbes declared 2020 as The Year of The Knowledge Workers and defined a knowledge worker as "Someone who generates value through their knowledge" (Ricard, 2020). The authors would expand this definition to include not only someone generating value through their knowledge but value by their access to data transformed to knowledge (such as a Customer Service Representative). These jobs tend to be very communications orientated.

VIEWING ORGANIZATIONS AS SYSTEMS

Systems are defined in terms of Input - Process - Output and a mechanism for feedback. For example, on an organizational level, consider a sales order as the starting input. The output of the sales order system may be input to fulfillment system which in turn becomes the input to order shipping system and the output of the shipping system, in turn, becomes the input to the billing system, which in turn then as input to the receivables system. The output of one system becomes the input for the next system. For a typical knowledge worker, the work flows the same way the same way. Some type of query transaction (Input) arrives via telephone, chat, email, Interactive Voice Response (IVR) system, computerized workflow manager, etc. The knowledge worker fulfils the information request (Process) or triggers the next activity (Output) – they process or transform inputs to outputs.

NODES ON A NETWORK

In the above-described workflow example, each of the departments and even the individual within those departments becomes a node on a network. Management monitors and shapes network traffic for volume and adjusts resources accordingly to optimize the flow of work. We measure efficiency as the ratio of output to input (velocity through the network) but effectiveness is based upon the how well the output meets the needs of the successive organizational function or customer.

Thus, the individuals become nodes on a network and each of the functional area (sales, fulfillment, shipping, etc.) may be considered a cluster of nodes (a group of individuals) whether physically together or remotely distributed. This is the same approach as outsourcing. Take payroll for an example. Payroll processing could be down the hall, in another building, or at another organizational location or the function could be outsourced to another company. In outsourcing, the entire cluster of nodes may be under the managerial control of another organization. Organizations can be virtual like plug and play in a "lego block" fashion such that if the outsourcing provider doesn't measure up to cost (efficiency) and quality (effectiveness) expectations, they are easily replaced with another provider by swapping one cluster of nodes for another or removing one Lego block and snapping in another. Such organizations are made up clusters of nodes. Part of the "coordinating" organization (or managerial cluster) or "operating" node serves as the feedback mechanism.

WHY HASN'T WORK FROM HOME CAUGHT ON FASTER?

Studies have shown manager hesitancy is the prime reason even considering the benefits for the organization (improved productivity, increased revenue, and better customer service) and the employee (increased satisfaction, improved recruitment and retention and less absenteeism) (Kavan & Saunders, 1998). If managers think telecommuting won't work, then it becomes a self-fulfilling prophesy. For decades, managers have been encouraged to manage by walking around to see if people "look busy." Managers utilizing this method are going to have a more difficult time evaluating remote employees. Rather than simply task-based busyness, the authors contend that organizations need to better define "job roles" based upon behaviors rather than tasks. The outcome of these behaviors can be measured (such as customer service survey). Inter-personal relationships, like teamwork, coaching and mentoring, need to be specifically addressed by the manager in a more virtual environment (Wang et al., 2021).

WHY IS SOME REMOTE WORK LIKELY TO STICK BECAUSE OF THE PANDEMIC?

After almost instant transition to remote work as a direct result of the pandemic, managers seem to have decided that the sky hasn't fallen and, although remote work isn't perfect, it is successful and there may even be more productivity. A lot has happened on the technology front since ATT's work at home push of the 1990's. There are many more technology options in terms of application availability. In the 90's, there was still a lot of information that was located physical files in offices that individuals needed to access. Today, organizations are further along with digitization resulting in less need to find the physical information at the office to respond to information needs. And finally, the advance of "the cloud" provides for both applications and repositories of information allowing greater access from remote locations. It is much easier for plug and play opportunities for remote workers or nodes (people and departments) on the network. The network is faster and easier to build. Speed and organizational agility are significantly enhanced.

NEW OPPORTUNITIES FOR LABOR – THE EXAMPLE OF A DIGITAL GIG WORKER

With nodes defined as individuals and "functional departments" as a cluster of nodes, new organizational approaches and forms are likely to develop. Consider a traditional customer service call center in a remote work environment where customer calls in, information is provided or assisted with a problem, and, as a result, something happens – a airline ticket is sold, a banking statement is explained, etc. Typically, in a physical environment, these customer service agents (nodes) are full time employees, and some may be part-time, some may be contract workers, and some may receive full benefits[5].

Now suppose you trained a non-traditional large pool of potential home workers (nodes) on a variety of applications and certified these individuals for specific capabilities. Suppose a "stay at home mom" only wants to work when their children are in school, or teachers want to work an off hours job, or future actors want to work between casting calls, or older workers that may be in assisted living facilities would like to supplement their savings, these certified individuals that are out of the current workforce could bid for time slots each month. This process is not unlike how flight attendants bid (based primarily on seniority) for different flight routes. These nodes could bid to perform as a knowledge worker for smaller chunks of time – this greatly expands the potential workforce and provides additional flexibility based on smaller time work schedule modules. Of course, the employer would specify what equipment, software, and security these digital workers would have to utilize, and the worker would be responsible for their own internet bandwidth. This is not unlike the "gig" economy – many Uber drivers have "regular jobs" but some don't, but most use their own vehicles subject to a minimum standard. All are nodes on a plug and play network. The work force is greatly expanded. The work force could be expanded yet further by going global. One could add spoken and written language certifications as a basis for cultural compatibility within markets. With digital workers potentially geographically dispersed, risks from environmental issues (hurricanes, flood, tornadoes, etc.) are significantly reduced.

THE CHANGING NATURE OF WORK

Innovation and the creation of new and applied knowledge has helped transform the American economy from an agrarian society through the industrial revolution to age of manufacturing and subsequently to the serviced based economy. With growth in the service sector, information about the service provided was recognized as a major component of customer service. This gave way to the information era and now into the digital age or the Forth Revolution as tagged by the World Economic Forum (Davos – 2017). With the digital age comes better toolsets with a variety distributed to support a different notion of work.

With the work at home resulting from the pandemic – workers, albeit knowledge workers, became nodes on this network – we can video with them, talk to them, observe them, monitor conversations, etc. Managers who managed by "walking around" now need a higher level of skills. This has put the management spotlight not on tasks accomplished by customer satisfaction – the ultimate revenue generator. Customer satisfaction is driven by behaviors not number of tasks accomplished.

Just as the economy transformed over these different areas of value creation, so did organizational forms. The movement to factories in the industrial revolution brough the need to differentiate and control the process (mom and dad on small farms didn't need formalized control mechanisms – they just expressed themselves). With this transition to factories, there was need to direct, control, and monitor workers. Hence the development of the concept of a manager. From a systems perspective, management became the feedback mechanism for the organizational system. And, the larger the company, the larger the managerial structure. A nodal approach to organizations requires a new and potentially different feedback mechanism. Additionally, each node needs to be defined in terms of three things – responsibilities (things they are to do), authorities (decisions that they may make), and accountability (results to be delivered). The flow of work between nodes may be managed by a Workflow system guided by Artificial Intelligence. Some nodes may be just fully automated processes.

MAJOR MANAGERIAL ISSUES

From a cost perspective, real estate (particularly in major cities) represents a significant cost that is not easily scalable (subject to lease constraints and availability). A digital nodal worker therefore provides significantly scalable and lower cost alternative. However, this approach is not without downsides to overcome. The most significant downside is the development of people. How do we onboard new hires not in the work accomplishment aspect, but from a cultural standpoint? In many call centers, nesting is used in the period after training to allow knowledge workers to sit in the middle of a cluster of workers to observe, ask questions of, have someone to go to lunch with, and relate too. All important aspects particularly as it comes to retention. Teams are built on trust – how do you instill trust in the nodal environment? How are managers developed – not the technical aspects of the job, but the coaching, mentoring, and insuring organizational visibility for potential future opportunities? With the nature of work changing, it is a significant opportunity to re-engineer the entire organization around workflow and networks.

CREATING THE FUTURE TOGETHER

Both individuals and organizations need to prepare for the continuation of the digital worker or hybrid environment trust upon us by the Pandemic. As author of *Who Moved My Cheese*, Spencer Johnson said, "if you do not change, you can become extinct" (Johnson, 2002). The purpose of this chapter was to introduce the readers to "food for thought" concerning digital work and digital workers (also referred to as telecommuters and home workers). Twenty years ago, when introducing the concept of networks to students in Management Information (MIS) classes, they understood the physical network concept as one that connected devices such as computer and phones. They struggled with the social network concept until applications like Multiply, Friendster, Myspace and Facebook came into existence. It is certainly easier to understand the power of networks now. That same network power can be used to create nodal presence on a network with clusters of nodes that we now call organizations and work flowing through it. The challenge will be moving to such forms while simultaneously servicing our customers (internal or external or just another node). It will be like trying to change the tire on a car going 80 miles an hour. But once "work" is reengineered, these nodes or clusters of nodes can be reconfigured very quickly to better compete in the global marketplace.

REFERENCES

Associated Press. (1994, September 15). Work at Home, AT&T Says. *New York Times*. https://www.nytimes.com/1994/09/15/business/work-at-home-at-t-says.html

Dingel, J. I., & Neiman, B. (2020). How many jobs can be done at home? *Journal of Public Economics*, *189*, 104235. doi:10.1016/j.jpubeco.2020.104235 PMID:32834177

Hsu, A. (2021, June 24). Millions of Workers Are Saying 'I Quit'. *NPR*. https://www.npr.org/2021/06/24/1007914455/as-the-pandemic-recedes-millions-of-workers-are-saying-i-quit

Johnson, S. (2002). *Who moved my cheese? An amazing way to deal with change in your work and in your life*. Putnam.

Kavan, C. B., & Saunders, C. S. (1998). Managers: A Key Ingredient to Alternative. *Journal of Organizational and End User Computing*, *10*(4), 23–32. doi:10.4018/joeuc.1998100103

Olson, M. H., & Primps, S. B. (1984). Working at home with computers: Work and nonwork issues. *The Journal of Social Issues*, *40*(3), 97–112. doi:10.1111/j.1540-4560.1984.tb00194.x

Ricard, S. (2020, December 10). *The Year of The Knowledge Worker.* Forbes Technology Council. https://www.forbes.com/sites/forbestechcouncil/2020/12/10/the-year-of-the-knowledge-worker/?sh=1f22e2d87fbb

Wang, B., Liu, Y., Qian, J., & Parker, S. K. (2021). Achieving effective remote working during the COVID-19 pandemic: A work design perspective. *Applied Psychology*, *70*(1), 16–59. doi:10.1111/apps.12290 PMID:33230359

Glossary

Affordable Care Act (ACA): The Affordable Care Act is a comprehensive health care reform law enacted in March 2010 (sometimes known as ACA, PPACA, or “Obamacare”).

Agile Manifesto: non prescriptive declaration introducing a more philosophical approach to work based on a set of guiding values and principals. The philosophy, however, applies to more than just technology teams. Any kind of team can adopt the same mindsets and approach work in a similar way.

Agility: Behaviors and mindsets required to ensure teams can pivot and adapt to a continuously changing world, in other words, part of a modern way of working.

Attitudes: The way people see the world and others and act on it.

Blue Cross Blue Shield: Since 1929, Blue Cross Blue Shield (BCBS) companies have provided health care coverage to members, allowing them to live free of worry, free of fear. In every ZIP code, Blue Cross Blue Shield offers a personalized approach to health care based on the needs of the communities where their members live and work.

Bricolage: A mix and match of different elements.

Collective Bargaining Agreement: Agreements typically negotiated between professional sports leagues and its players, covering subjects such as minimum and maximum salaries, benefits, health & safety protocols, revenue sharing, roster sizes, etc.

Command and Control: An outdated style of management. Typically found where trust is not. Employees are told what to do without regard for their input.

COVID-19: Coronavirus disease (COVID-19) is an infectious disease caused by the SARS-CoV-2 virus.

COVID-19 Vaccine: The COVID-19 vaccine is designed to prevent COVID-19 infection or reduce a person's risk of severe illness.

Esports: Name given to organized electronic sports, typically in the form of organized video game competitions. Over the past several years the global Esports market has grown to generate in excess of $1 billion annually.

Florida Blue: Florida Blue, the leading health insurer in Florida, has been providing health insurance to residents of Florida for more than 75 years. Driven by its mission of helping people and communities achieve better health, the company serves more than 5 million health care members across the state. In total, Florida Blue and its affiliated companies serve 16 million people in 29 states. Headquartered in Jacksonville, Fla., it is an independent licensee of the Blue Cross and Blue Shield Association.

Florida Blue Centers: Florida Blue Centers help our members navigate their health care and talk to someone face-to-face in their community. Each of our Florida Blue Centers offers a variety of programs, classes, and events.

Fluidity: A state of changeability.

Formula One Racing: One of the most popular sports in the world, Formula One Racing, commonly referred to as F1, is the premier level of open-wheel racing cars, with events taking place around the world. Its popularity is highest in Europe and South America, with rapidly growing audiences in North America and Asia.

Global Home: PGA TOUR's campus.

GuideWell: GuideWell and its family of forward-thinking companies are focused on helping people and communities achieve better health and are at the forefront in the transformation of health care. The not-for-profit mutual holding company includes Florida Blue, GuideWell Connect, GuideWell Health and Diversified Service Options, Inc.

Hybridity: A state of blended of characteristics.

Kanban: Japanese term, loosely translated as sign board. Also a tool for allowing teams to be transparent and manage/pull prioritized work in for completion.

Liquid Times: An era characterized by volatility and uncertainty.

Major Championships: In men's professional golf, The Open Championship, The Masters, United States Open and PGA Championship are considered golf's major championships. In women's professional golf, the major championships are Chevron Championships (sometimes referred to as the Dinah Shore), United States Women's Open, Women's PGA Championship, The Evian Championship and the Women's British Open.

Make Goods: Term used in sports marketing referring to situations when teams, leagues or athletes are unable to fulfill certain obligations of a sponsorship agreement, and provide "make good" provisions to the sponsor to account for lost sponsorship opportunities.

Medicare Advantage: Medicare Advantage plans include all the same benefits covered in Medicare Parts A and B, and many of these plans offer additional drug, vision, hearing, dental and wellness coverage.

oDNA: oDNA is the "backbone" of an organization, consisting of culture and strategy coiling around each other interdependently. The primary glue in this oDNA structure that keeps these coils aligned and connected, include leadership and agility.

Organizational Goals: Particular objectives aligned with the organization's mission and vision.

Pat Geraghty: Patrick "Pat" Geraghty is president and chief executive officer (CEO) of GuideWell Mutual Holding Corporation, Florida Blue and GuideWell Group, Inc.

Playoffs: Following the completion of a regular season, the highest performing teams compete in an elimination style tournament, ultimately culminating in a champion. Leagues vary on how they determine how many teams qualify for the playoffs, and the format of the tournament.

POTUS: President of The United States.

Psychological Safety: Ideas are embraced, voices are heard, failures are opportunities to learn and people feel safe to be their best.

RTO: Return to office.

Scrum: Agile Framework providing guardrails to teams, ensuring they focus on the same goals and move chunks of work together, in shorter iterations (typically 2-4 weeks).

Sports Sponsorship: Critical component of professional sports, where brands pay money to leagues, teams and/or athletes in exchange for recognition, promotion and/or hospitality. Common forms of sponsorships include venue naming rights, logo placement on jerseys or fields, player endorsements and media rights.

Talent and Culture: PGA TOUR's Human Resources department.

Traits: Particular qualities of people.

Virtual Care/Telehealth: Virtual care, or telehealth, allows patients to have health care visits with their doctors and other providers using technology.

WFH: Work from home.

Compilation of References

Agarwal, S., & Bhal, K. T. (2020). A multidimensional measure of responsible leadership: Integrating strategy and ethics. *Group & Organization Management, 45*(5), 637–673. doi:10.1177/1059601120930140

American Hospital Association. (2020, June 30). *New AHA Report Finds Losses Deepen for Hospitals and Health Systems Due to COVID-19*. Retrieved from https://www.aha.org/issue-brief/2020-06-30-new-aha-report-finds-losses-deepen-hospitals-and-health-systems-due-covid-19

Appelbaum, S. H., Audet, L., & Miller, J. (2003). Gender and leadership. *Leadership and Organization Development Journal, 24*(1), 43–51. doi:10.1108/01437730310457320

Arasli, H., Arici, H. E., & Kole, E. (2020). Constructive Leadership and Employee Innovative Behaviors: A Serial Mediation Model. *Sustainability, 12*(2592), 2592. doi:10.3390u12072592

Aschburner, S. (2020). *Silver, NBA Players seek 'new normal' in return to play amid pandemic*. https://www.nba.com/news/adam-silver-social-unrest-return-play-inside-nba

Askew, S. (2018, Oct. 31). *The Future of Innovation in the Supply Chain Industry*. Supply and Demand Chain Executive. https://www.sdcexec.com/software-technology/blog/21025509/the-future-of-innovation-in-the-supply-chain-industry

Associated Press. (1994, September 15). Work at Home, AT&T Says. *New York Times*. https://www.nytimes.com/1994/09/15/business/work-at-home-at-t-says.html

Aubert, B. A., & Kelsey, B. L. (2003). Further understanding of trust and performance in virtual teams. *Small Group Research, 34*(1), 575–618. doi:10.1177/1046496403256011

Aydogmus, C. (2019). Globally responsible intergenerational leadership. In Intergenerational Governance and Leadership in the Corporate World: Emerging Research and Opportunities (pp. 123-152). IGI Global. doi:10.4018/978-1-5225-8003-4.ch007

Ba, A., Ellerby, K., Green, D., Kinderman, D., Kauffman, S., Weinert, M., & Ali, S. H. (2019). Hybrid leadership councils: Envisioning inclusive and resilient governance. *European Journal of Futures Research, 7*(1), 1–10. doi:10.118640309-019-0155-2

Baker, D. (2021). *The future of work is hybrid: Could covid be the catalyst for organizations to implement a hybrid workplace model?* Academic Press.

Baker, E., Avery, G. C., & Crawford, J. D. (2007). Satisfaction and perceived productivity when professionals work from home. *Research and Practice in Human Resource Management, 15*(1), 37–62.

Balwant, P. T. (2021). Is There a Bright Side to Destructive Leadership? How Gordon Ramsay Leads Change in Nightmare Kitchens. *The Journal of Leadership Studies, 14*(4), 81–88. doi:10.1002/jls.21723

Barclays. (2013). *Talking About My Generation: Exploring the Benefits Engagement Challenge.* Barclays.

Barnakova, Y., & Krupp, S. (2021). *The work anywhere paradox: Love it or hate it, how leaders can optimize it.* Heidrick Consulting.

Bassett, P. (2020). Leadership: A Protean Institution of the Mind and of Civilization. *The Journal of Student Leadership, 3*(2), 15-21.

Bauman, Z. (2006). *Liquid Times: Living in an Age of Uncertainty.* Polity.

Bell, B. S., & Kozlowski, S. W. (2002). A typology of virtual teams: Implications for effective leadership. *Group & Organization Management, 27*(1), 14–49. doi:10.1177/1059601102027001003

Bem, S. L. (1974). The measurement of psychological androgyny. *Journal of Consulting and Clinical Psychology, 42*(2), 155–162. doi:10.1037/h0036215 PMID:4823550

Bentley, T. A., Teo, S. T. T., McLeod, L., Tan, F., Bosua, R., & Gloet, M. (2016). The role of organizational support in teleworker wellbeing: A socio-technical systems approach. *Applied Ergonomics, 52*, 207–215. doi:10.1016/j.apergo.2015.07.019 PMID:26360212

Bjorn, P., & Ngwenyama, O. (2009). Virtual team collaboration: Building shared meaning, resolving breakdowns and creating translucence. *Information Systems Journal, 19*(3), 227–253. doi:10.1111/j.1365-2575.2007.00281.x

Blake-Beard, S., Shapiro, M., & Ingols, C. (2020). Feminine? Masculine? Androgynous leadership as a necessity in COVID-19. *Gender in Management: An International Journal.*

Blanchard, K. H., & Sargent, A. G. (1984). The one-minute manager is an androgynous manager. *Training and Development Journal.*

Bloom, N., Liang, J., Roberts, J., & Yin, Z.-J. N. (2015). Does working from home work? Evidence from a Chinese experiment. *The Quarterly Journal of Economics, 130*(1), 165–218. doi:10.1093/qje/qju032

Boell, S. K., Cecez-Kecmanovic, D., & Campbell, J. (2016). Telework paradoxes and practices: The importance of the nature of work. *New Technology, Work and Employment, 31*(2), 114–131. doi:10.1111/ntwe.12063

Bohm, D. (2008). *On Dialogue*. Routledge Classics.

Bolden, R. (2011). *Distributed Leadership in Organizations: A Review of Theory and Research*. Academic Press.

Bourgeois, T. (2013). *The hybrid leader: Blending the best of the male and female leadership styles*. Oakhill Press.

Brandsen, T., Van de Donk, W., & Putters, K. (2005). Griffins or chameleons? Hybridity as a permanent and inevitable characteristic of the third sector. *International Journal of Public Administration, 28*(9-10), 749–765. doi:10.1081/PAD-200067320

British Broadcasting Corporation. (2020). *Why the future of work might be hybrid*. https://www.bbc.com/worklife/article/20200824-why-the-future-of-work-might-be-hybrid

Bryman, A., Collinson, D., Grintr, K., Jackson B., & Uhl Bien, M. (Eds.). (2011). The SAGE handbook of leadership. Sage Publications.

Buchen, I. H. (2011). *The Hybrid Leader: Evolving, Adaptable, Unfinished*. Rowman & Littlefield Education.

Buchen, I. H. (2012). Hybrid Futures Intelligence: Circular, Cyclical, and Convergent. *World Futures Review, 4*(3), 33–38. doi:10.1177/194675671200400307

Bureau of Labor Statistics. (2021). The Economics Daily, *Quits rate 6.6 percent in accommodation and food services in September 2021*. U.S. Bureau of Labor Statistics. https://www.bls.gov/opub/ted/2021/quits-rate-6-6-percent-in-accommodation-and-food-services-in-september-2021.htm

Bureau of Labor Statistics. (2021a). Business Employment Dynamics, *Establishment age and survival BED data for nation by major industry*. U.S. Bureau of Labor Statistics. https://www.bls.gov/bdm/us_age_naics_21_table1.txt

Centers for Disease Control and Prevention. (2017, July 3). *African-American Health article*. https://www.cdc.gov/vitalsigns/aahealth/index.html#:~:text=African%20Americans%20ages%2018%2D49,high%20blood%20pressure%20than%20whites

Chamorro-Premuzic, T., & Berg, K. (2021, August 3). Fostering a Culture of Belonging in the Hybrid Workplace. *Harvard Business Review*. Retrieved October 26, 2021, from https://hbr.org/2021/08/fostering-a-culture-of-belonging-in-the-hybrid-workplace

Chamorro-Premuzic, T. (2019). *Why do so many incompetent men become leaders?: (And how to fix it)*. Harvard Business Press.

Chatwani, N. (2018). *Distributed Leadership: The Dynamics of Balancing Leadership with Followership*. Spinger International Publishing. doi:10.1007/978-3-319-59581-8

Chénard-Poirier, L. A., Morin, A. J. S., Boudrias, J.-S., & Gillet, N. (2021). The combined effects of destructive and constructive leadership on thriving at work and behavioral empowerment. *Journal of Business and Psychology*. Advance online publication. doi:10.100710869-021-09734-7

Chong, D. (2020, April 20). *Deep Dive into Netflix's Recommender System.* Towards Data Science. https://towardsdatascience.com/deep-dive-into-netflixs-recommender-system-341806ae3b48

Christensen, C. M. (2010, July 1). How Will You Measure Your Life? *Harvard Business Review*. Retrieved October 29, 2021, from https://hbr.org/2010/07/how-will-you-measure-your-life

Clarke, J., & Newman, J. (1997). The managerial state. *Sage (Atlanta, Ga.)*.

Coenen, M., & Kok, R. A. W. (2014). Workplace flexibility and new product development performance: The role of telework and flexible work schedules. *European Management Journal*, *32*(4), 564–576. doi:10.1016/j.emj.2013.12.003

Collins, M. (2005). The (not so simple) case for teleworking: A study at Lloyd's of London. *New Technology, Work and Employment*, *20*(2), 115–132. doi:10.1111/j.1468-005X.2005.00148.x

CoreAxis. (2021). *Top Skills Checklist for Nurturing Hybrid Leadership*. https://coreaxis.com/wp-content/uploads/2021/06/CoreAxis-White-Paper-Nurturing-Hybrid-Leadership.pdf

Costikyan, N. (2021, August). *Conversation with Nancy Costikyan, Director of Work/Life at Harvard University.* Boston College Center for Work and Family. http://hdl.handle.net/10713/16574

Covey, S. R. (1999). *Principle-Centered Leadership*. Free Press.

Cox, C. (2020, December 9). *How Has the Pandemic Affected Health Coverage in the U.S.?* Kaiser Family Foundation. https://www.kff.org/policy-watch/how-has-the-pandemic-affected-health-coverage-in-the-u-s/

Crestcom. (2021). *Leading in the Hybrid Workplace*. https://crestcom.com/wp-content/uploads/2021/06/Crestcom_Leading-in-the-Hyrbid-Workplace.pdf

Crevani, L., Ekman, M., Lindgren, M., & Packendorff, J. (2015). Leadership cultures and discursive hybridisation: On the cultural production of leadership in higher education reforms. *International Journal of Public Leadership*, *11*(3/4), 147–165. doi:10.1108/IJPL-08-2015-0019

Cutway, A. (2020, September 25). *Timeline: The spread of coronavirus in Florida*. https://www.clickorlando.com/news/local/2020/03/20/timeline-the-spread-of-coronavirus-in-florida/

Davis, D. D., & Bryant, J. L. (2003). Influence at a distance: Leadership in global virtual teams. *Advances in Global Leadership*, *3*(1), 303–340. doi:10.1016/S1535-1203(02)03015-0

De Paoli, D., & Ropo, A. (2015). Open plan offices – the response to leadership challenges of virtual project work? *Journal of Corporate Real Estate*, *17*(1), 63–74. doi:10.1108/JCRE-08-2014-0020

De Smet, A., Lurie, M., & St. George, A. (2018). *Leading agile transformation: The new capabilities leaders need to build 21st-century organizations*. McKinsey. https://www.mckinsey.com/business-functions/people-and-organizational-performance/our-insights/leading-agile-transformation-the-new-capabilities-leaders-need-to-build-21st-century-organizations

De Smet, A., Pacthod, D., Relyea, C., & Sternfels, B. (2020). *Ready, set, go: Reinventing the organization for speed in the post-COVID-19 era.* McKinsey & Company.

DeFilippis, E., Impink, S. M., Singell, M., Polzer, J. T., & Sadun, R. (2020). *Collaborating during coronavirus: The impact of COVID-19 on the nature of work.* National Bureau of Economic Research (Working paper: 27612). doi:10.3386/w27612

DeGraff, J. (1999). How You Innovate Is What You Innovate: A Systematic Approach to Effectively Leading Enterprise Innovation. *The 2009 Pfeiffer Annual on Leadership Development*, 1-13.

Diffen. (n.d.). *Leadership vs. Management.* Retrieved from https://www.diffen.com/difference/Leadership_vs_Management#:~:text=%20Leadership%20vs.%20Management%20%201%20Summary.%20Managing,Often%20the%20same%20people%20play%20wear...%20More%20

Dingel, J. I., & Neiman, B. (2020). How many jobs can be done at home? *Journal of Public Economics, 189*, 104235. doi:10.1016/j.jpubeco.2020.104235 PMID:32834177

Dixon, E. (2020, June 19). *F1 Virtual Grand Prix pulls in 30m total viewers.* https://www.sportspromedia.com/news/f1-virtual-grands-prix-total-viewers-audience-tv-digital-social-esports/

Dose, J. J., & Klimoski, R. J. (1995). Doing the right thing in the workplace: Responsibility in the face of accountability. *Employee Responsibilities and Rights Journal, 8*(1), 35–36. doi:10.1007/BF02621254

Dosh, K. (2021). NCAA Has Confirmed Its Basketball Revenue Distribution Plan for 2021, But Impact of 2020 Will Linger. *Forbes.* https://www.forbes.com/sites/kristidosh/2021/02/28/ncaa-has-confirmed-its-basketball-revenue-distribution-plan-for-2021-but-impact-of-2020-will-last/?sh=104a721f391a

Duggal, N. (2022). *Leadership vs Management: Understanding the Key Difference.* Simplilearn. Retrieved from https://www.simplilearn.com/leadership-vs-management-difference-article

Duncan, R. D. (2018). Culture, Leadership, Performance: How Are They Linked? *Forbes.* https://www.forbes.com/sites/rodgerdeanduncan/2018/10/30/culture-leadership-performance-how-are-they-linked/?sh=4ddb55c85e44

Eagly, A. H., Johannesen-Schmidt, M. C., & Van Engen, M. L. (2003). Transformational, transactional, and laissez-faire leadership styles: A meta-analysis comparing women and men. *Psychological Bulletin, 129*(4), 569–591. doi:10.1037/0033-2909.129.4.569 PMID:12848221

Einarsen, S, Aasland, M. S., & Skogstad, A. (2007). *Destructive leadership behaviour: A definition and conceptual model.* doi:10.1016/j.leaqua.2007.03.002

Erçetin, Ş. Ş., & Kamacı, M. C. (2008). Quantum leadership paradigm. *World Applied Sciences Journal, 3*(6), 865–868.

Erickson, T., & Kellogg, W. A. (2000). Social translucence: An approach to the designing systems that support social processes. *ACM Transactions on Computer-Human Interaction, 7*(1), 59–83. doi:10.1145/344949.345004

Eti-Tofinga, B., Douglas, H., & Singh, G. (2017). Influence of evolving culture on leadership: A study of Fijian cooperatives. *European Business Review, 29*(5), 534–550. doi:10.1108/EBR-10-2015-0122

Evetts, J. (2014). The Concept of Professionalism: Professional Work, Professional Practice and Learning. In S. Billett, C. Harteis, & H. Gruber (Eds.), *International Handbook of Research in Professional and Practice-Based Learning* (pp. 29–56). Springer International Handbooks of Education. doi:10.1007/978-94-017-8902-8_2

Faizan, R., Nair, S. L. S., & Haque, A. U. (2018). The effectiveness of feminine and masculine leadership styles in relation to contrasting gender's performances. *Polish Journal of Management Studies, 17.*

Falayi, O. (2016). *American Nigerian Leadership: An Exploration into Hybrid Leadership* (Doctoral dissertation). The Chicago School of Professional Psychology. https://www.proquest.com/openview/27540781abcb80b439cf380f543ac149/1?pq-origsite=gscholar&cbl=18750

Felstead, A., & Henseke, G. (2017). Assessing the growth of remote working and its consequences for effort, well-being and work-life balance. *New Technology, Work and Employment, 32*(3), 195–212. doi:10.1111/ntwe.12097

Ferris, G. R., Mitchell, T. R., Canavan, P. J., Frink, D. D., & Hopper, H. (1995). Accountability in human resources systems. In G. R. Ferris, S. D. Rosen, & D. T. Basman (Eds.), *Handbook of human resource management* (pp. 175–196). Blackwell Business.

Florida Blue (2020). *Rewards to Help You with Premium Payments and Medical Expenses.* Retrieved from https://www.floridablue.com/blog/rewards-to-help-you

Florida Blue [@floridabluehealth]. (2020, September 4). #GetMaskedFL [Status update]. On *Facebook*. https://fb.watch/d69PU2i-eQ/.

Foster, P. A. (2010). *Leader-Follower Theory for the Learning Organization.* http://followership2.pbworks.com/f/Leader-Follower+Theory+for+the+Learning+Organization.pdf

Garbes, A. (2021). *What working parents really need from workplaces.* TED Series: The Way We Work. https://www.ted.com/talks/angela_garbes_what_working_parents_really_need_from_workplaces

Gartner. (2021). *Are you a hybrid workforce champion or a laggard?* https://www.gartner.com/smarterwithgartner/are-you-a-hybrid-workforce-champion-or-a-laggard

Goldsmith, M., & Reiter, M. (2015). *Triggers: Creating Behavior That Lasts, Becoming The Person You Want To Be.* Crown Publishing Group.

Goodwin, T. (2015). *The Battle Is For The Customer Interface.* TechCrunch. Retrieved from https://techcrunch.com/2015/03/03/in-the-age-of-disintermediation-the-battle-is-all-for-the-customer-interface/?guccounter=1&guce_referrer=aHR0cHM6Ly93d3cuZ29vZ2xlLmNvbS8&guce_referrer_sig=AQAAAGO_UNXdPwqBjUyp8vEIcHkeKHJ_KdsroYtuKzO0pP4NklYmP8xCX_3WA_qT2QX8qPzpEEAf_Vh77qQ36wXdFzfB2DPV3etgAQwDU1bjNzbpyka2JNEiynIKWnyNt2z5dQmmfwO0BMVAbavXKr4fgWDkjjoy8iF960xUVXkJFFnM

Górska, A. (2016). Gender differences in leadership. *Studia i Materiały, 1*(20), 136-144.

Gregory, S. (2020, April 29). German Soccer Fans are Putting Cardboard Cutouts of Themselves in the Stands to Avoid Games in 'Empty' Stadiums. *Time*. https://time.com/5828699/soccer-cardboard-cutouts/

Gronn, P. (2009). *Hybrid leadership*. Routledge.

GuideWell. (2020). *2021 GuideWell Social Impact Report*. Retrieved from https://www.floridablue.com/binaries/content/assets/floridablue/misc/2021-guidewell-social-impact-report.pdf

GuideWell. (2021). *Grand prize winners selected in $6M XPRIZE Rapid COVID Testing competition to create fast, frequent, cheap and easy-to-use solutions*. Retrieved from https://www.guidewell.com/tags/blog/xprize

GuideWell. (2021). *Pat Geraghty Full Transcript: Moments of Hope Show We're Turning a Corner*. Retrieved from https://www.guidewell.com/blog/pat-geraghty-full-transcript-moments-hope-show-were-turning-corner

GuideWell. (2022). *Who We Are*. Retrieved from https://www.guidewell.com/who-we-are

Hanine, S., & Nita, M. A. (2019). The paradigm of quantum leadership: Ontology, praxis and application to management. *Revue Internationale des Sciences de Gestion, 2*(2), 837–858.

Hatch, M. J. (2013). *Organization theory: Modern, symbolic, and postmodern perspectives*. Oxford University Press.

Heath, C., Svensson, M. S., Hindmarsh, J., Luff, P., & Lehn, D. (2002). Conðguring awareness. *Computer Supported Cooperative Work (CSCW) International Journal, 11*, 317–347.

Herrera, S., Fung, E., & Kapner, S. (2021, August 19). Amazon plans to open large retail locations akin to Department Stores. *The Wall Street Journal*. https://www.wsj.com/articles/amazon-retail-department-stores-11629330842

Hess, T., Matt, C., Benlian, A., & Wiesböck, F. (2016). Options for formulating a digital transformation strategy. *MIS Quarterly Executive, 15*(2).

Hoegl, M., Muethel, M., & Gemuenden, H. G. (2012). Leadership and teamwork in dispersed projects. In P. W. G. Morris, J. K. Pinto, & J. Söderlund (Eds.), *The Oxford Handbook of Project Management* (pp. 483–500). Oxford University Press.

Hognestad, K., & Boe, M. (2015). Leading site-based knowledge development: A mission impossible? Insights from a study from Norway. *Thinking and learning about leadership. Early childhood research from Australia, Finland, and Norway*, 210-228.

Hsu, A. (2021, June 24). Millions of Workers Are Saying 'I Quit'. *NPR*. https://www.npr.org/2021/06/24/1007914455/as-the-pandemic-recedes-millions-of-workers-are-saying-i-quit

Hudson, R. P. O. (2015). *The great generational shift*. https://eu.hudsonrpo.com/insights/thinking/the-great-generational-shift/

Jarvenpaa, S. L., & Leidner, D. E. (1999). Communication and trust in global virtual teams. *Organization Science*, *10*(1), 791–815. doi:10.1287/orsc.10.6.791

Jernigan, L. B. (2021, June 5). The mental health crisis: A toolkit for business leaders. *Psychology Today*. https://www.psychologytoday.com/us/blog/license-shine/202106/the-mental-health-crisis-toolkit-business-leaders

Johnson, S. (2002). *Who moved my cheese? An amazing way to deal with change in your work and in your life*. Putnam.

Jones, B. (2017, February 28). Great Leaders Show Genuine Care for Their Team. *Harvard Business Review*. https://hbr.org/sponsored/2017/02/great-leaders-show-genuine-care-for-their-teams

Jones, B. (1982). *Sleepers, Wake*. Oxford University Press.

Jones, H., & Hunter, K. O. (2016). A reflective hybrid approach to connecting leadership style and stakeholder perspective. *Challenging Organizations and Society.*, *5*(2), 950–1006.

Joshi, A., & Lazarova, M. B. (2005). Do 'global' teams need 'global' leaders? Identifying leadership competences in multinational teams. In D. L. Shapiro, M. A. Von Glinow, & J. L. C. Cheng (Eds.), *Managing Multinational Teams: Global Perspectives* (pp. 281–301). Elsevier. doi:10.1016/S0747-7929(05)18011-1

Kamouri, A., & Lister, K. (2020). *Survey reveals 76% of global office workers want to continue working from home post-COVID-19*. Global Workplace Analytics. https://globalworkplaceanalytics.com/brags/news-releases

Kasula, C. (2020, June 28). *Netflix Recommender System — A Big Data Case Study*. Towards data science. https://towardsdatascience.com/netflix-recommender-system-a-big-data-case-study-19cfa6d56ff5

Kavan, C. B., & Saunders, C. S. (1998). Managers: A Key Ingredient to Alternative. *Journal of Organizational and End User Computing*, *10*(4), 23–32. doi:10.4018/joeuc.1998100103

Kazekami, S. (2020). Mechanisms to improve labor productivity by performing telework. *Telecommunications Policy*, *44*(2), 101868. doi:10.1016/j.telpol.2019.101868

Keene, D. L., & Handrich, R. R. (2015). Loyalty, longevity and leadership: A multigenerational workforce update. *Journal of Expertise*, *27*, 34.

Kellerman, B. (2007). What Every Leader Needs to Know About Followers. *Harvard Business Review*. https://hbr.org/2007/12/what-every-leader-needs-to-know-about-followers

Keynes. (1930). Economic Possibilities for our Grandchildren. In *Essays in Persuasion*. New York: Harcourt Brace.

Kirkman, B. L., Rosen, B., Tesluk, P. E., & Gibson, C. B. (2004). The impact of team empowerment on virtual team performance: The moderating role of face-to-face interaction. *Academy of Management Journal*, *47*(2), 175–192.

Klotz, A. (2001, May 30). *The Covid vaccine means a return to work. And a wave of resignations: For everyone exiting the pandemic feeling burned out, know you are not alone.* NBC News. https://www.nbcnews.com/think/opinion/covid-vaccine-means-return-work-wave-resignations-ncna1269018

Knights, D., & McCabe, D. (2003). Governing through teamwork: Reconstituting subjectivity in a call centre. *Journal of Management Studies*, *40*(7), 1587–1619. doi:10.1111/1467-6486.00393

Kocolowski, M. D. (2010). Shared Leadership: Is it Time for a Change? *Emerging Leadership Journeys*, *3*(1), 22–32.

Korabik, K. (1990). Androgyny and leadership style. *Journal of Business Ethics*, *9*(4), 283–292. doi:10.1007/BF00380328

Kotera, Y., & Vione, K. (2020). Psychological impacts of the new ways of working (NWWW): A systematic review. *International Journal of Environmental Research and Public Health*, *17*(14), 5080. doi:10.3390/ijerph17145080 PMID:32674518

Kraidy, M. (2005). *Hybridity, or the Cultural Logic of Globalization.* Temple University. Press.

Krebs, S. A., Hobman, E. V., & Bordia, P. (2006). Virtual teams and group member dissimilarity: Consequences for the development of trust. *Small Group Research*, *37*(6), 721–741. doi:10.1177/1046496406294886

Kronfli, C. (2021). *Mental wellness in the workplace: A playbook for employers.* Ontario Chamber of Commerce.

Lacques, G. (2020, June 23). Major League Baseball implements 60-game 2020 season as players agree on safety protocols. *USA Today*. https://www.usatoday.com/story/sports/mlb/2020/06/23/mlb-implements-60-game-schedule-beginning-around-july-24/5308390002/

Latour, B. (1993). *We have never been modern.* Harvard University Press.

Lazaridou, A., & Fris, J. (n.d.). *Slipping the Yoke of the Heroic Paradigm: Looking for Quantum Leadership.* Education Resources Information Center. https://files.eric.ed.gov/fulltext/EJ940819.pdf

Leithwood, K., Mascall, B., & Strauss, T. (Eds.). (2009). *Distributed leadership according to the evidence.* Routledge. doi:10.4324/9780203868539

Lewin, K., Lippitt, R., & White, R. K. (1939). Patterns of aggressive behavior in experimentally created social climates. *The Journal of Social Psychology*, *10*(2), 271–301. doi:10.1080/00224545.1939.9713366

Lewis, R. D. (2006). *When cultures collide: Leading across cultures.* Nicholas Brealey.

Lister, K. (2021). *The business case for remote work – for employers, employees, the environment, and society.* Global Workplace Analytics. https://globalworkplaceanalytics.com/whitepapers

Lombardo, J. (2020, October 19). NBA preserved $1.5B in revenue at Disney, but losses are steep. *Sports Business Journal*. https://www.sportsbusinessjournal.com/Journal/Issues/2020/10/19/Leagues-and-Governing-Bodies/NBA-bubble.aspx

Maclagan, P. W. (1983). The concept of responsibility: Some implications for organizational behaviour and development. *Journal of Management Studies*, *20*(4), 411–423. doi:10.1111/j.1467-6486.1983.tb00216.x

Madsen, S. R. (2003). The effects of home-based teleworking on work-family conflict. *Human Resource Development Quarterly*, *14*(1), 35–58. doi:10.1002/hrdq.1049

Mahfoodh, H., Aleid, K., Bahzad, A., Matar, S., Shubbar, Z. S., & Mattar, E. (2021) *Sustaining work continuity through hybrid work environments: Tracking systems.* 2021 International Conference on Innovation and Intelligence for Informatics, Computing, and Technologies (3ICT), Zallaq, Bahrain. 10.1109/3ICT53449.2021.9581371

Maiorescu, R. D. (2016). Crisis management at General Motors and Toyota: An analysis of gender-specific communication and media coverage. *Public Relations Review*, *42*(4), 556–563. doi:10.1016/j.pubrev.2016.03.011

Maister, D. H., Green, C. H., & Galford, R. M. (2000). The Trusted Advisor. Free Press, An Imprint of Simon & Schuster.

Malloch, K., & Porter-O'Grady, T. (2009). *The quantum leader: Applications for the new world of work*. Jones & Bartlett Learning.

Manyika, L., Chui, B., & Woetzel, B. Ko, & Sanghvi. (2017). *Jobs lost, jobs gained: What the future of work will mean for jobs, skills, and wages.* McKinsey Global Institute. Retrieved from https://www.mckinsey.com/featured-insights/future-of-work/jobs-lost-jobs-gained-what-the-future-of-work-will-mean-for-jobs-skills-and-wages

Martinich, L. (2016). Excellent execution: Balancing top-down and bottom-up management. *IEEE Engineering Management Review*, *44*(2), 20–23. doi:10.1109/EMR.2016.2568720

Martin, J., Cormican, K., Sampaio, S., & Wu, Q. (2018). Shared leadership and team performance: An analysis of moderating factors. *Procedia Computer Science*, *138*, 671–679. doi:10.1016/j.procs.2018.10.089

Matson, K. M. (2014). Revisiting the past, revamping the future: The leadership edition. *Nursing Management*, *45*(8), 47–51. doi:10.1097/01.NUMA.0000452001.49343.29 PMID:25058534

Matt, C., Hess, T., & Benlian, A. (2015). Digital transformation strategies. *Business & Information Systems Engineering*, *57*(5), 339–343. doi:10.100712599-015-0401-5

Mautz, S. (2015, July 20). 6 Steps for Creating a Culture of Significance from the Ground Up. *Entrepreneur*. Retrieved October 28, 2021, from https://www.entrepreneur.com/article/248626

Maxwell, J. C. (1999). *The 21 Indispensable Qualities of a Leader: Becoming the Person Others Will Want to Follow*. HarperCollins Leadership.

McCloskey, D. W., & Igbaria, M. (2003). Does "out of sight" mean "out of mind?" An empirical investigation of career advancement prospects of telecommuters. *Information Resources Management Journal, 16*(2), 19–34. doi:10.4018/irmj.2003040102

McNally, K. (2017). Leading a Multigenerational Workforce. *Healthcare Executive, 32*(1), 58–61. PMID:30280532

Mendenhall, M. E., Reiche, B. S., Bird, A., & Osland, J. S. (2012). Defining the 'global' in global leadership. *Journal of World Business, 47*(1), 493–503. doi:10.1016/j.jwb.2012.01.003

Merriam-Webster. (2021). *Hybrid.* https://www.merriam-webster.com/dictionary/hybrid

Meyer, J. P., & Allen, N. J. (1991). A three-component conceptualization of organizational commitment. *Human Resource Management Review, 1*(1), 61–89. doi:10.1016/1053-4822(91)90011-Z

Mixon, E. (2021, Mar. 20). *Data Science at Netflix: How Advanced Data & Analytics Helps Netflix Generate Billions.* AI Data & Analytics Network. https://www.aidataanalytics.network/data-science-ai/articles/data-science-at-netflix-how-advanced-data-analytics-helped-netflix-generate-billions

Montaudon-Tomás, C. M., & Pinto-López, I. N. (2021). Developing a Metaphor for Self-Managed Organizations. In *Handbook of Research on International Business and Models for Global Purpose-Driven Companies* (pp. 65–85). IGI Global. doi:10.4018/978-1-7998-4909-4.ch004

Moretti, A., Menna, F., Aulicino, M., Paoletta, M., Liguori, S., & Iolascon, G. (2020). Characterization of home working population during COVID-19 emergency: A cross-sectional analysis. *International Journal of Environmental Research and Public Health, 17*(17), 6284. doi:10.3390/ijerph17176284 PMID:32872321

Muethel, M., & Hoegl, M. (2010). Cultural and societal influences on shared leadership in globally dispersed teams. *Journal of International Management, 16*(1), 234–246. doi:10.1016/j.intman.2010.06.003

Nanjundeswaraswamy T. S., & Swamy D. R. (2014). Leadership styles. *Advances in Management, 7*(2), 57-72.

Nassauer, S. (2021, Feb. 25). Best Buy Steps Up Digital Overhaul as Slowdown Looms. *The Wall Street Journal.* https://www.wsj.com/articles/best-buy-workers-powered-through-covid-19-pandemic-then-they-lost-their-jobs-11614256495

Nejatian, M., Zarei, M. H., Nejati, M., & Zanjirchi, S. M. (2018). A hybrid approach to achieve organizational agility. *Benchmarking, 25*(1), 201–234. doi:10.1108/BIJ-09-2016-0147

Neufeld, D. J., & Fang, Y. (2004). Predicting telecommuter productivity. *Proceedings from 37th Annual Hawaii International Conference on System Sciences.* 10.1109/HICSS.2004.1265160

Neufeld, D. J., & Fang, Y. (2005). Individual, social and situational determinants of telecommuter productivity. *Information & Management, 42*(7), 1037–1049. doi:10.1016/j.im.2004.12.001

Nigri, G., & Agulini, A. (2019). *Culture and consciousness toward quantum leadership.* Cultural Perspectives on Creativity, Innovation and Risk-Taking track IACCM-IÉSEG 2019 Congress, Paris, France.

Nikulina, I. E., Khomenko, I. V., Sediakina, A., & Kanov, V. (2016). A feminine style of management in the contemporary business world. In *SHS Web of Conferences. Vol. 28: Research Paradigms Transformation in Social Sciences (RPTSS 2015). Les Ulis, 2016* (*Vol. 282015*, p. 1153). EDP Sciences. 10.1051hsconf/20162801153

Olito, F. (2020). Rise and Fall of Blockbuster. *Business Insider.* Retrieved from https://www.businessinsider.com/rise-and-fall-of-blockbuster

Olson, M. H., & Primps, S. B. (1984). Working at home with computers: Work and nonwork issues. *The Journal of Social Issues*, *40*(3), 97–112. doi:10.1111/j.1540-4560.1984.tb00194.x

Panetta, K. (2018, Dec. 18). *Gartner Predicts 2019 for Supply Chain Operations.* Gartner. https://www.gartner.com/smarterwithgartner/gartner-predicts-2019-for-supply-chain-operations

Park, D. (1997). Androgynous leadership style: An integration rather than a polarization. *Leadership and Organization Development Journal*, *18*(3), 166–171. doi:10.1108/01437739710168643

Pauleen, D. J. (2004). An inductively derived model of leader-initiated relationship building with virtual team members. *Journal of Management Information Systems*, *20*(3), 227–256. doi:10.1080/07421222.2003.11045771

Peace, L. (2022, February 27). Florida health equity experts reflect on progress, setbacks two years into COVID. *The Tampa Bay Times.* https://www.tampabay.com/news/health/2022/02/27/florida-health-equity-experts-reflect-on-progress-setbacks-two-years-into-covid/

Peters, P., & den Dulk, L. (2003). Cross cultural differences in managers' support for home-based telework: A theoretical elaboration. *International Journal of Cross Cultural Management*, *3*(3), 329–346. doi:10.1177/1470595803003003005

Pichault, F., & McKeown, T. (2019). Autonomy at work in the gig economy: Analysing work status, work content and working conditions of independent professionals. *New Technology, Work and Employment*, *34*(1), 59–72. doi:10.1111/ntwe.12132

Pieterse, J. N. (2001). Hybridity, so what? *Theory, Culture & Society*, *18*(2-3), 219–245. doi:10.1177/026327640101800211

Pinchot, Gifford, & Pellman. (1999). Intrapreneuring In Action: A Handbook for Business Innovation. Berrett-Koehler Publishers, Inc.

Pink, D. (2011). *Drive.* Riverhead Harcover.

Psychology Tools. (2021, May 31). *Fight Or Flight Response.* Retrieved October 28, 2021, from https://www.psychologytools.com/resource/fight-or-flight-response/

Pugliese, G. (2017). Kantei diplomacy? Japan's hybrid leadership in foreign and security policy. *The Pacific Review*, *30*(2), 152–168. doi:10.1080/09512748.2016.1201131

Quinn, R. E., Cameron, K. S., Thakor, A. V., & DeGraff, J. (2006). *Competing Values Leadership: Creating Value In Organizations*. Edward Elgar Publishing, Inc.

Ramella, B. (2021). 5 Business Communication Issues in the workplace. *GetVoiP Blog*. Retrieved from https://gp1.com/5-business-communication-issues-in-the-workplace/

Revsine, D. (2021). 'What is going on here?': Three days in March 2020 when COVID-19 changed everything in sports. *Sporting News*. Retrieved from https://www.sportingnews.com/us/ncaa-basketball/news/covid-19-sports-march-2020/52218di40lv41vacngrwqofen

Ricard, S. (2020, December 10). *The Year of The Knowledge Worker.* Forbes Technology Council. https://www.forbes.com/sites/forbestechcouncil/2020/12/10/the-year-of-the-knowledge-worker/?sh=1f22e2d87fbb

Rugerinyange, N. (2016). *Traditional and hybrid leadership styles in Rwanda: examining the common leadership styles, influencing factors, and culture in post-genocide Rwanda* (Doctoral dissertation).

Salopeck, J. (2006). *Leadership for a New Age.* Trends. https://www.ngenperformance.com/pdf/articles/TandD.pdf

Sayegh, P. Y. (2008). *Cultural hybridity and modern binaries: Overcoming the opposition between identity and otherness?* Academic Press.

Schindler, J. (2021). Don't Underestimate The "Culture" In Corporate Cultures. *Forbes Magazine*. https://www.forbes.com/sites/forbescoachescouncil/2021/10/14/dont-underestimate-the-culture-in-corporate-culture/?sh=20657dd06f20

Seide, J. (2021, August 1). *A Brief History of Rinkside Advertising*. https://thehockeywriters.com/a-brief-history-of-rinkside-advertising/

Şenses, B., & Temoçin, P. (2016, October). An Interdisciplinary Study: *Quantum Leadership and Hybrid Leadership. In International Symposium on Chaos, Complexity, and Leadership* (pp. 547-559). Springer.

Shabbir, M. A., Ishtiaq, Z., & Zia-ud-Din, M. (2017). The Impact of Hybrid leadership on Employee performance in Textile Sector of Pakistan. *International Journal of Academic Research in Business & Social Sciences*, *7*(4), 359–374. doi:10.6007/IJARBSS/v7-i4/2815

Sims, P. (2012, July 30). *Pixar's Motto: Going From Suck to Nonsuck*. Fast Company. Retrieved October 29, 2021, from https://www.fastcompany.com/1742431/pixars-motto-going-suck-nonsuck

Sinek, S. (2009). *Start with Why: How Great Leaders Inspire Everyone to Take Action*. Penguin.

Snelling, I., Exworthy, M., & Ghezelayagh, S. (2020). The chief registrar role in the UK: Leadership capacity and development of hybrid leaders. *Journal of Health Organization and Management*, *34*(1), 1–15. doi:10.1108/JHOM-08-2019-0229 PMID:32018338

Spataro, J. (2021). *Hybrid work is here. Are you ready?* Microsoft. https://www.microsoft.com/en-us/microsoft-365/blog/2021/03/02/hybrid-work-is-here-are-you-ready/

Stafford, M. (2010). *The full-range leadership model: A brief primer*. Instructor Training Material, Squadron Officer School. https://www3.nd.edu/~jthomp19/AS300/1_Fall%20Semester/27%20Sep/Full_Range_Leadership_V1.pdf

Stanier, M. B. (2016). *The Coaching Habit: Say Less, Ask More & Change the Way You Lead Forever*. Box of Crayons P.

Statista Research Department. (2022). *Walmart – Statistic & Facts*. Retrieved from https://www.statista.com/topics/1451/walmart/#topicHeader__wrapper

Survey: 40% of Employees Are Thinking of Quitting Their Jobs. (2021). *World Economic Forum*. Retrieved October 20, 2021, from https://www.weforum.org/agenda/2021/06/remote-workers-burnout-covid-microsoft-survey/

Tait, B. (2020). Traditional Leadership Vs. Servant Leadership. *Forbes*. https://www.forbes.com/sites/forbescoachescouncil/2020/03/11/traditional-leadership-vs-servant-leadership/?sh=2cfe67f6451e

The Balance Careers. (2021). *The pros and cons of a flexible work schedule*. www.thebalancecareers.com/advantages-and-disadvantages-of-flexible-work-schedules-1917964

The Scientific Truth Behind 'Fake It Till You Make It'. (2018, December 5). *Cognition Today*. Retrieved October 28, 2021, from https://cognitiontoday.com/the-scientific-truth-behind-fake-it-till-you-make-it/

The World Bank. (2021). *Employment in agriculture (% of total employment)*. Retrieved from https://data.worldbank.org/indicator/SL.AGR.EMPL.ZS

Thomas, G. (n.d.). What is Modern Effective Leadership. *weLead*. Retrieved from https://www.leadingtoday.org/what-is-effective-modern-leadership/

Tian, Q. (2013). *Hybrid leadership: a study of the leadership (roles and characteristics) of nine Chinese university presidents with US experiences*. University of Illinois at Urbana-Champaign. https://www.ideals.illinois.edu/bitstream/handle/2142/44354/Qingyan_Tian.pdf?sequence=1&isAllowed=y

Tian, Q. (2020). *Glocalization and the Development of a Hybrid Leadership Model: A Study of Chinese University Presidency*. Routledge. doi:10.4324/9780429284960

Time Magazine. (1961). *The Automation Jobless*. Retrieved from https://content.time.com/time/subscriber/article/0,33009,828815,00.html

Tonini, D. C., Burbules, N. C., & Gunsalus, C. K. (2016). New Models of Hybrid Leadership in Global Higher Education. *Educational Considerations*, *43*(3), 37–46. doi:10.4148/0146-9282.1019

Townsend, A. (2015). Leading school networks: Hybrid leadership in action? *Educational Management Administration & Leadership*, *43*(5), 719–737. doi:10.1177/1741143214543205

Tully, S. (2007). What barriers hold women back. *The Chronicle of Higher Education*. https://www.chronicle.com/article/what-barriers-hold-women-back/

Turner, J. R., Thurlow, N., & Rivera, B. (2020). The Flow System: Practitioner Tools for Navigating Complexity. In Cases on Performance Improvement Innovation (pp. 248-273). IGI Global.

van der Lippe, T., & Lippényi, Z. (2019). Co-workers working from home and individual and team performance. *New Technology, Work and Employment*, *35*(1), 60–79. doi:10.1111/ntwe.12153 PMID:32214593

van Dyne, L., Kossek, E., & Lobal, S. (2007). Less need to be there: Cross-level effects of work practices that support work–life flexibility and enhance group processes and group-level OCB. *Human Relations*, *60*(8), 1123–1153. doi:10.1177/0018726707081657

Vann, B. A., Coleman, A. N., & Simpson, J. A. (2014). Development of the Vannsimpco leadership survey: A delineation of hybrid leadership styles. *Swiss Business School Journal of Applied Business Research*, *3*(1), 28–38.

Velumyan, N. (2020). Androgyny: An emerging trend in leadership. *Forbes Magazine*. https://www.forbes.com/sites/forbescoachescouncil/2020/10/28/androgyny-an-emerging-trend-in-leadership/?sh=3d2098095777

Vittersø, J., Akselsen, S., Evjemo, B., Julsrud, T., Yttri, B., & Bergvik, S. (2003). Impacts of home-based telework on quality of life for employees and their partners. Quantitative and qualitative results from a European survey. *Journal of Happiness Studies*, *4*(2), 201–233. doi:10.1023/A:1024490621548

Wajdi, B. N. (2017). The Differences Between Management and Leadership. *Sinergi*, *7*(2), 75–84.

Wakefield, R. L., Leidner, D. E., & Garrison, G. (2008). A model of conflict, leadership and performance in virtual teams. *Information Systems Research*, *19*(4), 434–455. doi:10.1287/isre.1070.0149

Waldorf, T. (n.d.). *Renew blue: Best buy's turnaround.* https://www.tjwaldorf.com/renew-blue-best-buys-turnaround/

Wang, B., Liu, Y., Qian, J., & Parker, S. K. (2021). Achieving effective remote working during the COVID-19 pandemic: A work design perspective. *Applied Psychology*, *70*(1), 16–59. doi:10.1111/apps.12290 PMID:33230359

Web of Science. (2021). *Hybrid Leadership*. https://www-webofscience-com.e-revistas.ugto.mx/wos?app=wos&Init=Yes&SrcApp=CR&locale=en-US&SID=7DMk6ld5yhZFbHZ8ncM

Weinert, C., Maier, C., Laumer, S., & Weitzel, T. (2014). Does teleworking negatively influence IT professionals? An empirical analysis of IT personnel's telework-enabled stress. *Proceedings of the 52nd ACM Conference on Computers and People Research*, 139–147. 10.1145/2599990.2600011

Wigston, S. (2019). *Followership in Leadership: The Role It Plays*. Eagle's Flight. https://www.eaglesflight.com/blog/the-critical-role-of-followership-in-leadership

Wikipedia. (n.d.). *Industrial Revolution*. Retrieved from https://en.wikipedia.org/wiki/Industrial_Revolution

Winter, R., & O'Donohue, W. (2011). *Understanding identity construction in hybrid organisations: A work ideologies perspective*. Australian National University.

World Health Organization. (2020). *Archived: WHO Timeline - COVID-19*. https://www.who.int/news/item/27-04-2020-who-timeline---covid-19

Zander, L., Mockaitis, A. I., & Butler, C. L. (2012). Leading global teams. *Journal of World Business*, *47*(4), 592–603. doi:10.1016/j.jwb.2012.01.012

Zhang, S., & Fjermestad, J. (2006). Bridging the gap between traditional leadership theories and virtual team leadership. *International Journal of Technology, Policy and Management*, *6*(3), 56–78.

Zigurs, I. (2002). Leadership in virtual teams: Oxymoron or opportunity? *Organizational Dynamics*, *31*(4), 339–351. doi:10.1016/S0090-2616(02)00132-8

Related References

To continue our tradition of advancing information science and technology research, we have compiled a list of recommended IGI Global readings. These references will provide additional information and guidance to further enrich your knowledge and assist you with your own research and future publications.

Abdul Razak, R., & Mansor, N. A. (2021). Instagram Influencers in Social Media-Induced Tourism: Rethinking Tourist Trust Towards Tourism Destination. In M. Dinis, L. Bonixe, S. Lamy, & Z. Breda (Eds.), *Impact of New Media in Tourism* (pp. 135-144). IGI Global. https://doi.org/10.4018/978-1-7998-7095-1.ch009

Abir, T., & Khan, M. Y. (2022). Importance of ICT Advancement and Culture of Adaptation in the Tourism and Hospitality Industry for Developing Countries. In C. Ramos, S. Quinteiro, & A. Gonçalves (Eds.), *ICT as Innovator Between Tourism and Culture* (pp. 30–41). IGI Global. https://doi.org/10.4018/978-1-7998-8165-0.ch003

Abir, T., & Khan, M. Y. (2022). Importance of ICT Advancement and Culture of Adaptation in the Tourism and Hospitality Industry for Developing Countries. In C. Ramos, S. Quinteiro, & A. Gonçalves (Eds.), *ICT as Innovator Between Tourism and Culture* (pp. 30–41). IGI Global. https://doi.org/10.4018/978-1-7998-8165-0.ch003

Abtahi, M. S., Behboudi, L., & Hasanabad, H. M. (2017). Factors Affecting Internet Advertising Adoption in Ad Agencies. *International Journal of Innovation in the Digital Economy*, *8*(4), 18–29. doi:10.4018/IJIDE.2017100102

Afenyo-Agbe, E., & Mensah, I. (2022). Principles, Benefits, and Barriers to Community-Based Tourism: Implications for Management. In I. Mensah & E. Afenyo-Agbe (Eds.), *Prospects and Challenges of Community-Based Tourism and Changing Demographics* (pp. 1–29). IGI Global. doi:10.4018/978-1-7998-7335-8.ch001

Agbo, V. M. (2022). Distributive Justice Issues in Community-Based Tourism. In I. Mensah & E. Afenyo-Agbe (Eds.), *Prospects and Challenges of Community-Based Tourism and Changing Demographics* (pp. 107–129). IGI Global. https://doi.org/10.4018/978-1-7998-7335-8.ch005

Agrawal, S. (2017). The Impact of Emerging Technologies and Social Media on Different Business(es): Marketing and Management. In O. Rishi & A. Sharma (Eds.), *Maximizing Business Performance and Efficiency Through Intelligent Systems* (pp. 37–49). Hershey, PA: IGI Global. doi:10.4018/978-1-5225-2234-8.ch002

Ahmad, A., & Johari, S. (2022). Georgetown as a Gastronomy Tourism Destination: Visitor Awareness Towards Revisit Intention of Nasi Kandar Restaurant. In M. Valeri (Ed.), *New Governance and Management in Touristic Destinations* (pp. 71–83). IGI Global. https://doi.org/10.4018/978-1-6684-3889-3.ch005

Alkhatib, G., & Bayouq, S. T. (2021). A TAM-Based Model of Technological Factors Affecting Use of E-Tourism. *International Journal of Tourism and Hospitality Management in the Digital Age*, *5*(2), 50–67. https://doi.org/10.4018/IJTHMDA.20210701.oa1

Altinay Ozdemir, M. (2021). Virtual Reality (VR) and Augmented Reality (AR) Technologies for Accessibility and Marketing in the Tourism Industry. In C. Eusébio, L. Teixeira, & M. Carneiro (Eds.), *ICT Tools and Applications for Accessible Tourism* (pp. 277-301). IGI Global. https://doi.org/10.4018/978-1-7998-6428-8.ch013

Anantharaman, R. N., Rajeswari, K. S., Angusamy, A., & Kuppusamy, J. (2017). Role of Self-Efficacy and Collective Efficacy as Moderators of Occupational Stress Among Software Development Professionals. *International Journal of Human Capital and Information Technology Professionals*, *8*(2), 45–58. doi:10.4018/IJHCITP.2017040103

Aninze, F., El-Gohary, H., & Hussain, J. (2018). The Role of Microfinance to Empower Women: The Case of Developing Countries. *International Journal of Customer Relationship Marketing and Management*, *9*(1), 54–78. doi:10.4018/IJCRMM.2018010104

Antosova, G., Sabogal-Salamanca, M., & Krizova, E. (2021). Human Capital in Tourism: A Practical Model of Endogenous and Exogenous Territorial Tourism Planning in Bahía Solano, Colombia. In V. Costa, A. Moura, & M. Mira (Eds.), *Handbook of Research on Human Capital and People Management in the Tourism Industry* (pp. 282–302). IGI Global. https://doi.org/10.4018/978-1-7998-4318-4.ch014

Arsenijević, O. M., Orčić, D., & Kastratović, E. (2017). Development of an Optimization Tool for Intangibles in SMEs: A Case Study from Serbia with a Pilot Research in the Prestige by Milka Company. In M. Vemić (Ed.), *Optimal Management Strategies in Small and Medium Enterprises* (pp. 320–347). Hershey, PA: IGI Global. doi:10.4018/978-1-5225-1949-2.ch015

Aryanto, V. D., Wismantoro, Y., & Widyatmoko, K. (2018). Implementing Eco-Innovation by Utilizing the Internet to Enhance Firm's Marketing Performance: Study of Green Batik Small and Medium Enterprises in Indonesia. *International Journal of E-Business Research, 14*(1), 21–36. doi:10.4018/IJEBR.2018010102

Asero, V., & Billi, S. (2022). New Perspective of Networking in the DMO Model. In M. Valeri (Ed.), *New Governance and Management in Touristic Destinations* (pp. 105–118). IGI Global. https://doi.org/10.4018/978-1-6684-3889-3.ch007

Atiku, S. O., & Fields, Z. (2017). Multicultural Orientations for 21st Century Global Leadership. In N. Baporikar (Ed.), *Management Education for Global Leadership* (pp. 28–51). Hershey, PA: IGI Global. doi:10.4018/978-1-5225-1013-0.ch002

Atiku, S. O., & Fields, Z. (2018). Organisational Learning Dimensions and Talent Retention Strategies for the Service Industries. In N. Baporikar (Ed.), *Global Practices in Knowledge Management for Societal and Organizational Development* (pp. 358–381). Hershey, PA: IGI Global. doi:10.4018/978-1-5225-3009-1.ch017

Atsa'am, D. D., & Kuset Bodur, E. (2021). Pattern Mining on How Organizational Tenure Affects the Psychological Capital of Employees Within the Hospitality and Tourism Industry: Linking Employees' Organizational Tenure With PsyCap. *International Journal of Tourism and Hospitality Management in the Digital Age, 5*(2), 17–28. https://doi.org/10.4018/IJTHMDA.2021070102

Ávila, L., & Teixeira, L. (2018). The Main Concepts Behind the Dematerialization of Business Processes. In M. Khosrow-Pour, D.B.A. (Ed.), Encyclopedia of Information Science and Technology, Fourth Edition (pp. 888-898). Hershey, PA: IGI Global. https://doi.org/ doi:10.4018/978-1-5225-2255-3.ch076

Ayorekire, J., Mugizi, F., Obua, J., & Ampaire, G. (2022). Community-Based Tourism and Local People's Perceptions Towards Conservation: The Case of Queen Elizabeth Conservation Area, Uganda. In I. Mensah & E. Afenyo-Agbe (Eds.), *Prospects and Challenges of Community-Based Tourism and Changing Demographics* (pp. 56–82). IGI Global. https://doi.org/10.4018/978-1-7998-7335-8.ch003

Baleiro, R. (2022). Tourist Literature and the Architecture of Travel in Olga Tokarczuk and Patti Smith. In R. Baleiro & R. Pereira (Eds.), *Global Perspectives on Literary Tourism and Film-Induced Tourism* (pp. 202-216). IGI Global. https://doi.org/10.4018/978-1-7998-8262-6.ch011

Barat, S. (2021). Looking at the Future of Medical Tourism in Asia. *International Journal of Tourism and Hospitality Management in the Digital Age*, *5*(1), 19–33. https://doi.org/10.4018/IJTHMDA.2021010102

Barbosa, C. A., Magalhães, M., & Nunes, M. R. (2021). Travel Instagramability: A Way of Choosing a Destination? In M. Dinis, L. Bonixe, S. Lamy, & Z. Breda (Eds.), *Impact of New Media in Tourism* (pp. 173-190). IGI Global. https://doi.org/10.4018/978-1-7998-7095-1.ch011

Bari, M. W., & Khan, Q. (2021). Pakistan as a Destination of Religious Tourism. In E. Alaverdov & M. Bari (Eds.), *Global Development of Religious Tourism* (pp. 1-10). IGI Global. https://doi.org/10.4018/978-1-7998-5792-1.ch001

Bartens, Y., Chunpir, H. I., Schulte, F., & Voß, S. (2017). Business/IT Alignment in Two-Sided Markets: A COBIT 5 Analysis for Media Streaming Business Models. In S. De Haes & W. Van Grembergen (Eds.), *Strategic IT Governance and Alignment in Business Settings* (pp. 82–111). Hershey, PA: IGI Global. doi:10.4018/978-1-5225-0861-8.ch004

Bashayreh, A. M. (2018). Organizational Culture and Organizational Performance. In W. Lee & F. Sabetzadeh (Eds.), *Contemporary Knowledge and Systems Science* (pp. 50–69). Hershey, PA: IGI Global. doi:10.4018/978-1-5225-5655-8.ch003

Bechthold, L., Lude, M., & Prügl, R. (2021). Crisis Favors the Prepared Firm: How Organizational Ambidexterity Relates to Perceptions of Organizational Resilience. In A. Zehrer, G. Glowka, K. Schwaiger, & V. Ranacher-Lackner (Eds.), *Resiliency Models and Addressing Future Risks for Family Firms in the Tourism Industry* (pp. 178–205). IGI Global. https://doi.org/10.4018/978-1-7998-7352-5.ch008

Bedford, D. A. (2018). Sustainable Knowledge Management Strategies: Aligning Business Capabilities and Knowledge Management Goals. In N. Baporikar (Ed.), *Global Practices in Knowledge Management for Societal and Organizational Development* (pp. 46–73). Hershey, PA: IGI Global. doi:10.4018/978-1-5225-3009-1.ch003

Bekjanov, D., & Matyusupov, B. (2021). Influence of Innovative Processes in the Competitiveness of Tourist Destination. In J. Soares (Ed.), *Innovation and Entrepreneurial Opportunities in Community Tourism* (pp. 243–263). IGI Global. https://doi.org/10.4018/978-1-7998-4855-4.ch014

Bharwani, S., & Musunuri, D. (2018). Reflection as a Process From Theory to Practice. In M. Khosrow-Pour, D.B.A. (Ed.), Encyclopedia of Information Science and Technology, Fourth Edition (pp. 1529-1539). Hershey, PA: IGI Global. doi:10.4018/978-1-5225-2255-3.ch132

Bhatt, G. D., Wang, Z., & Rodger, J. A. (2017). Information Systems Capabilities and Their Effects on Competitive Advantages: A Study of Chinese Companies. *Information Resources Management Journal, 30*(3), 41–57. doi:10.4018/IRMJ.2017070103

Bhushan, M., & Yadav, A. (2017). Concept of Cloud Computing in ESB. In R. Bhadoria, N. Chaudhari, G. Tomar, & S. Singh (Eds.), *Exploring Enterprise Service Bus in the Service-Oriented Architecture Paradigm* (pp. 116–127). Hershey, PA: IGI Global. doi:10.4018/978-1-5225-2157-0.ch008

Bhushan, S. (2017). System Dynamics Base-Model of Humanitarian Supply Chain (HSCM) in Disaster Prone Eco-Communities of India: A Discussion on Simulation and Scenario Results. *International Journal of System Dynamics Applications, 6*(3), 20–37. doi:10.4018/IJSDA.2017070102

Binder, D., & Miller, J. W. (2021). A Generations' Perspective on Employer Branding in Tourism. In V. Costa, A. Moura, & M. Mira (Eds.), *Handbook of Research on Human Capital and People Management in the Tourism Industry* (pp. 152–174). IGI Global. https://doi.org/10.4018/978-1-7998-4318-4.ch008

Birch Freeman, A. A., Mensah, I., & Antwi, K. B. (2022). Smiling vs. Frowning Faces: Community Participation for Sustainable Tourism in Ghanaian Communities. In I. Mensah & E. Afenyo-Agbe (Eds.), *Prospects and Challenges of Community-Based Tourism and Changing Demographics* (pp. 83–106). IGI Global. https://doi.org/10.4018/978-1-7998-7335-8.ch004

Biswas, A., & De, A. K. (2017). On Development of a Fuzzy Stochastic Programming Model with Its Application to Business Management. In S. Trivedi, S. Dey, A. Kumar, & T. Panda (Eds.), *Handbook of Research on Advanced Data Mining Techniques and Applications for Business Intelligence* (pp. 353–378). Hershey, PA: IGI Global. doi:10.4018/978-1-5225-2031-3.ch021

Boragnio, A., & Faracce Macia, C. (2021). "Taking Care of Yourself at Home": Use of E-Commerce About Food and Care During the COVID-19 Pandemic in the City of Buenos Aires. In M. Korstanje (Ed.), *Socio-Economic Effects and Recovery Efforts for the Rental Industry: Post-COVID-19 Strategies* (pp. 45–71). IGI Global. https://doi.org/10.4018/978-1-7998-7287-0.ch003

Borges, V. D. (2021). Happiness: The Basis for Public Policy in Tourism. In A. Perinotto, V. Mayer, & J. Soares (Eds.), *Rebuilding and Restructuring the Tourism Industry: Infusion of Happiness and Quality of Life* (pp. 1–25). IGI Global. https://doi.org/10.4018/978-1-7998-7239-9.ch001

Bücker, J., & Ernste, K. (2018). Use of Brand Heroes in Strategic Reputation Management: The Case of Bacardi, Adidas, and Daimler. In A. Erdemir (Ed.), *Reputation Management Techniques in Public Relations* (pp. 126–150). Hershey, PA: IGI Global. doi:10.4018/978-1-5225-3619-2.ch007

Buluk Eşitti, B. (2021). COVID-19 and Alternative Tourism: New Destinations and New Tourism Products. In M. Demir, A. Dalgıç, & F. Ergen (Eds.), *Handbook of Research on the Impacts and Implications of COVID-19 on the Tourism Industry* (pp. 786–805). IGI Global. https://doi.org/10.4018/978-1-7998-8231-2.ch038

Bureš, V. (2018). Industry 4.0 From the Systems Engineering Perspective: Alternative Holistic Framework Development. In R. Brunet-Thornton & F. Martinez (Eds.), *Analyzing the Impacts of Industry 4.0 in Modern Business Environments* (pp. 199–223). Hershey, PA: IGI Global. doi:10.4018/978-1-5225-3468-6.ch011

Buzady, Z. (2017). Resolving the Magic Cube of Effective Case Teaching: Benchmarking Case Teaching Practices in Emerging Markets – Insights from the Central European University Business School, Hungary. In D. Latusek (Ed.), *Case Studies as a Teaching Tool in Management Education* (pp. 79–103). Hershey, PA: IGI Global. doi:10.4018/978-1-5225-0770-3.ch005

Camillo, A. (2021). *Legal Matters, Risk Management, and Risk Prevention: From Forming a Business to Legal Representation*. IGI Global. doi:10.4018/978-1-7998-4342-9.ch004

Căpusneanu, S., & Topor, D. I. (2018). Business Ethics and Cost Management in SMEs: Theories of Business Ethics and Cost Management Ethos. In I. Oncioiu (Ed.), *Ethics and Decision-Making for Sustainable Business Practices* (pp. 109–127). Hershey, PA: IGI Global. doi:10.4018/978-1-5225-3773-1.ch007

Chan, R. L., Mo, P. L., & Moon, K. K. (2018). Strategic and Tactical Measures in Managing Enterprise Risks: A Study of the Textile and Apparel Industry. In K. Strang, M. Korstanje, & N. Vajjhala (Eds.), *Research, Practices, and Innovations in Global Risk and Contingency Management* (pp. 1–19). Hershey, PA: IGI Global. doi:10.4018/978-1-5225-4754-9.ch001

Charlier, S. D., Burke-Smalley, L. A., & Fisher, S. L. (2018). Undergraduate Programs in the U.S: A Contextual and Content-Based Analysis. In J. Mendy (Ed.), *Teaching Human Resources and Organizational Behavior at the College Level* (pp. 26–57). Hershey, PA: IGI Global. doi:10.4018/978-1-5225-2820-3.ch002

Chumillas, J., Güell, M., & Quer, P. (2022). The Use of ICT in Tourist and Educational Literary Routes: The Role of the Guide. In C. Ramos, S. Quinteiro, & A. Gonçalves (Eds.), *ICT as Innovator Between Tourism and Culture* (pp. 15–29). IGI Global. https://doi.org/10.4018/978-1-7998-8165-0.ch002

Dahlberg, T., Kivijärvi, H., & Saarinen, T. (2017). IT Investment Consistency and Other Factors Influencing the Success of IT Performance. In S. De Haes & W. Van Grembergen (Eds.), *Strategic IT Governance and Alignment in Business Settings* (pp. 176–208). Hershey, PA: IGI Global. doi:10.4018/978-1-5225-0861-8.ch007

Damnjanović, A. M. (2017). Knowledge Management Optimization through IT and E-Business Utilization: A Qualitative Study on Serbian SMEs. In M. Vemić (Ed.), *Optimal Management Strategies in Small and Medium Enterprises* (pp. 249–267). Hershey, PA: IGI Global. doi:10.4018/978-1-5225-1949-2.ch012

Daneshpour, H. (2017). Integrating Sustainable Development into Project Portfolio Management through Application of Open Innovation. In M. Vemić (Ed.), *Optimal Management Strategies in Small and Medium Enterprises* (pp. 370–387). Hershey, PA: IGI Global. doi:10.4018/978-1-5225-1949-2.ch017

Daniel, A. D., & Reis de Castro, V. (2018). Entrepreneurship Education: How to Measure the Impact on Nascent Entrepreneurs. In A. Carrizo Moreira, J. Guilherme Leitão Dantas, & F. Manuel Valente (Eds.), *Nascent Entrepreneurship and Successful New Venture Creation* (pp. 85–110). Hershey, PA: IGI Global. doi:10.4018/978-1-5225-2936-1.ch004

David, R., Swami, B. N., & Tangirala, S. (2018). Ethics Impact on Knowledge Management in Organizational Development: A Case Study. In N. Baporikar (Ed.), *Global Practices in Knowledge Management for Societal and Organizational Development* (pp. 19–45). Hershey, PA: IGI Global. doi:10.4018/978-1-5225-3009-1.ch002

De Uña-Álvarez, E., & Villarino-Pérez, M. (2022). Fostering Ecocultural Resources, Identity, and Tourism in Inland Territories (Galicia, NW Spain). In G. Fernandes (Ed.), *Challenges and New Opportunities for Tourism in Inland Territories: Ecocultural Resources and Sustainable Initiatives* (pp. 1-16). IGI Global. https://doi.org/10.4018/978-1-7998-7339-6.ch001

Delias, P., & Lakiotaki, K. (2018). Discovering Process Horizontal Boundaries to Facilitate Process Comprehension. *International Journal of Operations Research and Information Systems*, *9*(2), 1–31. doi:10.4018/IJORIS.2018040101

Denholm, J., & Lee-Davies, L. (2018). Success Factors for Games in Business and Project Management. In *Enhancing Education and Training Initiatives Through Serious Games* (pp. 34–68). Hershey, PA: IGI Global. doi:10.4018/978-1-5225-3689-5.ch002

Deshpande, M. (2017). Best Practices in Management Institutions for Global Leadership: Policy Aspects. In N. Baporikar (Ed.), *Management Education for Global Leadership* (pp. 1–27). Hershey, PA: IGI Global. doi:10.4018/978-1-5225-1013-0.ch001

Deshpande, M. (2018). Policy Perspectives for SMEs Knowledge Management. In N. Baporikar (Ed.), *Knowledge Integration Strategies for Entrepreneurship and Sustainability* (pp. 23–46). Hershey, PA: IGI Global. doi:10.4018/978-1-5225-5115-7.ch002

Dezdar, S. (2017). ERP Implementation Projects in Asian Countries: A Comparative Study on Iran and China. *International Journal of Information Technology Project Management*, *8*(3), 52–68. doi:10.4018/IJITPM.2017070104

Domingos, D., Respício, A., & Martinho, R. (2017). Reliability of IoT-Aware BPMN Healthcare Processes. In C. Reis & M. Maximiano (Eds.), *Internet of Things and Advanced Application in Healthcare* (pp. 214–248). Hershey, PA: IGI Global. doi:10.4018/978-1-5225-1820-4.ch008

Dosumu, O., Hussain, J., & El-Gohary, H. (2017). An Exploratory Study of the Impact of Government Policies on the Development of Small and Medium Enterprises in Developing Countries: The Case of Nigeria. *International Journal of Customer Relationship Marketing and Management*, *8*(4), 51–62. doi:10.4018/IJCRMM.2017100104

Durst, S., Bruns, G., & Edvardsson, I. R. (2017). Retaining Knowledge in Smaller Building and Construction Firms. *International Journal of Knowledge and Systems Science*, *8*(3), 1–12. doi:10.4018/IJKSS.2017070101

Edvardsson, I. R., & Durst, S. (2017). Outsourcing, Knowledge, and Learning: A Critical Review. *International Journal of Knowledge-Based Organizations*, *7*(2), 13–26. doi:10.4018/IJKBO.2017040102

Edwards, J. S. (2018). Integrating Knowledge Management and Business Processes. In M. Khosrow-Pour, D.B.A. (Ed.), Encyclopedia of Information Science and Technology, Fourth Edition (pp. 5046-5055). Hershey, PA: IGI Global. doi:10.4018/978-1-5225-2255-3.ch437

Eichelberger, S., & Peters, M. (2021). Family Firm Management in Turbulent Times: Opportunities for Responsible Tourism. In A. Zehrer, G. Glowka, K. Schwaiger, & V. Ranacher-Lackner (Eds.), *Resiliency Models and Addressing Future Risks for Family Firms in the Tourism Industry* (pp. 103–124). IGI Global. https://doi.org/10.4018/978-1-7998-7352-5.ch005

Eide, D., Hjalager, A., & Hansen, M. (2022). Innovative Certifications in Adventure Tourism: Attributes and Diffusion. In R. Augusto Costa, F. Brandão, Z. Breda, & C. Costa (Eds.), *Planning and Managing the Experience Economy in Tourism* (pp. 161-175). IGI Global. https://doi.org/10.4018/978-1-7998-8775-1.ch009

Ejiogu, A. O. (2018). Economics of Farm Management. In *Agricultural Finance and Opportunities for Investment and Expansion* (pp. 56–72). Hershey, PA: IGI Global. doi:10.4018/978-1-5225-3059-6.ch003

Ekanem, I., & Abiade, G. E. (2018). Factors Influencing the Use of E-Commerce by Small Enterprises in Nigeria. *International Journal of ICT Research in Africa and the Middle East*, *7*(1), 37–53. doi:10.4018/IJICTRAME.2018010103

Ekanem, I., & Alrossais, L. A. (2017). Succession Challenges Facing Family Businesses in Saudi Arabia. In P. Zgheib (Ed.), *Entrepreneurship and Business Innovation in the Middle East* (pp. 122–146). Hershey, PA: IGI Global. doi:10.4018/978-1-5225-2066-5.ch007

El Faquih, L., & Fredj, M. (2017). Ontology-Based Framework for Quality in Configurable Process Models. *Journal of Electronic Commerce in Organizations*, *15*(2), 48–60. doi:10.4018/JECO.2017040104

Faisal, M. N., & Talib, F. (2017). Building Ambidextrous Supply Chains in SMEs: How to Tackle the Barriers? *International Journal of Information Systems and Supply Chain Management*, *10*(4), 80–100. doi:10.4018/IJISSCM.2017100105

Fernandes, T. M., Gomes, J., & Romão, M. (2017). Investments in E-Government: A Benefit Management Case Study. *International Journal of Electronic Government Research*, *13*(3), 1–17. doi:10.4018/IJEGR.2017070101

Figueira, L. M., Honrado, G. R., & Dionísio, M. S. (2021). Human Capital Management in the Tourism Industry in Portugal. In V. Costa, A. Moura, & M. Mira (Eds.), *Handbook of Research on Human Capital and People Management in the Tourism Industry* (pp. 1–19). IGI Global. doi:10.4018/978-1-7998-4318-4.ch001

Gao, S. S., Oreal, S., & Zhang, J. (2018). Contemporary Financial Risk Management Perceptions and Practices of Small-Sized Chinese Businesses. In I. Management Association (Ed.), Global Business Expansion: Concepts, Methodologies, Tools, and Applications (pp. 917-931). Hershey, PA: IGI Global. doi:10.4018/978-1-5225-5481-3.ch041

Garg, R., & Berning, S. C. (2017). Indigenous Chinese Management Philosophies: Key Concepts and Relevance for Modern Chinese Firms. In B. Christiansen & G. Koc (Eds.), *Transcontinental Strategies for Industrial Development and Economic Growth* (pp. 43–57). Hershey, PA: IGI Global. doi:10.4018/978-1-5225-2160-0.ch003

Gencer, Y. G. (2017). Supply Chain Management in Retailing Business. In U. Akkucuk (Ed.), *Ethics and Sustainability in Global Supply Chain Management* (pp. 197–210). Hershey, PA: IGI Global. doi:10.4018/978-1-5225-2036-8.ch011

Gera, R., Arora, S., & Malik, S. (2021). Emotional Labor in the Tourism Industry: Strategies, Antecedents, and Outcomes. In V. Costa, A. Moura, & M. Mira (Eds.), *Handbook of Research on Human Capital and People Management in the Tourism Industry* (pp. 73–91). IGI Global. https://doi.org/10.4018/978-1-7998-4318-4.ch004

Giacosa, E. (2018). The Increasing of the Regional Development Thanks to the Luxury Business Innovation. In L. Carvalho (Ed.), *Handbook of Research on Entrepreneurial Ecosystems and Social Dynamics in a Globalized World* (pp. 260–273). Hershey, PA: IGI Global. doi:10.4018/978-1-5225-3525-6.ch011

Glowka, G., Tusch, M., & Zehrer, A. (2021). The Risk Perception of Family Business Owner-Manager in the Tourism Industry: A Qualitative Comparison of the Intra-Firm Senior and Junior Generation. In A. Zehrer, G. Glowka, K. Schwaiger, & V. Ranacher-Lackner (Eds.), *Resiliency Models and Addressing Future Risks for Family Firms in the Tourism Industry* (pp. 126–153). IGI Global. https://doi.org/10.4018/978-1-7998-7352-5.ch006

Glykas, M., & George, J. (2017). Quality and Process Management Systems in the UAE Maritime Industry. *International Journal of Productivity Management and Assessment Technologies*, *5*(1), 20–39. doi:10.4018/IJPMAT.2017010102

Glykas, M., Valiris, G., Kokkinaki, A., & Koutsoukou, Z. (2018). Banking Business Process Management Implementation. *International Journal of Productivity Management and Assessment Technologies*, *6*(1), 50–69. doi:10.4018/IJPMAT.2018010104

Gomes, J., & Romão, M. (2017). The Balanced Scorecard: Keeping Updated and Aligned with Today's Business Trends. *International Journal of Productivity Management and Assessment Technologies*, *5*(2), 1–15. doi:10.4018/IJPMAT.2017070101

Gomes, J., & Romão, M. (2017). Aligning Information Systems and Technology with Benefit Management and Balanced Scorecard. In S. De Haes & W. Van Grembergen (Eds.), *Strategic IT Governance and Alignment in Business Settings* (pp. 112–131). Hershey, PA: IGI Global. doi:10.4018/978-1-5225-0861-8.ch005

Goyal, A. (2021). Communicating and Building Destination Brands With New Media. In M. Dinis, L. Bonixe, S. Lamy, & Z. Breda (Eds.), *Impact of New Media in Tourism* (pp. 1-20). IGI Global. https://doi.org/10.4018/978-1-7998-7095-1.ch001

Grefen, P., & Turetken, O. (2017). Advanced Business Process Management in Networked E-Business Scenarios. *International Journal of E-Business Research*, *13*(4), 70–104. doi:10.4018/IJEBR.2017100105

Guasca, M., Van Broeck, A. M., & Vanneste, D. (2021). Tourism and the Social Reintegration of Colombian Ex-Combatants. In J. da Silva, Z. Breda, & F. Carbone (Eds.), *Role and Impact of Tourism in Peacebuilding and Conflict Transformation* (pp. 66-86). IGI Global. https://doi.org/10.4018/978-1-7998-5053-3.ch005

Haider, A., & Saetang, S. (2017). Strategic IT Alignment in Service Sector. In S. Rozenes & Y. Cohen (Eds.), *Handbook of Research on Strategic Alliances and Value Co-Creation in the Service Industry* (pp. 231–258). Hershey, PA: IGI Global. doi:10.4018/978-1-5225-2084-9.ch012

Hajilari, A. B., Ghadaksaz, M., & Fasghandis, G. S. (2017). Assessing Organizational Readiness for Implementing ERP System Using Fuzzy Expert System Approach. *International Journal of Enterprise Information Systems*, *13*(1), 67–85. doi:10.4018/IJEIS.2017010105

Haldorai, A., Ramu, A., & Murugan, S. (2018). Social Aware Cognitive Radio Networks: Effectiveness of Social Networks as a Strategic Tool for Organizational Business Management. In H. Bansal, G. Shrivastava, G. Nguyen, & L. Stanciu (Eds.), *Social Network Analytics for Contemporary Business Organizations* (pp. 188–202). Hershey, PA: IGI Global. doi:10.4018/978-1-5225-5097-6.ch010

Hall, O. P. Jr. (2017). Social Media Driven Management Education. *International Journal of Knowledge-Based Organizations*, *7*(2), 43–59. doi:10.4018/IJKBO.2017040104

Hanifah, H., Halim, H. A., Ahmad, N. H., & Vafaei-Zadeh, A. (2017). Innovation Culture as a Mediator Between Specific Human Capital and Innovation Performance Among Bumiputera SMEs in Malaysia. In N. Ahmad, T. Ramayah, H. Halim, & S. Rahman (Eds.), *Handbook of Research on Small and Medium Enterprises in Developing Countries* (pp. 261–279). Hershey, PA: IGI Global. doi:10.4018/978-1-5225-2165-5.ch012

Hartlieb, S., & Silvius, G. (2017). Handling Uncertainty in Project Management and Business Development: Similarities and Differences. In Y. Raydugin (Ed.), *Handbook of Research on Leveraging Risk and Uncertainties for Effective Project Management* (pp. 337–362). Hershey, PA: IGI Global. doi:10.4018/978-1-5225-1790-0.ch016

Hass, K. B. (2017). Living on the Edge: Managing Project Complexity. In Y. Raydugin (Ed.), *Handbook of Research on Leveraging Risk and Uncertainties for Effective Project Management* (pp. 177–201). Hershey, PA: IGI Global. doi:10.4018/978-1-5225-1790-0.ch009

Hawking, P., & Carmine Sellitto, C. (2017). Developing an Effective Strategy for Organizational Business Intelligence. In M. Tavana (Ed.), *Enterprise Information Systems and the Digitalization of Business Functions* (pp. 222–237). Hershey, PA: IGI Global. doi:10.4018/978-1-5225-2382-6.ch010

Hawking, P., & Sellitto, C. (2017). A Fast-Moving Consumer Goods Company and Business Intelligence Strategy Development. *International Journal of Enterprise Information Systems*, *13*(2), 22–33. doi:10.4018/IJEIS.2017040102

Hawking, P., & Sellitto, C. (2017). Business Intelligence Strategy: Two Case Studies. *International Journal of Business Intelligence Research*, *8*(2), 17–30. doi:10.4018/IJBIR.2017070102

Hee, W. J., Jalleh, G., Lai, H., & Lin, C. (2017). E-Commerce and IT Projects: Evaluation and Management Issues in Australian and Taiwanese Hospitals. *International Journal of Public Health Management and Ethics*, *2*(1), 69–90. doi:10.4018/IJPHME.2017010104

Hernandez, A. A. (2018). Exploring the Factors to Green IT Adoption of SMEs in the Philippines. *Journal of Cases on Information Technology*, *20*(2), 49–66. doi:10.4018/JCIT.2018040104

Hollman, A., Bickford, S., & Hollman, T. (2017). Cyber InSecurity: A Post-Mortem Attempt to Assess Cyber Problems from IT and Business Management Perspectives. *Journal of Cases on Information Technology*, *19*(3), 42–70. doi:10.4018/JCIT.2017070104

Ibrahim, F., & Zainin, N. M. (2021). Exploring the Technological Impacts: The Case of Museums in Brunei Darussalam. *International Journal of Tourism and Hospitality Management in the Digital Age*, *5*(1), 1–18. https://doi.org/10.4018/IJTHMDA.2021010101

Igbinakhase, I. (2017). Responsible and Sustainable Management Practices in Developing and Developed Business Environments. In Z. Fields (Ed.), *Collective Creativity for Responsible and Sustainable Business Practice* (pp. 180–207). Hershey, PA: IGI Global. doi:10.4018/978-1-5225-1823-5.ch010

Iwata, J. J., & Hoskins, R. G. (2017). Managing Indigenous Knowledge in Tanzania: A Business Perspective. In P. Jain & N. Mnjama (Eds.), *Managing Knowledge Resources and Records in Modern Organizations* (pp. 198–214). Hershey, PA: IGI Global. doi:10.4018/978-1-5225-1965-2.ch012

Jain, P. (2017). Ethical and Legal Issues in Knowledge Management Life-Cycle in Business. In P. Jain & N. Mnjama (Eds.), *Managing Knowledge Resources and Records in Modern Organizations* (pp. 82–101). Hershey, PA: IGI Global. doi:10.4018/978-1-5225-1965-2.ch006

James, S., & Hauli, E. (2017). Holistic Management Education at Tanzanian Rural Development Planning Institute. In N. Baporikar (Ed.), *Management Education for Global Leadership* (pp. 112–136). Hershey, PA: IGI Global. doi:10.4018/978-1-5225-1013-0.ch006

Janošková, M., Csikósová, A., & Čulková, K. (2018). Measurement of Company Performance as Part of Its Strategic Management. In R. Leon (Ed.), *Managerial Strategies for Business Sustainability During Turbulent Times* (pp. 309–335). Hershey, PA: IGI Global. doi:10.4018/978-1-5225-2716-9.ch017

Jean-Vasile, A., & Alecu, A. (2017). Theoretical and Practical Approaches in Understanding the Influences of Cost-Productivity-Profit Trinomial in Contemporary Enterprises. In A. Jean Vasile & D. Nicolò (Eds.), *Sustainable Entrepreneurship and Investments in the Green Economy* (pp. 28–62). Hershey, PA: IGI Global. doi:10.4018/978-1-5225-2075-7.ch002

Joia, L. A., & Correia, J. C. (2018). CIO Competencies From the IT Professional Perspective: Insights From Brazil. *Journal of Global Information Management*, *26*(2), 74–103. doi:10.4018/JGIM.2018040104

Juma, A., & Mzera, N. (2017). Knowledge Management and Records Management and Competitive Advantage in Business. In P. Jain & N. Mnjama (Eds.), *Managing Knowledge Resources and Records in Modern Organizations* (pp. 15–28). Hershey, PA: IGI Global. doi:10.4018/978-1-5225-1965-2.ch002

K., I., & A, V. (2018). Monitoring and Auditing in the Cloud. In K. Munir (Ed.), *Cloud Computing Technologies for Green Enterprises* (pp. 318-350). Hershey, PA: IGI Global. https://doi.org/ doi:10.4018/978-1-5225-3038-1.ch013

Kabra, G., Ghosh, V., & Ramesh, A. (2018). Enterprise Integrated Business Process Management and Business Intelligence Framework for Business Process Sustainability. In A. Paul, D. Bhattacharyya, & S. Anand (Eds.), *Green Initiatives for Business Sustainability and Value Creation* (pp. 228–238). Hershey, PA: IGI Global. doi:10.4018/978-1-5225-2662-9.ch010

Kaoud, M. (2017). Investigation of Customer Knowledge Management: A Case Study Research. *International Journal of Service Science, Management, Engineering, and Technology*, *8*(2), 12–22. doi:10.4018/IJSSMET.2017040102

Katuu, S. (2018). A Comparative Assessment of Enterprise Content Management Maturity Models. In N. Gwangwava & M. Mutingi (Eds.), *E-Manufacturing and E-Service Strategies in Contemporary Organizations* (pp. 93–118). Hershey, PA: IGI Global. doi:10.4018/978-1-5225-3628-4.ch005

Khan, M. Y., & Abir, T. (2022). The Role of Social Media Marketing in the Tourism and Hospitality Industry: A Conceptual Study on Bangladesh. In C. Ramos, S. Quinteiro, & A. Gonçalves (Eds.), *ICT as Innovator Between Tourism and Culture* (pp. 213–229). IGI Global. https://doi.org/10.4018/978-1-7998-8165-0.ch013

Kinnunen, S., Ylä-Kujala, A., Marttonen-Arola, S., Kärri, T., & Baglee, D. (2018). Internet of Things in Asset Management: Insights from Industrial Professionals and Academia. *International Journal of Service Science, Management, Engineering, and Technology*, *9*(2), 104–119. doi:10.4018/IJSSMET.2018040105

Klein, A. Z., Sabino de Freitas, A., Machado, L., Freitas, J. C. Jr, Graziola, P. G. Jr, & Schlemmer, E. (2017). Virtual Worlds Applications for Management Education. In L. Tomei (Ed.), *Exploring the New Era of Technology-Infused Education* (pp. 279–299). Hershey, PA: IGI Global. doi:10.4018/978-1-5225-1709-2.ch017

Kővári, E., Saleh, M., & Steinbachné Hajmásy, G. (2022). The Impact of Corporate Digital Responsibility (CDR) on Internal Stakeholders' Satisfaction in Hungarian Upscale Hotels. In M. Valeri (Ed.), *New Governance and Management in Touristic Destinations* (pp. 35–51). IGI Global. https://doi.org/10.4018/978-1-6684-3889-3.ch003

Kożuch, B., & Jabłoński, A. (2017). Adopting the Concept of Business Models in Public Management. In M. Lewandowski & B. Kożuch (Eds.), *Public Sector Entrepreneurship and the Integration of Innovative Business Models* (pp. 10–46). Hershey, PA: IGI Global. doi:10.4018/978-1-5225-2215-7.ch002

Kumar, J., Adhikary, A., & Jha, A. (2017). Small Active Investors' Perceptions and Preferences Towards Tax Saving Mutual Fund Schemes in Eastern India: An Empirical Note. *International Journal of Asian Business and Information Management*, *8*(2), 35–45. doi:10.4018/IJABIM.2017040103

Latusi, S., & Fissore, M. (2021). Pilgrimage Routes to Happiness: Comparing the Camino de Santiago and Via Francigena. In A. Perinotto, V. Mayer, & J. Soares (Eds.), *Rebuilding and Restructuring the Tourism Industry: Infusion of Happiness and Quality of Life* (pp. 157–182). IGI Global. https://doi.org/10.4018/978-1-7998-7239-9.ch008

Lavassani, K. M., & Movahedi, B. (2017). Applications Driven Information Systems: Beyond Networks toward Business Ecosystems. *International Journal of Innovation in the Digital Economy*, *8*(1), 61–75. doi:10.4018/IJIDE.2017010104

Lazzareschi, V. H., & Brito, M. S. (2017). Strategic Information Management: Proposal of Business Project Model. In G. Jamil, A. Soares, & C. Pessoa (Eds.), *Handbook of Research on Information Management for Effective Logistics and Supply Chains* (pp. 59–88). Hershey, PA: IGI Global. doi:10.4018/978-1-5225-0973-8.ch004

Lechuga Sancho, M. P., & Martín Navarro, A. (2022). Evolution of the Literature on Social Responsibility in the Tourism Sector: A Systematic Literature Review. In G. Fernandes (Ed.), *Challenges and New Opportunities for Tourism in Inland Territories: Ecocultural Resources and Sustainable Initiatives* (pp. 169–186). IGI Global. https://doi.org/10.4018/978-1-7998-7339-6.ch010

Lederer, M., Kurz, M., & Lazarov, P. (2017). Usage and Suitability of Methods for Strategic Business Process Initiatives: A Multi Case Study Research. *International Journal of Productivity Management and Assessment Technologies*, *5*(1), 40–51. doi:10.4018/IJPMAT.2017010103

Lee, I. (2017). A Social Enterprise Business Model and a Case Study of Pacific Community Ventures (PCV). In V. Potocan, M. Ünğan, & Z. Nedelko (Eds.), *Handbook of Research on Managerial Solutions in Non-Profit Organizations* (pp. 182–204). Hershey, PA: IGI Global. doi:10.4018/978-1-5225-0731-4.ch009

Leon, L. A., Seal, K. C., Przasnyski, Z. H., & Wiedenman, I. (2017). Skills and Competencies Required for Jobs in Business Analytics: A Content Analysis of Job Advertisements Using Text Mining. *International Journal of Business Intelligence Research, 8*(1), 1–25. doi:10.4018/IJBIR.2017010101

Levy, C. L., & Elias, N. I. (2017). SOHO Users' Perceptions of Reliability and Continuity of Cloud-Based Services. In M. Moore (Ed.), *Cybersecurity Breaches and Issues Surrounding Online Threat Protection* (pp. 248–287). Hershey, PA: IGI Global. doi:10.4018/978-1-5225-1941-6.ch011

Levy, M. (2018). Change Management Serving Knowledge Management and Organizational Development: Reflections and Review. In N. Baporikar (Ed.), *Global Practices in Knowledge Management for Societal and Organizational Development* (pp. 256–270). Hershey, PA: IGI Global. doi:10.4018/978-1-5225-3009-1.ch012

Lewandowski, M. (2017). Public Organizations and Business Model Innovation: The Role of Public Service Design. In M. Lewandowski & B. Kożuch (Eds.), *Public Sector Entrepreneurship and the Integration of Innovative Business Models* (pp. 47–72). Hershey, PA: IGI Global. doi:10.4018/978-1-5225-2215-7.ch003

Lhannaoui, H., Kabbaj, M. I., & Bakkoury, Z. (2017). A Survey of Risk-Aware Business Process Modelling. *International Journal of Risk and Contingency Management, 6*(3), 14–26. doi:10.4018/IJRCM.2017070102

Li, J., Sun, W., Jiang, W., Yang, H., & Zhang, L. (2017). How the Nature of Exogenous Shocks and Crises Impact Company Performance?: The Effects of Industry Characteristics. *International Journal of Risk and Contingency Management, 6*(4), 40–55. doi:10.4018/IJRCM.2017100103

Lopez-Fernandez, M., Perez-Perez, M., Serrano-Bedia, A., & Cobo-Gonzalez, A. (2021). Small and Medium Tourism Enterprise Survival in Times of Crisis: "El Capricho de Gaudí. In D. Toubes & N. Araújo-Vila (Eds.), *Risk, Crisis, and Disaster Management in Small and Medium-Sized Tourism Enterprises* (pp. 103–129). IGI Global. doi:10.4018/978-1-7998-6996-2.ch005

Mahajan, A., Maidullah, S., & Hossain, M. R. (2022). Experience Toward Smart Tour Guide Apps in Travelling: An Analysis of Users' Reviews on Audio Odigos and Trip My Way. In R. Augusto Costa, F. Brandão, Z. Breda, & C. Costa (Eds.), *Planning and Managing the Experience Economy in Tourism* (pp. 255-273). IGI Global. https://doi.org/10.4018/978-1-7998-8775-1.ch014

Malega, P. (2017). Small and Medium Enterprises in the Slovak Republic: Status and Competitiveness of SMEs in the Global Markets and Possibilities of Optimization. In M. Vemić (Ed.), *Optimal Management Strategies in Small and Medium Enterprises* (pp. 102–124). Hershey, PA: IGI Global. doi:10.4018/978-1-5225-1949-2.ch006

Malewska, K. M. (2017). Intuition in Decision-Making on the Example of a Non-Profit Organization. In V. Potocan, M. Üngan, & Z. Nedelko (Eds.), *Handbook of Research on Managerial Solutions in Non-Profit Organizations* (pp. 378–399). Hershey, PA: IGI Global. doi:10.4018/978-1-5225-0731-4.ch018

Maroofi, F. (2017). Entrepreneurial Orientation and Organizational Learning Ability Analysis for Innovation and Firm Performance. In N. Baporikar (Ed.), *Innovation and Shifting Perspectives in Management Education* (pp. 144–165). Hershey, PA: IGI Global. doi:10.4018/978-1-5225-1019-2.ch007

Marques, M., Moleiro, D., Brito, T. M., & Marques, T. (2021). Customer Relationship Management as an Important Relationship Marketing Tool: The Case of the Hospitality Industry in Estoril Coast. In M. Dinis, L. Bonixe, S. Lamy, & Z. Breda (Eds.), Impact of New Media in Tourism (pp. 39-56). IGI Global. https://doi.org/doi:10.4018/978-1-7998-7095-1.ch003

Martins, P. V., & Zacarias, M. (2017). A Web-based Tool for Business Process Improvement. *International Journal of Web Portals*, *9*(2), 68–84. doi:10.4018/IJWP.2017070104

Matthies, B., & Coners, A. (2017). Exploring the Conceptual Nature of e-Business Projects. *Journal of Electronic Commerce in Organizations*, *15*(3), 33–63. doi:10.4018/JECO.2017070103

Mayer, V. F., Fraga, C. C., & Silva, L. C. (2021). Contributions of Neurosciences to Studies of Well-Being in Tourism. In A. Perinotto, V. Mayer, & J. Soares (Eds.), *Rebuilding and Restructuring the Tourism Industry: Infusion of Happiness and Quality of Life* (pp. 108–128). IGI Global. https://doi.org/10.4018/978-1-7998-7239-9.ch006

McKee, J. (2018). Architecture as a Tool to Solve Business Planning Problems. In M. Khosrow-Pour, D.B.A. (Ed.), Encyclopedia of Information Science and Technology, Fourth Edition (pp. 573-586). Hershey, PA: IGI Global. doi:10.4018/978-1-5225-2255-3.ch050

McMurray, A. J., Cross, J., & Caponecchia, C. (2018). The Risk Management Profession in Australia: Business Continuity Plan Practices. In N. Bajgoric (Ed.), *Always-On Enterprise Information Systems for Modern Organizations* (pp. 112–129). Hershey, PA: IGI Global. doi:10.4018/978-1-5225-3704-5.ch006

Meddah, I. H., & Belkadi, K. (2018). Mining Patterns Using Business Process Management. In R. Hamou (Ed.), *Handbook of Research on Biomimicry in Information Retrieval and Knowledge Management* (pp. 78–89). Hershey, PA: IGI Global. doi:10.4018/978-1-5225-3004-6.ch005

Melian, A. G., & Camprubí, R. (2021). The Accessibility of Museum Websites: The Case of Barcelona. In C. Eusébio, L. Teixeira, & M. Carneiro (Eds.), *ICT Tools and Applications for Accessible Tourism* (pp. 234–255). IGI Global. https://doi.org/10.4018/978-1-7998-6428-8.ch011

Mendes, L. (2017). TQM and Knowledge Management: An Integrated Approach Towards Tacit Knowledge Management. In D. Jaziri-Bouagina & G. Jamil (Eds.), *Handbook of Research on Tacit Knowledge Management for Organizational Success* (pp. 236–263). Hershey, PA: IGI Global. doi:10.4018/978-1-5225-2394-9.ch009

Menezes, V. D., & Cavagnaro, E. (2021). Communicating Sustainable Initiatives in the Hotel Industry: The Case of the Hotel Jakarta Amsterdam. In F. Brandão, Z. Breda, R. Costa, & C. Costa (Eds.), *Handbook of Research on the Role of Tourism in Achieving Sustainable Development Goals* (pp. 224-234). IGI Global. https://doi.org/10.4018/978-1-7998-5691-7.ch013

Menezes, V. D., & Cavagnaro, E. (2021). Communicating Sustainable Initiatives in the Hotel Industry: The Case of the Hotel Jakarta Amsterdam. In F. Brandão, Z. Breda, R. Costa, & C. Costa (Eds.), *Handbook of Research on the Role of Tourism in Achieving Sustainable Development Goals* (pp. 224-234). IGI Global. https://doi.org/10.4018/978-1-7998-5691-7.ch013

Mitas, O., Bastiaansen, M., & Boode, W. (2022). If You're Happy, I'm Happy: Emotion Contagion at a Tourist Information Center. In R. Augusto Costa, F. Brandão, Z. Breda, & C. Costa (Eds.), *Planning and Managing the Experience Economy in Tourism* (pp. 122-140). IGI Global. https://doi.org/10.4018/978-1-7998-8775-1.ch007

Mnjama, N. M. (2017). Preservation of Recorded Information in Public and Private Sector Organizations. In P. Jain & N. Mnjama (Eds.), *Managing Knowledge Resources and Records in Modern Organizations* (pp. 149–167). Hershey, PA: IGI Global. doi:10.4018/978-1-5225-1965-2.ch009

Mokoqama, M., & Fields, Z. (2017). Principles of Responsible Management Education (PRME): Call for Responsible Management Education. In Z. Fields (Ed.), *Collective Creativity for Responsible and Sustainable Business Practice* (pp. 229–241). Hershey, PA: IGI Global. doi:10.4018/978-1-5225-1823-5.ch012

Monteiro, A., Lopes, S., & Carbone, F. (2021). Academic Mobility: Bridging Tourism and Peace Education. In J. da Silva, Z. Breda, & F. Carbone (Eds.), *Role and Impact of Tourism in Peacebuilding and Conflict Transformation* (pp. 275-301). IGI Global. https://doi.org/10.4018/978-1-7998-5053-3.ch016

Muniapan, B. (2017). Philosophy and Management: The Relevance of Vedanta in Management. In P. Ordóñez de Pablos (Ed.), *Managerial Strategies and Solutions for Business Success in Asia* (pp. 124–139). Hershey, PA: IGI Global. doi:10.4018/978-1-5225-1886-0.ch007

Murad, S. E., & Dowaji, S. (2017). Using Value-Based Approach for Managing Cloud-Based Services. In A. Turuk, B. Sahoo, & S. Addya (Eds.), *Resource Management and Efficiency in Cloud Computing Environments* (pp. 33–60). Hershey, PA: IGI Global. doi:10.4018/978-1-5225-1721-4.ch002

Mutahar, A. M., Daud, N. M., Thurasamy, R., Isaac, O., & Abdulsalam, R. (2018). The Mediating of Perceived Usefulness and Perceived Ease of Use: The Case of Mobile Banking in Yemen. *International Journal of Technology Diffusion*, *9*(2), 21–40. doi:10.4018/IJTD.2018040102

Naidoo, V. (2017). E-Learning and Management Education at African Universities. In N. Baporikar (Ed.), *Management Education for Global Leadership* (pp. 181–201). Hershey, PA: IGI Global. doi:10.4018/978-1-5225-1013-0.ch009

Naidoo, V., & Igbinakhase, I. (2018). Opportunities and Challenges of Knowledge Retention in SMEs. In N. Baporikar (Ed.), *Knowledge Integration Strategies for Entrepreneurship and Sustainability* (pp. 70–94). Hershey, PA: IGI Global. doi:10.4018/978-1-5225-5115-7.ch004

Naumov, N., & Costandachi, G. (2021). Creativity and Entrepreneurship: Gastronomic Tourism in Mexico. In J. Soares (Ed.), *Innovation and Entrepreneurial Opportunities in Community Tourism* (pp. 90–108). IGI Global. https://doi.org/10.4018/978-1-7998-4855-4.ch006

Nayak, S., & Prabhu, N. (2017). Paradigm Shift in Management Education: Need for a Cross Functional Perspective. In N. Baporikar (Ed.), *Management Education for Global Leadership* (pp. 241–255). Hershey, PA: IGI Global. doi:10.4018/978-1-5225-1013-0.ch012

Nedelko, Z., & Potocan, V. (2017). Management Solutions in Non-Profit Organizations: Case of Slovenia. In V. Potocan, M. Ünğan, & Z. Nedelko (Eds.), *Handbook of Research on Managerial Solutions in Non-Profit Organizations* (pp. 1–22). Hershey, PA: IGI Global. doi:10.4018/978-1-5225-0731-4.ch001

Nedelko, Z., & Potocan, V. (2017). Priority of Management Tools Utilization among Managers: International Comparison. In V. Wang (Ed.), *Encyclopedia of Strategic Leadership and Management* (pp. 1083–1094). Hershey, PA: IGI Global. doi:10.4018/978-1-5225-1049-9.ch075

Nedelko, Z., Raudeliūnienė, J., & Črešnar, R. (2018). Knowledge Dynamics in Supply Chain Management. In N. Baporikar (Ed.), *Knowledge Integration Strategies for Entrepreneurship and Sustainability* (pp. 150–166). Hershey, PA: IGI Global. doi:10.4018/978-1-5225-5115-7.ch008

Nguyen, H. T., & Hipsher, S. A. (2018). Innovation and Creativity Used by Private Sector Firms in a Resources-Constrained Environment. In S. Hipsher (Ed.), *Examining the Private Sector's Role in Wealth Creation and Poverty Reduction* (pp. 219–238). Hershey, PA: IGI Global. doi:10.4018/978-1-5225-3117-3.ch010

Obicci, P. A. (2017). Risk Sharing in a Partnership. In *Risk Management Strategies in Public-Private Partnerships* (pp. 115–152). Hershey, PA: IGI Global. doi:10.4018/978-1-5225-2503-5.ch004

Obidallah, W. J., & Raahemi, B. (2017). Managing Changes in Service Oriented Virtual Organizations: A Structural and Procedural Framework to Facilitate the Process of Change. *Journal of Electronic Commerce in Organizations*, *15*(1), 59–83. doi:10.4018/JECO.2017010104

Ojo, O. (2017). Impact of Innovation on the Entrepreneurial Success in Selected Business Enterprises in South-West Nigeria. *International Journal of Innovation in the Digital Economy*, *8*(2), 29–38. doi:10.4018/IJIDE.2017040103

Okdinawati, L., Simatupang, T. M., & Sunitiyoso, Y. (2017). Multi-Agent Reinforcement Learning for Value Co-Creation of Collaborative Transportation Management (CTM). *International Journal of Information Systems and Supply Chain Management*, *10*(3), 84–95. doi:10.4018/IJISSCM.2017070105

Olivera, V. A., & Carrillo, I. M. (2021). Organizational Culture: A Key Element for the Development of Mexican Micro and Small Tourist Companies. In J. Soares (Ed.), *Innovation and Entrepreneurial Opportunities in Community Tourism* (pp. 227–242). IGI Global. doi:10.4018/978-1-7998-4855-4.ch013

Ossorio, M. (2022). Corporate Museum Experiences in Enogastronomic Tourism. In R. Augusto Costa, F. Brandão, Z. Breda, & C. Costa (Eds.), Planning and Managing the Experience Economy in Tourism (pp. 107-121). IGI Global. https://doi.org/doi:10.4018/978-1-7998-8775-1.ch006

Ossorio, M. (2022). Enogastronomic Tourism in Times of Pandemic. In G. Fernandes (Ed.), *Challenges and New Opportunities for Tourism in Inland Territories: Ecocultural Resources and Sustainable Initiatives* (pp. 241–255). IGI Global. https://doi.org/10.4018/978-1-7998-7339-6.ch014

Özekici, Y. K. (2022). ICT as an Acculturative Agent and Its Role in the Tourism Context: Introduction, Acculturation Theory, Progress of the Acculturation Theory in Extant Literature. In C. Ramos, S. Quinteiro, & A. Gonçalves (Eds.), *ICT as Innovator Between Tourism and Culture* (pp. 42–66). IGI Global. https://doi.org/10.4018/978-1-7998-8165-0.ch004

Pal, K. (2018). Building High Quality Big Data-Based Applications in Supply Chains. In A. Kumar & S. Saurav (Eds.), *Supply Chain Management Strategies and Risk Assessment in Retail Environments* (pp. 1–24). Hershey, PA: IGI Global. doi:10.4018/978-1-5225-3056-5.ch001

Palos-Sanchez, P. R., & Correia, M. B. (2018). Perspectives of the Adoption of Cloud Computing in the Tourism Sector. In J. Rodrigues, C. Ramos, P. Cardoso, & C. Henriques (Eds.), *Handbook of Research on Technological Developments for Cultural Heritage and eTourism Applications* (pp. 377–400). Hershey, PA: IGI Global. doi:10.4018/978-1-5225-2927-9.ch018

Papadopoulou, G. (2021). Promoting Gender Equality and Women Empowerment in the Tourism Sector. In F. Brandão, Z. Breda, R. Costa, & C. Costa (Eds.), Handbook of Research on the Role of Tourism in Achieving Sustainable Development Goals (pp. 152-174). IGI Global. https://doi.org/ doi:10.4018/978-1-7998-5691-7.ch009

Papp-Váry, Á. F., & Tóth, T. Z. (2022). Analysis of Budapest as a Film Tourism Destination. In R. Baleiro & R. Pereira (Eds.), *Global Perspectives on Literary Tourism and Film-Induced Tourism* (pp. 257-279). IGI Global. https://doi.org/10.4018/978-1-7998-8262-6.ch014

Patiño, B. E. (2017). New Generation Management by Convergence and Individual Identity: A Systemic and Human-Oriented Approach. In N. Baporikar (Ed.), *Innovation and Shifting Perspectives in Management Education* (pp. 119–143). Hershey, PA: IGI Global. doi:10.4018/978-1-5225-1019-2.ch006

Patro, C. S. (2021). Digital Tourism: Influence of E-Marketing Technology. In M. Dinis, L. Bonixe, S. Lamy, & Z. Breda (Eds.), *Impact of New Media in Tourism* (pp. 234-254). IGI Global. https://doi.org/10.4018/978-1-7998-7095-1.ch014

Pawliczek, A., & Rössler, M. (2017). Knowledge of Management Tools and Systems in SMEs: Knowledge Transfer in Management. In A. Bencsik (Ed.), *Knowledge Management Initiatives and Strategies in Small and Medium Enterprises* (pp. 180–203). Hershey, PA: IGI Global. doi:10.4018/978-1-5225-1642-2.ch009

Pejic-Bach, M., Omazic, M. A., Aleksic, A., & Zoroja, J. (2018). Knowledge-Based Decision Making: A Multi-Case Analysis. In R. Leon (Ed.), *Managerial Strategies for Business Sustainability During Turbulent Times* (pp. 160–184). Hershey, PA: IGI Global. doi:10.4018/978-1-5225-2716-9.ch009

Perano, M., Hysa, X., & Calabrese, M. (2018). Strategic Planning, Cultural Context, and Business Continuity Management: Business Cases in the City of Shkoder. In A. Presenza & L. Sheehan (Eds.), *Geopolitics and Strategic Management in the Global Economy* (pp. 57–77). Hershey, PA: IGI Global. doi:10.4018/978-1-5225-2673-5.ch004

Pereira, R., Mira da Silva, M., & Lapão, L. V. (2017). IT Governance Maturity Patterns in Portuguese Healthcare. In S. De Haes & W. Van Grembergen (Eds.), *Strategic IT Governance and Alignment in Business Settings* (pp. 24–52). Hershey, PA: IGI Global. doi:10.4018/978-1-5225-0861-8.ch002

Pérez-Uribe, R. I., Torres, D. A., Jurado, S. P., & Prada, D. M. (2018). Cloud Tools for the Development of Project Management in SMEs. In R. Perez-Uribe, C. Salcedo-Perez, & D. Ocampo-Guzman (Eds.), *Handbook of Research on Intrapreneurship and Organizational Sustainability in SMEs* (pp. 95–120). Hershey, PA: IGI Global. doi:10.4018/978-1-5225-3543-0.ch005

Petrisor, I., & Cozmiuc, D. (2017). Global Supply Chain Management Organization at Siemens in the Advent of Industry 4.0. In L. Saglietto & C. Cezanne (Eds.), *Global Intermediation and Logistics Service Providers* (pp. 123–142). Hershey, PA: IGI Global. doi:10.4018/978-1-5225-2133-4.ch007

Pierce, J. M., Velliaris, D. M., & Edwards, J. (2017). A Living Case Study: A Journey Not a Destination. In N. Silton (Ed.), *Exploring the Benefits of Creativity in Education, Media, and the Arts* (pp. 158–178). Hershey, PA: IGI Global. doi:10.4018/978-1-5225-0504-4.ch008

Pipia, S., & Pipia, S. (2021). Challenges of Religious Tourism in the Conflict Region: An Example of Jerusalem. In E. Alaverdov & M. Bari (Eds.), *Global Development of Religious Tourism* (pp. 135-148). IGI Global. https://doi.org/10.4018/978-1-7998-5792-1.ch009

Poulaki, P., Kritikos, A., Vasilakis, N., & Valeri, M. (2022). The Contribution of Female Creativity to the Development of Gastronomic Tourism in Greece: The Case of the Island of Naxos in the South Aegean Region. In M. Valeri (Ed.), *New Governance and Management in Touristic Destinations* (pp. 246–258). IGI Global. https://doi.org/10.4018/978-1-6684-3889-3.ch015

Radosavljevic, M., & Andjelkovic, A. (2017). Multi-Criteria Decision Making Approach for Choosing Business Process for the Improvement: Upgrading of the Six Sigma Methodology. In J. Stanković, P. Delias, S. Marinković, & S. Rochhia (Eds.), *Tools and Techniques for Economic Decision Analysis* (pp. 225–247). Hershey, PA: IGI Global. doi:10.4018/978-1-5225-0959-2.ch011

Radovic, V. M. (2017). Corporate Sustainability and Responsibility and Disaster Risk Reduction: A Serbian Overview. In M. Camilleri (Ed.), *CSR 2.0 and the New Era of Corporate Citizenship* (pp. 147–164). Hershey, PA: IGI Global. doi:10.4018/978-1-5225-1842-6.ch008

Raghunath, K. M., Devi, S. L., & Patro, C. S. (2018). Impact of Risk Assessment Models on Risk Factors: A Holistic Outlook. In K. Strang, M. Korstanje, & N. Vajjhala (Eds.), *Research, Practices, and Innovations in Global Risk and Contingency Management* (pp. 134–153). Hershey, PA: IGI Global. doi:10.4018/978-1-5225-4754-9.ch008

Raman, A., & Goyal, D. P. (2017). Extending IMPLEMENT Framework for Enterprise Information Systems Implementation to Information System Innovation. In M. Tavana (Ed.), *Enterprise Information Systems and the Digitalization of Business Functions* (pp. 137–177). Hershey, PA: IGI Global. doi:10.4018/978-1-5225-2382-6.ch007

Rao, Y., & Zhang, Y. (2017). The Construction and Development of Academic Library Digital Special Subject Databases. In L. Ruan, Q. Zhu, & Y. Ye (Eds.), *Academic Library Development and Administration in China* (pp. 163–183). Hershey, PA: IGI Global. doi:10.4018/978-1-5225-0550-1.ch010

Ravasan, A. Z., Mohammadi, M. M., & Hamidi, H. (2018). An Investigation Into the Critical Success Factors of Implementing Information Technology Service Management Frameworks. In K. Jakobs (Ed.), *Corporate and Global Standardization Initiatives in Contemporary Society* (pp. 200–218). Hershey, PA: IGI Global. doi:10.4018/978-1-5225-5320-5.ch009

Rezaie, S., Mirabedini, S. J., & Abtahi, A. (2018). Designing a Model for Implementation of Business Intelligence in the Banking Industry. *International Journal of Enterprise Information Systems*, *14*(1), 77–103. doi:10.4018/IJEIS.2018010105

Richards, V., Matthews, N., Williams, O. J., & Khan, Z. (2021). The Challenges of Accessible Tourism Information Systems for Tourists With Vision Impairment: Sensory Communications Beyond the Screen. In C. Eusébio, L. Teixeira, & M. Carneiro (Eds.), *ICT Tools and Applications for Accessible Tourism* (pp. 26–54). IGI Global. https://doi.org/10.4018/978-1-7998-6428-8.ch002

Rodrigues de Souza Neto, V., & Marques, O. (2021). Rural Tourism Fostering Welfare Through Sustainable Development: A Conceptual Approach. In A. Perinotto, V. Mayer, & J. Soares (Eds.), *Rebuilding and Restructuring the Tourism Industry: Infusion of Happiness and Quality of Life* (pp. 38–57). IGI Global. https://doi.org/10.4018/978-1-7998-7239-9.ch003

Romano, L., Grimaldi, R., & Colasuonno, F. S. (2017). Demand Management as a Success Factor in Project Portfolio Management. In L. Romano (Ed.), *Project Portfolio Management Strategies for Effective Organizational Operations* (pp. 202–219). Hershey, PA: IGI Global. doi:10.4018/978-1-5225-2151-8.ch008

Rubio-Escuderos, L., & García-Andreu, H. (2021). Competitiveness Factors of Accessible Tourism E-Travel Agencies. In C. Eusébio, L. Teixeira, & M. Carneiro (Eds.), *ICT Tools and Applications for Accessible Tourism* (pp. 196–217). IGI Global. https://doi.org/10.4018/978-1-7998-6428-8.ch009

Rucci, A. C., Porto, N., Darcy, S., & Becka, L. (2021). Smart and Accessible Cities?: Not Always – The Case for Accessible Tourism Initiatives in Buenos Aries and Sydney. In C. Eusébio, L. Teixeira, & M. Carneiro (Eds.), *ICT Tools and Applications for Accessible Tourism* (pp. 115–145). IGI Global. https://doi.org/10.4018/978-1-7998-6428-8.ch006

Ruhi, U. (2018). Towards an Interdisciplinary Socio-Technical Definition of Virtual Communities. In M. Khosrow-Pour, D.B.A. (Ed.), Encyclopedia of Information Science and Technology, Fourth Edition (pp. 4278-4295). Hershey, PA: IGI Global. doi:10.4018/978-1-5225-2255-3.ch371

Ryan, L., Catena, M., Ros, P., & Stephens, S. (2021). Designing Entrepreneurial Ecosystems to Support Resource Management in the Tourism Industry. In V. Costa, A. Moura, & M. Mira (Eds.), *Handbook of Research on Human Capital and People Management in the Tourism Industry* (pp. 265–281). IGI Global. https://doi.org/10.4018/978-1-7998-4318-4.ch013

Sabuncu, I. (2021). Understanding Tourist Perceptions and Expectations During Pandemic Through Social Media Big Data. In M. Demir, A. Dalgıç, & F. Ergen (Eds.), *Handbook of Research on the Impacts and Implications of COVID-19 on the Tourism Industry* (pp. 330–350). IGI Global. https://doi.org/10.4018/978-1-7998-8231-2.ch016

Safari, M. R., & Jiang, Q. (2018). The Theory and Practice of IT Governance Maturity and Strategies Alignment: Evidence From Banking Industry. *Journal of Global Information Management*, *26*(2), 127–146. doi:10.4018/JGIM.2018040106

Sahoo, J., Pati, B., & Mohanty, B. (2017). Knowledge Management as an Academic Discipline: An Assessment. In B. Gunjal (Ed.), *Managing Knowledge and Scholarly Assets in Academic Libraries* (pp. 99–126). Hershey, PA: IGI Global. doi:10.4018/978-1-5225-1741-2.ch005

Saini, D. (2017). Relevance of Teaching Values and Ethics in Management Education. In N. Baporikar (Ed.), *Management Education for Global Leadership* (pp. 90–111). Hershey, PA: IGI Global. doi:10.4018/978-1-5225-1013-0.ch005

Sambhanthan, A. (2017). Assessing and Benchmarking Sustainability in Organisations: An Integrated Conceptual Model. *International Journal of Systems and Service-Oriented Engineering*, *7*(4), 22–43. doi:10.4018/IJSSOE.2017100102

Sambhanthan, A., & Potdar, V. (2017). A Study of the Parameters Impacting Sustainability in Information Technology Organizations. *International Journal of Knowledge-Based Organizations*, *7*(3), 27–39. doi:10.4018/IJKBO.2017070103

Sánchez-Fernández, M. D., & Manríquez, M. R. (2018). The Entrepreneurial Spirit Based on Social Values: The Digital Generation. In P. Isaias & L. Carvalho (Eds.), *User Innovation and the Entrepreneurship Phenomenon in the Digital Economy* (pp. 173–193). Hershey, PA: IGI Global. doi:10.4018/978-1-5225-2826-5.ch009

Sanchez-Ruiz, L., & Blanco, B. (2017). Process Management for SMEs: Barriers, Enablers, and Benefits. In M. Vemić (Ed.), *Optimal Management Strategies in Small and Medium Enterprises* (pp. 293–319). Hershey, PA: IGI Global. doi:10.4018/978-1-5225-1949-2.ch014

Sanz, L. F., Gómez-Pérez, J., & Castillo-Martinez, A. (2018). Analysis of the European ICT Competence Frameworks. In V. Ahuja & S. Rathore (Eds.), *Multidisciplinary Perspectives on Human Capital and Information Technology Professionals* (pp. 225–245). Hershey, PA: IGI Global. doi:10.4018/978-1-5225-5297-0.ch012

Sarvepalli, A., & Godin, J. (2017). Business Process Management in the Classroom. *Journal of Cases on Information Technology*, *19*(2), 17–28. doi:10.4018/JCIT.2017040102

Saxena, G. G., & Saxena, A. (2021). Host Community Role in Medical Tourism Development. In M. Singh & S. Kumaran (Eds.), *Growth of the Medical Tourism Industry and Its Impact on Society: Emerging Research and Opportunities* (pp. 105–127). IGI Global. https://doi.org/10.4018/978-1-7998-3427-4.ch006

Saygili, E. E., Ozturkoglu, Y., & Kocakulah, M. C. (2017). End Users' Perceptions of Critical Success Factors in ERP Applications. *International Journal of Enterprise Information Systems, 13*(4), 58–75. doi:10.4018/IJEIS.2017100104

Saygili, E. E., & Saygili, A. T. (2017). Contemporary Issues in Enterprise Information Systems: A Critical Review of CSFs in ERP Implementations. In M. Tavana (Ed.), *Enterprise Information Systems and the Digitalization of Business Functions* (pp. 120–136). Hershey, PA: IGI Global. doi:10.4018/978-1-5225-2382-6.ch006

Schwaiger, K. M., & Zehrer, A. (2021). The COVID-19 Pandemic and Organizational Resilience in Hospitality Family Firms: A Qualitative Approach. In A. Zehrer, G. Glowka, K. Schwaiger, & V. Ranacher-Lackner (Eds.), *Resiliency Models and Addressing Future Risks for Family Firms in the Tourism Industry* (pp. 32–49). IGI Global. https://doi.org/10.4018/978-1-7998-7352-5.ch002

Scott, N., & Campos, A. C. (2022). Cognitive Science of Tourism Experiences. In R. Augusto Costa, F. Brandão, Z. Breda, & C. Costa (Eds.), Planning and Managing the Experience Economy in Tourism (pp. 1-21). IGI Global. https://doi.org/ doi:10.4018/978-1-7998-8775-1.ch001

Seidenstricker, S., & Antonino, A. (2018). Business Model Innovation-Oriented Technology Management for Emergent Technologies. In M. Khosrow-Pour, D.B.A. (Ed.), Encyclopedia of Information Science and Technology, Fourth Edition (pp. 4560-4569). Hershey, PA: IGI Global. doi:10.4018/978-1-5225-2255-3.ch396

Selvi, M. S. (2021). Changes in Tourism Sales and Marketing Post COVID-19. In M. Demir, A. Dalgıç, & F. Ergen (Eds.), *Handbook of Research on the Impacts and Implications of COVID-19 on the Tourism Industry* (pp. 437–460). IGI Global. doi:10.4018/978-1-7998-8231-2.ch021

Senaratne, S., & Gunarathne, A. D. (2017). Excellence Perspective for Management Education from a Global Accountants' Hub in Asia. In N. Baporikar (Ed.), *Management Education for Global Leadership* (pp. 158–180). Hershey, PA: IGI Global. doi:10.4018/978-1-5225-1013-0.ch008

Sensuse, D. I., & Cahyaningsih, E. (2018). Knowledge Management Models: A Summative Review. *International Journal of Information Systems in the Service Sector, 10*(1), 71–100. doi:10.4018/IJISSS.2018010105

Seth, M., Goyal, D., & Kiran, R. (2017). Diminution of Impediments in Implementation of Supply Chain Management Information System for Enhancing its Effectiveness in Indian Automobile Industry. *Journal of Global Information Management, 25*(3), 1–20. doi:10.4018/JGIM.2017070101

Seyal, A. H., & Rahman, M. N. (2017). Investigating Impact of Inter-Organizational Factors in Measuring ERP Systems Success: Bruneian Perspectives. In M. Tavana (Ed.), *Enterprise Information Systems and the Digitalization of Business Functions* (pp. 178–204). Hershey, PA: IGI Global. doi:10.4018/978-1-5225-2382-6.ch008

Shaqrah, A. A. (2018). Analyzing Business Intelligence Systems Based on 7s Model of McKinsey. *International Journal of Business Intelligence Research*, *9*(1), 53–63. doi:10.4018/IJBIR.2018010104

Sharma, A. J. (2017). Enhancing Sustainability through Experiential Learning in Management Education. In N. Baporikar (Ed.), *Management Education for Global Leadership* (pp. 256–274). Hershey, PA: IGI Global. doi:10.4018/978-1-5225-1013-0.ch013

Shetty, K. P. (2017). Responsible Global Leadership: Ethical Challenges in Management Education. In N. Baporikar (Ed.), *Innovation and Shifting Perspectives in Management Education* (pp. 194–223). Hershey, PA: IGI Global. doi:10.4018/978-1-5225-1019-2.ch009

Sinthupundaja, J., & Kohda, Y. (2017). Effects of Corporate Social Responsibility and Creating Shared Value on Sustainability. *International Journal of Sustainable Entrepreneurship and Corporate Social Responsibility*, *2*(1), 27–38. doi:10.4018/IJSECSR.2017010103

Škarica, I., & Hrgović, A. V. (2018). Implementation of Total Quality Management Principles in Public Health Institutes in the Republic of Croatia. *International Journal of Productivity Management and Assessment Technologies*, *6*(1), 1–16. doi:10.4018/IJPMAT.2018010101

Skokic, V. (2021). How Small Hotel Owners Practice Resilience: Longitudinal Study Among Small Family Hotels in Croatia. In A. Zehrer, G. Glowka, K. Schwaiger, & V. Ranacher-Lackner (Eds.), *Resiliency Models and Addressing Future Risks for Family Firms in the Tourism Industry* (pp. 50–73). IGI Global. doi:10.4018/978-1-7998-7352-5.ch003

Smuts, H., Kotzé, P., Van der Merwe, A., & Loock, M. (2017). Framework for Managing Shared Knowledge in an Information Systems Outsourcing Context. *International Journal of Knowledge Management*, *13*(4), 1–30. doi:10.4018/IJKM.2017100101

Sousa, M. J., Cruz, R., Dias, I., & Caracol, C. (2017). Information Management Systems in the Supply Chain. In G. Jamil, A. Soares, & C. Pessoa (Eds.), *Handbook of Research on Information Management for Effective Logistics and Supply Chains* (pp. 469–485). Hershey, PA: IGI Global. doi:10.4018/978-1-5225-0973-8.ch025

Spremic, M., Turulja, L., & Bajgoric, N. (2018). Two Approaches in Assessing Business Continuity Management Attitudes in the Organizational Context. In N. Bajgoric (Ed.), *Always-On Enterprise Information Systems for Modern Organizations* (pp. 159–183). Hershey, PA: IGI Global. doi:10.4018/978-1-5225-3704-5.ch008

Steenkamp, A. L. (2018). Some Insights in Computer Science and Information Technology. In *Examining the Changing Role of Supervision in Doctoral Research Projects: Emerging Research and Opportunities* (pp. 113–133). Hershey, PA: IGI Global. doi:10.4018/978-1-5225-2610-0.ch005

Stipanović, C., Rudan, E., & Zubović, V. (2022). Reaching the New Tourist Through Creativity: Sustainable Development Challenges in Croatian Coastal Towns. In M. Valeri (Ed.), *New Governance and Management in Touristic Destinations* (pp. 231–245). IGI Global. https://doi.org/10.4018/978-1-6684-3889-3.ch014

Tabach, A., & Croteau, A. (2017). Configurations of Information Technology Governance Practices and Business Unit Performance. *International Journal of IT/Business Alignment and Governance*, *8*(2), 1–27. doi:10.4018/IJITBAG.2017070101

Talaue, G. M., & Iqbal, T. (2017). Assessment of e-Business Mode of Selected Private Universities in the Philippines and Pakistan. *International Journal of Online Marketing*, *7*(4), 63–77. doi:10.4018/IJOM.2017100105

Tam, G. C. (2017). Project Manager Sustainability Competence. In *Managerial Strategies and Green Solutions for Project Sustainability* (pp. 178–207). Hershey, PA: IGI Global. doi:10.4018/978-1-5225-2371-0.ch008

Tambo, T. (2018). Fashion Retail Innovation: About Context, Antecedents, and Outcome in Technological Change Projects. In I. Management Association (Ed.), Fashion and Textiles: Breakthroughs in Research and Practice (pp. 233-260). Hershey, PA: IGI Global. https://doi.org/ doi:10.4018/978-1-5225-3432-7.ch010

Tantau, A. D., & Frăţilă, L. C. (2018). Information and Management System for Renewable Energy Business. In *Entrepreneurship and Business Development in the Renewable Energy Sector* (pp. 200–244). Hershey, PA: IGI Global. doi:10.4018/978-1-5225-3625-3.ch006

Teixeira, N., Pardal, P. N., & Rafael, B. G. (2018). Internationalization, Financial Performance, and Organizational Challenges: A Success Case in Portugal. In L. Carvalho (Ed.), *Handbook of Research on Entrepreneurial Ecosystems and Social Dynamics in a Globalized World* (pp. 379–423). Hershey, PA: IGI Global. doi:10.4018/978-1-5225-3525-6.ch017

Teixeira, P., Teixeira, L., Eusébio, C., Silva, S., & Teixeira, A. (2021). The Impact of ICTs on Accessible Tourism: Evidence Based on a Systematic Literature Review. In C. Eusébio, L. Teixeira, & M. Carneiro (Eds.), *ICT Tools and Applications for Accessible Tourism* (pp. 1–25). IGI Global. doi:10.4018/978-1-7998-6428-8.ch001

Trad, A., & Kalpić, D. (2018). The Business Transformation Framework, Agile Project and Change Management. In M. Khosrow-Pour, D.B.A. (Ed.), Encyclopedia of Information Science and Technology, Fourth Edition (pp. 620-635). Hershey, PA: IGI Global. https://doi.org/ doi:10.4018/978-1-5225-2255-3.ch054

Trad, A., & Kalpić, D. (2018). The Business Transformation and Enterprise Architecture Framework: The Financial Engineering E-Risk Management and E-Law Integration. In B. Sergi, F. Fidanoski, M. Ziolo, & V. Naumovski (Eds.), *Regaining Global Stability After the Financial Crisis* (pp. 46–65). Hershey, PA: IGI Global. doi:10.4018/978-1-5225-4026-7.ch003

Trengereid, V. (2022). Conditions of Network Engagement: The Quest for a Common Good. In R. Augusto Costa, F. Brandão, Z. Breda, & C. Costa (Eds.), *Planning and Managing the Experience Economy in Tourism* (pp. 69-84). IGI Global. https://doi.org/10.4018/978-1-7998-8775-1.ch004

Turulja, L., & Bajgoric, N. (2018). Business Continuity and Information Systems: A Systematic Literature Review. In N. Bajgoric (Ed.), *Always-On Enterprise Information Systems for Modern Organizations* (pp. 60–87). Hershey, PA: IGI Global. doi:10.4018/978-1-5225-3704-5.ch004

Vargas-Hernández, J. G. (2017). Professional Integrity in Business Management Education. In N. Baporikar (Ed.), *Management Education for Global Leadership* (pp. 70–89). Hershey, PA: IGI Global. doi:10.4018/978-1-5225-1013-0.ch004

Varnacı Uzun, F. (2021). The Destination Preferences of Foreign Tourists During the COVID-19 Pandemic and Attitudes Towards: Marmaris, Turkey. In M. Demir, A. Dalgıç, & F. Ergen (Eds.), *Handbook of Research on the Impacts and Implications of COVID-19 on the Tourism Industry* (pp. 285–306). IGI Global. https://doi.org/10.4018/978-1-7998-8231-2.ch014

Vasista, T. G., & AlAbdullatif, A. M. (2017). Role of Electronic Customer Relationship Management in Demand Chain Management: A Predictive Analytic Approach. *International Journal of Information Systems and Supply Chain Management, 10*(1), 53–67. doi:10.4018/IJISSCM.2017010104

Vieru, D., & Bourdeau, S. (2017). Survival in the Digital Era: A Digital Competence-Based Multi-Case Study in the Canadian SME Clothing Industry. *International Journal of Social and Organizational Dynamics in IT*, *6*(1), 17–34. doi:10.4018/IJSODIT.2017010102

Vijayan, G., & Kamarulzaman, N. H. (2017). An Introduction to Sustainable Supply Chain Management and Business Implications. In M. Khan, M. Hussain, & M. Ajmal (Eds.), *Green Supply Chain Management for Sustainable Business Practice* (pp. 27–50). Hershey, PA: IGI Global. doi:10.4018/978-1-5225-0635-5.ch002

Vlachvei, A., & Notta, O. (2017). Firm Competitiveness: Theories, Evidence, and Measurement. In A. Vlachvei, O. Notta, K. Karantininis, & N. Tsounis (Eds.), *Factors Affecting Firm Competitiveness and Performance in the Modern Business World* (pp. 1–42). Hershey, PA: IGI Global. doi:10.4018/978-1-5225-0843-4.ch001

Wang, C., Schofield, M., Li, X., & Ou, X. (2017). Do Chinese Students in Public and Private Higher Education Institutes Perform at Different Level in One of the Leadership Skills: Critical Thinking?: An Exploratory Comparison. In V. Wang (Ed.), *Encyclopedia of Strategic Leadership and Management* (pp. 160–181). Hershey, PA: IGI Global. doi:10.4018/978-1-5225-1049-9.ch013

Wang, J. (2017). Multi-Agent based Production Management Decision System Modelling for the Textile Enterprise. *Journal of Global Information Management*, *25*(4), 1–15. doi:10.4018/JGIM.2017100101

Wiedemann, A., & Gewald, H. (2017). Examining Cross-Domain Alignment: The Correlation of Business Strategy, IT Management, and IT Business Value. *International Journal of IT/Business Alignment and Governance*, *8*(1), 17–31. doi:10.4018/IJITBAG.2017010102

Wolf, R., & Thiel, M. (2018). Advancing Global Business Ethics in China: Reducing Poverty Through Human and Social Welfare. In S. Hipsher (Ed.), *Examining the Private Sector's Role in Wealth Creation and Poverty Reduction* (pp. 67–84). Hershey, PA: IGI Global. doi:10.4018/978-1-5225-3117-3.ch004

Yablonsky, S. (2018). Innovation Platforms: Data and Analytics Platforms. In *Multi-Sided Platforms (MSPs) and Sharing Strategies in the Digital Economy: Emerging Research and Opportunities* (pp. 72–95). Hershey, PA: IGI Global. doi:10.4018/978-1-5225-5457-8.ch003

Yaşar, B. (2021). The Impact of COVID-19 on Volatility of Tourism Stocks: Evidence From BIST Tourism Index. In M. Demir, A. Dalgıç, & F. Ergen (Eds.), *Handbook of Research on the Impacts and Implications of COVID-19 on the Tourism Industry* (pp. 23–44). IGI Global. https://doi.org/10.4018/978-1-7998-8231-2.ch002

Yusoff, A., Ahmad, N. H., & Halim, H. A. (2017). Agropreneurship among Gen Y in Malaysia: The Role of Academic Institutions. In N. Ahmad, T. Ramayah, H. Halim, & S. Rahman (Eds.), *Handbook of Research on Small and Medium Enterprises in Developing Countries* (pp. 23–47). Hershey, PA: IGI Global. doi:10.4018/978-1-5225-2165-5.ch002

Zacher, D., & Pechlaner, H. (2021). Resilience as an Opportunity Approach: Challenges and Perspectives for Private Sector Participation on a Community Level. In A. Zehrer, G. Glowka, K. Schwaiger, & V. Ranacher-Lackner (Eds.), *Resiliency Models and Addressing Future Risks for Family Firms in the Tourism Industry* (pp. 75–102). IGI Global. https://doi.org/10.4018/978-1-7998-7352-5.ch004

Zanin, F., Comuzzi, E., & Costantini, A. (2018). The Effect of Business Strategy and Stock Market Listing on the Use of Risk Assessment Tools. In *Management Control Systems in Complex Settings: Emerging Research and Opportunities* (pp. 145–168). Hershey, PA: IGI Global. doi:10.4018/978-1-5225-3987-2.ch007

Zgheib, P. W. (2017). Corporate Innovation and Intrapreneurship in the Middle East. In P. Zgheib (Ed.), *Entrepreneurship and Business Innovation in the Middle East* (pp. 37–56). Hershey, PA: IGI Global. doi:10.4018/978-1-5225-2066-5.ch003

About the Contributors

Matthew Ohlson, Ph.D., is the Director of the Taylor Leadership Institute and Associate Professor of Leadership at the University of North Florida. A former teacher and administrator in the Boston Public Schools and the Florida Virtual School, Dr. Ohlson earned his Ph.D. in Organizational Leadership from the University of Florida and has served as a Leadership Coach to 7 Olympians, 15 professional athletes, and more than 500 educational leaders throughout the nation. Dr. Ohlson's research and community engagement work has been focused on collaborating with K12schools, athletic teams, nonprofits, and businesses to increase recruitment, retention, and achievement using leadership development as a catalyst for increased outcomes. For his efforts, Dr. Ohlson has received more than 23 external grants and has been awarded the Florida College Access Network (FCAN) Innovator Award, NPR American Graduate Champion, National Jefferson Award for Public Service, the Gender Equity Award and the Work of Heart Award from United Way. Dr. Ohlson also serves as the Leadership Advisor to UNF Athletics and serves on the Board of the Ronald McDonald House and Franklin Covey Higher Education.

Lakshmi Goel, Ph.D., is an associate professor of information systems and Associate Dean at the Coggin College of Business, teaches Management of Information Technology, Social Media and Business Analytics and E-Business Strategy. Goel's current research focuses on IT ecosystems in innovation networks, IT-facilitated learning environments and social media for small and medium enterprises. Goel received her Ph.D. in Decision and Information Sciences from the University of Houston. Her research works are published in various conferences such as International Conference on Information Systems and the Americas Conference on Information Systems, to name a few, as well as numerous journals including Management Information Systems Quarterly and Journal of the Association of Information Systems.

* * *

Anna Amsler is an independent consultant and researcher affiliated to the Observatory of Competitiveness and New Ways of Working. She holds a Bachelor's Degree in International Relations and a Master's in Political Communication and Marketing, having worked in private and public institutions in areas related to public policy, strategic planning and project evaluation.

Deepak Arora is the Vice President of Corporate Strategy at Crowley Maritime Corporation.

Michelle Broadbent is a seasoned IT professional, certified Agile Leader and Coach. My apex superpower is helping teams and change- makers, get from point A to point B seamlessly, overcoming obstacles along the way through strategic planning and diversity of thought. I partner with executives to build high-functioning Agile teams who find pleasure in their daily grind, seeking out joy-filled moments in the workspace and collaborating to use the most effective, results-driven methods to streamline processes, accelerate growth and achieve exceptional results.

Jill Callinan is a seasoned Program Manager, Scrum Master & Agile Coach with 20+ years experience in software development; the last 10 years focused on building highly effective Agile teams to master software delivery through the Scrum & Kanban frameworks.

Dave Cordero is a Southern California native with more than 20 years of public relations experience and expertise in media relations, internal & corporate communications, consumer marketing, social and digital media.

Doug Dawson is a thought leader in sales strategy and organizational culture. He holds a Bachelor of Business Administration from Belmont University, and Certificates from Harvard Business School in Sustainable Business Strategy and Disruptive Strategy. Doug is a Veteran of the United States Air Force and has held key leadership positions in the Financial Services Industry for over 20 Years.

Greg Gutkowski has over 25 years of multidisciplinary global business experience spanning marketing, sales, and IT management, as well as Internet software development, IoT, advanced data analytics, and journalism. Greg has earned the following advanced degrees: MBA in IT Management, MS in Economics, MS in Journalism. He currently runs the business analytics software company 3CLICKS.US and teaches business analytics and digital strategies at the University of North Florida Coggin College of Business. Greg has worked over the years with customers from various industries. He has helped, among others: Allstate, American Express, Aon/

Hewitt, AT Kearney, AT&T, Blue Cross Blue Shield of Illinois, Charmer-Sunbelt, Continental Bank, Dean Foods, Exxon- Mobil, First Bank, John Alden Life, Ralph Polo, United Stationers, and the University of North Florida. He has also designed analytics systems for several K-12 public and private school districts across the U.S. to assist them in evaluating the effectiveness of various education programs. His analytic software have been implemented by many leading U.S. school districts.

Ben Hippeli teaches Professional Selling and Sales Management at University of North Florida, leads the UNF Professional Selling Advisory Council, and is the founder of Benchmark Training, a firm dedicated to helping companies build a strong sales culture through recruiting, training, and coaching. Ben's customer-centric sales approach has been the secret to his success as a 4-time start-up entrepreneur and as the Executive Director of a national non-profit. He learned early in his career that great sales professionals are not born, but are trained and nurtured and considers building great sales teams a must in order to succeed in any business. Ben received his BBA from Georgia State University, his MBA from the University of North Florida and his sales trainer certification from Florida State University's Sales Trainer Academy and is a member of the HandsOn Jacksonville Blueprint for Leadership Cohort. He brings his real-world experience, combined with a collegiate educational background, and hands-on sales coaching techniques to sales leaders and professionals across the world to assure success in various industries and markets.

Cynthia Montaudon-Tomas is a full-time professor and a business consultant at the Business School at UPAEP. Since September 2018, she became head of the Observatory on Competitiveness and New Ways of Working, which deals with numerous issues related to social problems and creates awareness about current and future social needs. She has obtained a Post Doctorate Certificate In Organizational Leadership from Regent University in Virginia, USA; a Ph.D. in Strategic Planning and Technology Management from UPAEP, in Puebla, Mexico; a Ph.D. in Business from the University of Lincoln in Lincolnshire, UK, and three masters degrees: one in Quality Engineering from the Universidad Iberoamericana in Puebla, Mexico, another in Communication and media from the Jean Moulin, Lyon II University in Lyon, France, and the last one in Business Administration from the Tec de Monterrey in Mexico.

Ingrid Pinto López is a university professor, researcher and consultor at Business School of UPAEP University, recognized by the National System of Researchers (SNI Conacyt). Ph.D. in Strategic Planning and Technology Management. Currently coordinator of the competitiveness observatory and new forms of work, coordinator of the international arbitration of the Latin American Association of Accounting and Administration Schools ALAFEC, member of Barcelona Economics Network and the Illustrious Latin American Academy of doctors.

Amy Ruth is Senior Vice President, Human Services Group and Chief Human Resource Officer GuideWell, United States.

Kirsten Sabia is a 25-year veteran of the golf industry with experience in marketing and communications. Graduate of Dickinson College (Carlisle, PA).

Justin Sipes is the Acting Director of the Center for Community-Based Learning at the University of North Florida (UNF). In this role, he oversees the office and its employees and works collaboratively across the institution to enhance the breadth and depth of community engagement activities. This includes monitoring progress on the institution's community engagement efforts and preparing the campus for its Carnegie Elective Community Engagement Classification process. He received his doctorate from the University of North Florida in Educational Leadership with a focus on higher education, where his dissertation was on the pre-college expectations of first-generation college students. Dr. Sipes has almost two decades of experience in higher education in various functional areas (community engagement, faculty development, fraternity & sorority life, student organizations, housing and residence life, and leadership programs), and led and supervised various teams of professionals, paraprofessionals, and volunteers. He worked in public higher education the overwhelming majority of this career, particularly at regional comprehensive institutions. His research interests are first-generation college students, mid-level professionals, professional competencies, and assessment in student affairs. Dr. Sipes holds a B.S. in Biochemistry and Molecular Biology from the University of Maryland, Baltimore County, and an M.A. in College Student Personnel from Bowling Green State University. He is an active member of NASPA - Student Affairs Administrators in Higher Education, where he is involved at the national and regional levels as an award and program proposal reviewer and frequent attendee of various conferences and institutes. Often, Dr. Sipes presents on community engagement, community-based learning, faculty development, and first-generation students at regional and national conferences. Specifically, within the community engagement realm, Dr. Sipes is a co-facilitator of a national community of practice on Supporting Engaged Faculty Development with Campus Compact and the UNF campus lead for the International Association for Research in Service-Learning and Community Engagement Alliance. In addition, he is an executive member and assessment chair of the Gulf-South Summit, a regional community engagement and a service-learning entity that conducts an annual conference. Finally, Dr. Sipes is an inaugural certified consultant with the American Council on Education for the Carnegie Elective Community Engagement Classification. Dr. Sipes resides in Jacksonville, FL with his wife and daughter. Annually, he volunteers with THE PLAYERS Championship Golf Tournament hosted at TPC-Sawgrass in Ponte Vedra, Florida. He is an avid comic book collector, coffee consumer, and Old Bay seasoner. He is below average golfer and tennis player. Dr. Sipes grew up in Baltimore, MD, and is adamant that Maryland has the best state flag.

Dan Stotz is the Founder and Managing Partner of The Leadership Collaborative (TLC), a consulting and coaching firm that helps organizations develop, inspire, and retain their best people. He is a popular executive coach, keynote speaker, an award-winning program designer, and a highly-rated university instructor. Dan founded TLC after he retired from a 35-year career in higher education; most recently serving as both a faculty member and an Assistant Dean at Kennesaw State University. He now serves as an executive education instructor for the Coggin College of Business at the University of North Florida.

Breann Waiters is a graduate student at the University of North Florida. She is receiving a Master of Science in Management degree and a Master of Science in Business Administration degree with a concentration in Marketing. She currently works as a Graduate Assistant aiding professors in their research endeavors.

Brodie Waters has an extensive career in sports that spans more than twenty years at the executive level, working with some of the premier leagues, athletes and media outlets in the industry. During his career he has represented athletes in the NFL and PGA TOUR, as well as consulted for professional sports teams, media outlets and technology companies involved in sports. A former collegiate athlete at the University of North Florida, he currently resides in Saint Johns, FL with his wife and three children.

Index

H

I

J

K

L

M

N

O

P

Q

R

S

T

V

W

www.ingramcontent.com/pod-product-compliance
Lightning Source LLC
LaVergne TN
LVHW081326300926
849161LV00008B/1884